# Lecture Notes in Computer Science 8075

*Commenced Publication in 1973*
Founding and Former Series Editors:
Gerhard Goos, Juris Hartmanis, and Jan van Leeuwen

Maria A. Wimmer   Efthimios Tambouris
Ann Macintosh (Eds.)

# Electronic Participation

5th IFIP WG 8.5 International Conference, ePart 2013
Koblenz, Germany, September 17-19, 2013
Proceedings

 Springer

Volume Editors

Maria A. Wimmer
University of Koblenz-Landau
Institute for IS Research
Universitätsstrasse 1, 56070 Koblenz, Germany
E-mail: wimmer@uni-koblenz.de

Efthimios Tambouris
University of Macedonia
Applied Informatics Department
156 Egnatia Street, 54006 Thessaloniki, Greece
E-mail: tambouris@uom.gr

Ann Macintosh
University of Leeds
Institute of Communications Studies
Leeds, LS2 9JT, UK
E-mail: a.macintosh@leeds.ac.uk

ISSN 0302-9743                           e-ISSN 1611-3349
ISBN 978-3-642-40345-3                   e-ISBN 978-3-642-40346-0
DOI 10.1007/978-3-642-40346-0
Springer Heidelberg New York Dordrecht London

Library of Congress Control Number: 2013945410

CR Subject Classification (1998): K.4, K.5, J.1, H.3, H.4, H.5

LNCS Sublibrary: SL 3 – Information Systems and Application, incl. Internet/Web
and HCI

*Typesetting:* Camera-ready by author, data conversion by Scientific Publishing Services, Chennai, India

Printed on acid-free paper

Springer is part of Springer Science+Business Media (www.springer.com)

# Preface

The annual international IFIP electronic participation conference (ePart) aims to bring together researchers of distinct disciplines in order to present and discuss advances of eParticipation research. As the field of eParticipation is multidisciplinary in nature, ePart provides an excellent opportunity for researchers and practitioners with different disciplinary backgrounds to share and discuss current research on foundations, theories, methods, tools, and innovative applications of eParticipation. ePart also provides a fruitful ground to nurture and plan future cooperation.

The conference also provides an excellent platform for those who wish to learn about or update themselves on research advances in eParticipation, understand how other groups are applying advanced tools and techniques, and exchange ideas with leading international experts in the field. The 5th ePart was organized by members of IFIP Working Group 8.5 and it was supported by a multidisciplinary Program Committee from all over the globe.

As in previous years, ePart was co-located with IFIP EGOV 2013, the IFIP conference on electronic government. Co-location of both conferences intentionally allows for exchange and cross-fertilization between the two domains of study, and hence the chairs of both conferences are committed to continuing the co-location of IFIP ePart and IFIP EGOV. In 2013, ePart was also co-located with Informatik 2013, which is the German Computer Society's major annual conference. This way, German-speaking computer science and related information governance scholars were welcome to network with e-government and e-participation researchers and practitioners. Both conferences are supported by IFIP WG 8.5 (International Federation for Information Processing Working Group 8.5 on Information Systems in Public Administration).

The scope of ePart 2013 covered the whole range of research in eParticipation. Its principal aim was to review research advances in both social and technological scientific domains, seeking to demonstrate new theories, concepts, methods, and styles of eParticipation with the support of innovative ICT. The IFIP ePart 2013 Call for Papers attracted a wide range of topics with 30 paper submissions. In all, 13 papers were accepted for Springer's LNCS proceedings. These papers have been clustered under the following headings:

- Research Directions
- Social Media and eParticipation
- Online Deliberation

All ePart papers were blindly peer reviewed by at least three reviewers from the ePart 2013 Program Committee with the assistance of additional reviewers. We would like to acknowledge their professionalism and rigor, which resulted in these high-quality papers. Papers submitted to the ongoing research, poster abstracts, as well as workshop and panel abstracts were published in a complementary proceedings volume of *GI Lecture Notes in Informatics*. The proceedings cover contributions from both conferences, IFIP EGOV and IFIP ePart.

For the second time and per recommendation of the Paper Awards Committee, led by Committee Chair Prof. Olivier Glassey of IDHEAP, Lausanne, Switzerland, the IFIP ePart 2013 Organizing Committee granted an outstanding paper award. The winners were awarded in the ceremony at the conference dinner, which has become a highlight of each ePart conference. The name of the winner is announced on the conference website: `http://www.epart-conference.org/`

Many people make large events like this conference happen. We thank the 48 members of the ePart 2013 Program Committee and the additional reviewers for their great efforts in reviewing the submitted papers. Roman Weber of the University of Koblenz-Landau (Germany) supported us in the administrative management and in compiling the proceedings of ePart 2013. Particular thanks go also to the conference organization of Informatik 2013 — colleagues and staff of the University of Koblenz-Landau, who organized the conference system, the room management, the catering and the social events for the whole conference cluster.

The host of IFIP ePart 2013 was the University of Koblenz-Landau in Koblenz, Germany. The Faculty of Computer Science has over 20 professors and consists of four institutes, each with four to six research groups. The faculty researches and teaches various strands of core and applied computer science, including e-government. In the winter term of 2012–2013, the faculty introduced a new Master of Science program in e-government, a unique curriculum in Germany to be offered at a technical faculty. E-government is one of the four key research priorities of the faculty. Research and teaching cover investigations in strategic, analytical, managerial, conceptual, and technical aspects of introducing ICT in the public sector (administration and politics). Interdisciplinarity in design and analysis of study aspects is a central paradigm, particularly in the e-government research group, which is chaired by Maria A. Wimmer.

ePart 2013 took place in the lovely city of Koblenz. Koblenz is situated in the northern end of the famous world cultural heritage area of Upper Middle-Rhine Valley. The city has taken its name from the Roman word "confluentes," which stands for the intersection of the Rhine and Mosel rivers. Koblenz claims to have the only "real" German Corner — the Deutsches Eck. Since the German horticultural show in 2011, Koblenz has become a lovely city with an exciting lifestyle, culinary heritage, and culture. The city's long history with changing Roman and French occupation has created a rich cultural setting with numerous sites of interest in Koblenz and its surroundings. We are pleased to have had the pleasure of holding ePart 2013 in such a special place.

September 2013                                              Maria A. Wimmer
                                                        Efthimios Tambouris
                                                          Ann Macintosh

# Organization

## Executive Committee

| | |
|---|---|
| Maria A. Wimmer | University of Koblenz-Landau, Germany |
| Efthimios Tambouris | University of Macedonia, Greece |
| Ann Macintosh | University of Leeds, UK |

## Program Committee

| | |
|---|---|
| Georg Aichholzer | Austrian Academy of Sciences, Austria |
| Steffen Albrecht | Dresden University of Technology, Germany |
| Joachim Åström | Örebro University, Sweden |
| Lasse Berntzen | Vestfold University College, Norway |
| Yannis Charalabidis | University of the Aegean, Greece |
| Todd Davies | Stanford University, USA |
| Sharon Dawes | University at Albany, USA |
| Fiorella De Cindio | University of Milan, Italy |
| Anna De Liddo | Open University, UK |
| Annelie Ekelin | Linnnaeus University, Sweden |
| Leif Skiftenes Flak | University of Agder, Norway |
| Olivier Glassey | IDHEAP Lausanne, Switzerland |
| Tom Gordon | Fraunhofer Fokus, Germany |
| Dimitris Gouscos | University of Athens, Greece |
| Ake Grönlund | Örebro University, Sweden |
| Johann Höchtl | Danube University Krems, Austria |
| Nikos Karacapilidis | University of Patras, Greece |
| Vangelis Karkaletsis | National Centre for Scientific Research Demokritos, Greece |
| Roman Klinger | Universität Bielefeld, Germany |
| Euripidis Loukis | University of the Aegean, Greece |
| Rui Pedro Lourenço | University of Coimbra, Portugal |
| Cristiano Maciel | Universidade Federal de Mato Grosso, Brazil |
| Ann Macintosh | University of Leeds, UK |
| Rony Medaglia | Copenhagen Business School, Denmark |
| Yuri Misnikov | Belarus |
| Laurence Monnoyer-Smith | Technical University Compiegne, France |
| Panos Panagiotopoulos | Brunel University, UK |
| Eleni Panopoulou | University of Macedonia, Greece |
| Marco Prandini | University of Bologna, Italy |
| Andrea Resca | Luiss "Guido Carli" University, Italy |
| Øystein Sæbø | University of Agder, Norway |

Sabrina Scherer                 University of Koblenz-Landau, Germany
Douglas Schuler                 Evergreen State College, USA
Toramatsu Shintani              Nagoya Institute of Technology, Japan
Stefan Strauss                  Austrian Academy of Sciences, Austria
Efthimios Tambouris             University of Macedonia, Greece
Konstantinos Tarabanis          University of Macedonia, Greece
Ella Taylor-Smith               Edinburgh Napier University, UK
Peter Teufl                     Technical University of Graz, Austria
Daniela Tiscornia               National Research Centre CNR - ITTIG, Italy
Yanina Welp                     Swiss-Latin American Center at the University
                                of St. Gallen, Switzerland
Bridgette Wessels               The University of Sheffield, UK
Maria A. Wimmer                 University of Koblenz-Landau, Germany
Adam Wyner                      University of Aberdeen, UK

## Additional Reviewers

Sebastian Alsbach, Germany          Martin Karlsson, Sweden
Jordi Cucurull, Spain               Catherine G. Mkude, Germany
Asbjørn Følstad, Norway             Azi Lev-On, Israel
Vigneswara Ilavarasan, India        Anthony Patterson, Ireland

# Table of Contents

# Online Deliberation

# Mobile Participation: Exploring Mobile Tools in E-Participation

Maria A. Wimmer, Rüdiger Grimm, Nico Jahn, and J. Felix Hampe

University of Koblenz-Landau, Institute for IS Research, Koblenz, Germany
{wimmer,grimm,jahn,hampe}@uni-koblenz.de

**Abstract.** In this contribution, we investigate the use of mobile technology in e-participation contexts and we define grounds for mobile participation. Mobile participation (mPart) requires the support by tools comprising mobile digital client equipment, mobile access to the Internet, and service support of the related communication. This allows for new types of engagement of citizens in political decision-making at any time wherever citizens physically are. Different participation scenarios require different types of mPart tools. Information gathering, opinion polls, posts to political discussions in social media and in standard e-participation platforms, quick feedback forms, and group and event cooperation are some examples of participation scenarios, which we regard as mPart applications. In this paper, we examine different projects exploiting mobile technology for citizen participation – with a focus on e-participation – and we describe mPart applications and related tools that are developed and evaluated by the authors in a project. The mPart tools are embedded in a layered mPart architecture that allows a flexible integration of tools over an underlying secure communication infrastructure. The architecture serves as a reference architecture for integrating mPart tools.

**Keywords:** Mobile participation, mPart, e-participation, mPart tools, mPart-API framework.

## 1 Introduction

Mobile phones have reached a penetration of 125 % in Europe in 2009. Also the smartphone penetration is growing more and more. However, main use of mobile and in particular smartphone technology is currently recognized in private consumer use. While different attempts of introducing mobile technology in government contexts are known for nearly a decade (so-called m-government), mobile features are not so extensively exploited in e-participation contexts. This is astonishing especially since e-participation is striving for reaching out widely to citizens, and mobile technology is widespread in many developed and even in some developing countries.

Some e-participation projects have begun to allow smartphones to have access to their communication services. However, these are only a few, and the integration is rather ad-hoc. There is no standard strategy or architecture to build up mobile participation with respect to important requirements such as user-friendliness,

M.A. Wimmer, E. Tambouris, and A. Macintosh (Eds.): ePart 2013, LNCS 8075, pp. 1–13, 2013.
© IFIP International Federation for Information Processing 2013

scalability, security, and seamless cooperation with other participation means. We will use the acronym 'mPart' in short for 'm-participation' or 'mobile participation'.

In order to allow mPart tools to be integrated in a flexible way in different e-participation contexts, we suggest an architecture that separates the user functions from an underlying communication infrastructure, especially from the Internet. The architecture is based on an mPart-API framework that provides well defined interfaces to the user tools as well as secure communication channels on top of the underlying infrastructure. The architecture provides a reference framework for integrating various mPart tools into a common architectural environment.

The paper is structured as follows: Chapter 2 investigates the state of the art of e-participation literature. Chapter 3 provides an overview of related work on important mPart projects and their tools. Chapter 4 outlines the project and mPart applications with related research aims of an interdisciplinary project on communication, media and politics. The mPart tools we developed are described in chapter 5, together with a report of initial responses by users. Conclusions and an outlook on further research are given in chapter 6.

## 2     Setting Grounds for Mobile Participation: Foundations and Related Work on E-Participation

As a generic and widespread understanding, e-participation is referred to as the use of Information and Communication Technologies (ICT) in political participation (see e.g. [11, 12, 18, 23]). Macintosh argues that innovative tools and technology provide people with the capacity to participate and influence political decision-making [10]. Scholars investigating e-participation have made an attempt to structure and systematize the field of study through frameworks (e.g. [18, 23]) and differentiation among separate e-participation areas, such as information provision, consultation, deliberation, mediation, petitioning, spatial planning, participatory budgeting, etc. (see e.g. 26, 27]).

An important evolution of the field has been observed since the revolution of the Internet as a participatory web, where everyone can communicate through Web 2.0 technologies [7]. The potential of using electronic means to reach the wider citizenry opened up new possibilities for political participation via electronic means [13]. Since then, a number of e-participation tools have been developed in various projects through the support of the European Commission and through governments of different countries. An assessment of such programs and projects to spur innovation and to advance solutions for citizen participation via online means in different e-participation areas is e.g. available in [16, 23, 28]. Also, the United Nations have defined an e-participation index along their annual e-government surveys, which *'assesses the quality and usefulness of information and services provided by a country for the purpose of engaging its citizens in public policy making'[1]*. The index evaluates the capacity and willingness of a State to explore *'deliberative, participatory decision-making in public*

---

[1] http://unpan3.un.org/egovkb/egovernment_overview/
eparticipation.htm (last access: 24/03/2013).

*policy'* and whether a State reaches the objectives of *'its own socially inclusive governance program'*[2]. In the 2012 survey, Germany scored 0.7632, while Netherlands and South Korea reached the maximum of 1.000 [26, p. 134].

E-participation is also driven by technology development to support citizen participation in political decision-making. A categorization of ICT tools supporting e-participation endeavors is e.g. given in [21, 23]. Tambouris et al distinguish e.g. among rather simple tools such as weblogs and web portals and more sophisticated consultation platforms, argument visualization tools and natural language interfaces. Technologies include e.g. messaging, semantic web, filtering methods and ontologies. In a study the authors performed 2007 on nineteen EC funded research projects of the field seven projects using mobile technologies have been identified [23]. Half a decade later, social media on the one hand and the use of mobile technologies on the other hand, have become prime means for interaction among citizens and governments in e-government and e-participation initiatives[3]. Recent EUROSTAT data indicate that more than half of the Internet users in Europe post to social media[4].

While mobile government has reached attention as an extension or supplement of e-government [24], mobile participation has so far not reached wide attention as a concept. We therefore define mobile participation (or m-participation, in short mPart), as an extension of the concepts of e-participation – relying on above described foundations of e-participation. mPart refers to the extensive use of mobile technologies and mobile applications in e-participation contexts. Nowadays, Internet, broadband access and mobile phones are more widespread in Europe. In 2012, Eurostat reports an internet penetration in households of 76 % in EU27, with Germany reaching 85 %; broadband access being recorded with 82 % in EU27 and 82 % in Germany[5]. Statistics on mobile phone penetration showed already in 2009 a penetration of 125 % in EU27 and of 137 % in Germany[6]. Also the use of smartphones is catching up quickly – 47.6% of people in the EU5 (UK, Spain, Italy, France and Germany) are reported to use a smartphone in Q1 2012, with Germany scoring last among these top 5 with 41%.[7] Hence, the provision of mobile applications to engage citizens in policy processes and democratic decision-making of

---

[2] ibid.

[3] e.g., see publications in collective volume in [4] and in the International Journal of Electronic Government Research (IJEGR), volume 8, issue 3 in 2012.

[4] http://epp.eurostat.ec.europa.eu/cache/ITY_PUBLIC/4-18122012-AP/EN/4-18122012-AP-EN.PDF (last access 24/03/2013).

[5] ibid.

[6] Figures calculated based on numbers of population (http://epp.eurostat.ec.europa.eu/tgm/table.do?tab=table&init=1&language=de&pcode=tps00001&plugin=1) and mobile phone contracts (http://epp.eurostat.ec.europa.eu/tgm/table.do?tab=table&plugin=1&language=de &pcode=tin00059) in 2009 http://epp.eurostat.ec.europa.eu/cache/ITY_PUBLIC/4-18122012-AP/EN/4-18122012-AP-EN.PDF (last access 24/03/2013).

[7] http://www.onbile.com/info/mobile-penetration-in-europe/ (last access 24/03/2013).

States through mobile phones and smartphones is a natural and consequent evolution. To set the grounds for mobile participation, the next section investigates the use of mobile applications, tools and technologies in e-participation contexts of existing projects.

## 3    The Use of Mobile Technology in Government Projects: An Investigation of the Current State of Projects

Mobile technology has been explored in several projects of e-government and e-participation. Among the first projects funded in the scope of framework program 6 of the EC, use-me.gov researched mobile government solutions around 2005. Its aim was to advance three crucial developments for mobile solutions: (1) an *Open Service Platform for Mobile Government* meeting the most critical usability, interoperability and scalability requirements as well as supporting shared use between public organizations and respective departments, (2) *Comprehensive Business Models for Mobile Government* compiling interests and roles of relevant stakeholders and correlating their roles and interests in distinct service and business scenarios, and (3) *Recommendations for Service Planning* including aspects of technology, standards and business operation to serve as an example for "others" when planning similar services [1, 15].

After use-me.gov, several projects have investigated the usage of mobile technology for providing on-the-spot information to governments such as damages on infrastructure in cities, where photos are made with mobile phones and are then sent to government sites via MMS or emails through smartphones or through uploads to a web site. The most known project in this regard is FixMyStreet in UK[8]. Also in Germany, similar examples exist such as Märker Brandenburg[9] or "Sag's uns" of the city of Cologne, which is part of the city's mobile app[10]. The main features of the mobile part of these solutions are MMS or email communication to a government site with a server in the backend to integrate the mobile communication entries into the government solution of complaints management. Some sites are now beginning to integrate mobile access via smartphones (e.g. Cologne's app).

Besides reporting on damages in public spaces and other misconceptions on infrastructures of a city, cities are also launching mobile apps to provide information about the city and for tourists via smartphones. Examples to name but a few are: the Cologne service app, which provides up-to-date information and options for contacting the city with questions or feedback by the citizens[11]; various apps for visitors to the London city (either for download before visiting or accessible through numerous free wireless networks in the city of London)[12]; or the Stuttgart App, which

---

[8]  http://www.fixmystreet.com/ (last access 28/03/2013).
[9]  http://maerker.brandenburg.de/brandenburg (last access 28/03/2013).
[10]  http://www.stadt-koeln.de/1/verwaltung/10425/ (last access 28/03/2013).
[11]  Ibid.
[12]  http://www.visitlondon.com/traveller-information/getting-around-london/london-maps-and-guides/apps (last access 28/03/2013).

provides citizens and visitors with relevant information about the city and its tourism and traffic, as well as some e-government services[13].

With the evolution of open government data, a vast amount of mobile apps have evolved to provide users of smartphones information about cities or particular aspects of public interest. A good example of providing such mobile apps based on open government data is apps for Vienna with the objective to providing citizens, tourists and businesses with relevant information[14]. To spur the developments of the use of open government data in Germany, a contest was launched to bring forward mobile apps for informing citizens and businesses on issues of interest. The Apps4Deutschland brought forward 77 apps (among which many are for smartphones) providing useful information and services to citizens and other users by building on open government data sets[15]. There are many more examples where governments are providing their data to enable added-value services via smartphones to citizens. An overview of examples in the US is e.g. given in [2].

It is to be noted that most of afore mentioned solutions are largely targeting e-government contexts, while the use of mobile apps and tools in the context of e-participation is still rare. Examples of such projects are Padgets and urbanAPI, which are briefly introduced hereafter (both funded in framework program 7 of the EC).

PADGETS (Policy Gadgets Mashing Underlying Group Knowledge in Web 2.0 Media)[16] introduces the concept of Policy Gadgets (Padgets). These are applications on top of web 2.0 technology to describe and control the interaction between a user's web software and others. The project targets integration of this concept in the established social media platforms to acquire a large number of people and uses social platforms for new services. It thereby also integrates smartphone technology for the interaction among citizens and policy makers [5].

urbanAPI (Urban Agile Policy Implementation) targets and uses virtual representations of planning decisions. Models of the real world display ideas about spatial planning. These models are 3D-models of blocks of houses and 2D-maps for visual representation of socioeconomic activity and a region-wide development simulation addressing urban growth and change. Mobile communication services allow the exploration of communication traces, describing human sojourn and activity patterns. [17]

To conclude, searching for projects of e-participation employing mobile technology shows that this development is still in its infancy. The few projects we came across do employ mobile technology, even though not all fully focus on e-participation. Moreover, there is no standard strategy or architecture to build up mobile participation with respect of different challenges such as user-friendliness, acceptance, extensibility, scalability, seamless cooperation with other participation means, etc. To date, mobile tools are integrated rather in an ad-hoc manner However, the penetration of mobile phones and the trends towards more mobile access to services demands for much more research and investment in developing tools and

---

[13] http://www.stuttgart.de/item/show/168768 (last access 28/03/2013).

[14] http://data.wien.gv.at/apps/ (last access 28/03/2013).

[15] http://apps4deutschland.de/category/apps/ (last access 28/03/2013).

[16] http://www.padgets.eu (last access 25/03/2013).

[17] http://www.urbanapi.eu (last access 2013-06-03).

applications for mobile participation. The State of Rhineland-Palatinate has therefore launched a project where different research disciplines are to work together to foster developments of mobile participation among others. The project is introduced in the next chapter.

## 4    The Research Initiative 'Communication, Media and Politics' and Its mPart Project in the State Rhineland-Palatinate

In the period of 2012-2015, the State Rhineland-Palatinate is supporting a new research strand at the University of Koblenz-Landau, which addresses "Communication, Media and Politics" (KoMePol). The initiative brings together different research disciplines to study various concepts of the use of media in politics and how communication is impacted by the use of a particular media type. Finally, modern ICT and the use of mobile communication facilities are explored and studied in e-participation contexts. The initiative is also investigating the building of trust in communicating via innovative media in political contexts (directly or indirectly). The participation of social science, political theory and psychology allows to do research on trust in political systems and their actors. The participation of computer science and communication theory enables studying phenomena of trust in computer systems and communication via mobile devices, mobile communication infrastructures and open networks. The initiative is divided into ten sub-projects, which all help to achieve the accomplishment of the overall research focus. These ten sub-projects are:

1. "Political communication via smartphone" targeting the question of how political information is consumed by the citizen in everyday life.
2. "Para-social Relationship to political actors" studying the impact of trust in the popularity of politicians.
3. "Mobile participation of citizens with protection of privacy" designing tools and services for mobile participation systems that respect privacy and security needs in order to allow the users to trust the technical system for mobile participation.
4. "Televised Debates in Germany" studying recipients real-time feedback while watching televised debates. Research targets are knowledge about politicians' argumentation templates and the impact at recipients' side.
5. "Mobilization of right-wing parties against Europe" focusing on the impact of right-wing parties activities on citizens.
6. "Personalization of political communication" investigating the change of relevance of a single political person and a whole party.
7. "Moral misbehavior of politicians" addressing the sacrifice of cooperativeness empowered by politicians' behavior and reports of them.
8. "Representation, Democracy and Trust" examining the type and relevance of interaction relationships, based on Web 2.0 technology, between a representative and citizens.
9. "Statistical and semantic analysis of political communication in social media" aiming to develop computer-based methods, which push transparency in political communication.

10. "Usage motives for of social media" targeting motives of political information and communication in social media and studying the reliability of political information in social media.

The mobile participation tools and applications developed along the initiative support the projects 3) "Mobile participation of citizens with protection of privacy", 4) "Televised Debates in Germany", 5) "Mobilization of right-wing parties against Europe" and 6) "Personalization of political communication". Other sub-projects outside our research focus are also supported by realizing smartphone-based test infrastructures with the use of a survey tool and special measurement tools under our development, which are described in the next chapter.

# 5    mPart Tools in E-Participation Contexts

In this section, we specify the mPart tools under our development and examine the advantages over existing mPart tools. We differentiate between mPart tools themselves, which are directly used for participation as described in subsection 5.2, software components cooperating with an underlying infrastructure as outlined in subsection 5.3, and online survey tools used for research in other projects of our research focus as depicted in subsection 5.4. How these features work together is outlined in the overall mPart system architecture in subsection 5.1.

## 5.1    mPart System Architecture

In order to achieve a flexible and maintainable software architecture, the mPart system architecture is separated in a framework of components ( as e.g. argued in [19, p. 394]), which are grouped and related to one another by well-defined interfaces as shown in fig. 1. The specification of the interface architecture of the mPart-API-Framework can be used for a basic evaluation of some generic properties like a generic approach, flexibility for anonymous usage and for different authentication and authorization functions, for extensibility by more modules, and for independence of end-device connections like e.g. trusted servers and simple-transport clients (see sub-section 5.3). A major advantage of the architecture is that it is open for the developer community, because it supports an easy integration of new modules and special mPart tool implementations. It is also meant to be a generic framework that can be extended and adapted to special needs.

To ease system maintenance and especially to control the security features, "mPart tools" are separated from the "mPart-API framework": While mPart tools are directly invoked by users, the components of the mPart-API framework build an underlying communication infrastructure with related security and privacy support services. Some of these tools, like a mobile survey tool and a helper to secure users' privacy, enable participation directly. Others, like online survey tools, are special research tools to support researchers in their subprojects. They will work on top of the common mPart tools.

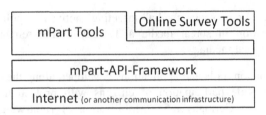

**Fig. 1.** Layers of the mPart System

## 5.2    mPart Tools

In this subsection, we outline the set of mPart tools developed within our project:

**Mobile Survey.** To run a survey is an efficient way to analyze the opinion of a bigger group of individuals, like the public opinion. A related survey tool is an essential mPart tool. We are developing an own survey system, which is already used by our project partners to collect research data. A first implementation was done by the student project "mPartOnCampus". They developed an approach for a participation platform for the relatives of our university, where we find also a complex political system. The main advantages of developing an own implementation, instead of using one from a third party, are the possibility to fulfill special requirements and integration in an application, which works on top of our own developed underlying infrastructure. For example, LimeSurvey[18] is an often used survey tool. It lacks a usable interface for mobile devices and for special needs, like retriggering survey participants, when a study is ongoing over time.

**Mobile Consultation.** Consultation in the context of e-participation is described by Macintosh as *"a two-way relationship in which citizens provide feedback to government. It is based on the prior definition of information. Governments define the issues for consultation, set the questions and manage the process, while citizens are invited to contribute their views and opinions"* [11]. Consultation has been classified as an e-participation area and a number of tools have emerged to support public consultation in political decision-making (general consultation, policy consultation or consultation in lawmaking) (see e.g. [16, 18, 23, 28]). Since existing projects on consultation in political decision-making barely use mobile devices, we have developed a mobile consultation tool, which enables consultation with respect of specific consultation needs. Among others these could be the request for feedback regarding measures taken or the discussion about measures to take in the future. The mobile survey implementation will as well be used as a tool within the mobile consultation tool. First prototypes for such a tool have been implemented in the project "mPartOnCampus" at the University of Koblenz-Landau. The tool will be advanced in iterative steps.

**Privacy Navigator.** Security requires both, functional support by a well-designed working system, and user awareness based on a sufficient knowledge about the risks and a cautious way of acting. A typical example is trust into website operators.

---

[18] http://www.limesurvey.org - last seen on 2012-13-03.

Although a channel between a visitor of a website and a webserver is protected end-to-end by SSL and certificate validation is supported by a browser, the user could circumvent the protection and manually accept untrustworthy websites. The Privacy Navigator supports user awareness of security and privacy. It offers a context-sensitive adaptation of the user and its issue to adequately secure communication channels, by choosing the channel type on the basis of the type of participation, a pragmatic analysis of the participation issue and of course additional user inputs. The design follows a simple scale for intensity of privacy, which is understood by unskilled users. Our research aim is twofold: firstly we implement the Privacy Navigator in all mPart tools in order to learn an effective way of privacy enhancing technology for mPart functions. Secondly, we will study the way of change in user behavior in order to learn how users trust the system.

### 5.3    mPart-API Framework

mPart tools do not directly use common Internet channels. We interpose an underlying infrastructure between the mPart tools and the Internet, as shown in fig. 1, encapsulated by the mPart-API framework. The mPart-API framework's tasks are

1. decouple the user functions of the mPart tools from an underlying communication infrastructure, especially from the Internet,
2. establish secure communication channels on top of the underlying infrastructure,
3. provide well defined interfaces, which are used by the mPart tools or other nodes of the mPart-API framework.

The mPart-API framework is composed of a set of interface specifications, used for implementation of the collaborating nodes and agents within the mPart system. Nodes are transmitting via machines that build an overlay network. In some cases they use other overlay networks between an underlying communication structure and themselves to establish communication channels. The design of the system allows an easy integration of new modules, which can establish communication channels on top of other communication structures.

A prototypical implementation of the framework shows the effectiveness of the architecture with an implementation on top of different communication networks. For example, I2P [19] is an overlay network for anonymous communication and thus supports the privacy of the communication partners. [4] used an implementation of I2P, which is encapsulated in a generalized communication module within the mPart-API-Framework, to realize a so called Trusted Server. A Trusted Server contains a whole implementation of the mPart-API, thus it is a part of the underlying mPart-Infrastructure, consisting of many cooperating mPart nodes. It can be used as a gateway for Mobile Clients or other applications, which have no (No-Transport-Client) or no complete (Simple-Transport-Client) implementation of the mPart-API, as shown in fig. 2. We evaluated the usability of the Trusted Server within the student project "mPartOnCampus".

---

[19] http://www.i2p2.de - last seen 2013-08-03.

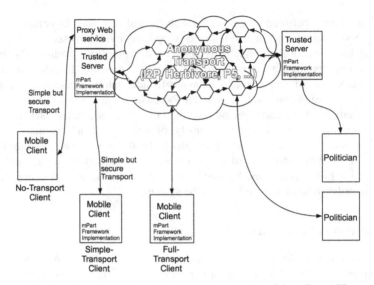

**Fig. 2.** mPart Usage Scenario - an implementation of the mPart-API

## 5.4    Online Survey Tools

In some subprojects of disciplines within our research focus (psychology, political theory and communication sciences), computer-aided measurement tools are used by a test-lab setup to measure human behavior by capturing user input. The following software tools are developed for this purpose:

**Affective Misattribution Procedure.** A psychological hypothesis supposes that recipients can be influenced by unconsciously consumed information [17]. The subprojects 5) "Mobilization of right-wing parties against Europe" and 6) "Personalization of political communication" aim to prove this effect by measuring a change of behavior. By their measurement they want to determine, which context-sensitive information results in a certain change of behavior. One method to examine this effect is the Affective Misattribution Procedure (AMP) described in [8]. We realized an AMP tool with connectivity to different survey systems, so that this procedure can be used directly in the context of a running survey.

**Real Time Response Measurement.** The concept of Real Time Response Measurement means immediate capturing of recipients' perception while consuming information. This method is explained and analyzed in [14]. The test environment of the subproject 4) "Televised Debates in Germany" is going to be the TV duel of the chancellor candidates in Germany in September 2013. It is suspected that investigation of data in a laboratory environment affects measurement of direct perception [3]. Our invention is the execution of such tests in a natural reception situation, e.g. respondents participate from their home being on the sofa. We will create a mobile app that provides a proper user interface for such measurements. It is expected that the study in this real-life environment will omit unwanted side-effect of a test-lab atmosphere and will make the test-results more reliable.

All our mPart tools are currently under development. As mentioned above, the online survey tools will be used by the subprojects 5) and 6) and by other projects outside our research focus. For the time being, they are used in a first test phase by the developers. We have received first feed-back reports by the users within our research project. They report that our mPart survey tools are running more stable and produce more reliable response data than the older Flash tools they used before. For example, they appreciate that our AMP has an online interface for integration in other survey systems like, for example, the GfK system[20], which implemented the surveys. Also with respect to RTR, the applicants report that their first impressions promise superior user convenience and more reliable results. A particular advantage is that larger sample sizes can be handled with less effort.

This is an indication, that we will be able to fulfill the requirements flexibility, robustness and performance. In the next project phase, a systematic evaluation will be performed including quantitative test methods.

## 6    Conclusions

The paper at hand shows that a few projects have already started to integrate the use of smartphones in e-participation applications. However, this happens in an ad-hoc way without a strategic design. We have presented an architecture that allows a flexible integration of mPart tools in an mPart-API framework. The framework offers infrastructure services such as overlay networks for anonymous communication (if needed) or authorization services (if needed) etc. through a standardized API to mPart tools. The framework is generic to enable extension of the mPart toolset with further implementations.

Examples of mPart tools under development are introduced with first reports by users (researchers in the overall multi-disciplinary project KoMePol).

Beside the technical development of the framework and the tools, our next important steps are to perform a systematic evaluation of the existing tools against the requirements: user-friendliness, acceptance, extensibility, scalability, and seamless cooperation with other participation means; and to extend the architecture with adding complementary mPart tools. Further research will be conducted to amend the architecture towards a comprehensive reference architecture for mobile participation.

**Acknowledgement.** This work was partially funded by the KoMePol project, which is funded by the Research Initiative (Stage II) of the State Rhineland-Palatinate. The authors express their gratitude for this interdisciplinary research opportunity.

## References

1. Abramowicz, W., Karsenty, L., Moore Olmstead, P., Peinel, G., Tilsner, D., Wisniewski, M.: USE-ME.GOV (USability-drivEn open platform for MobilE GOVernment). In: Kushchu, I. (ed.) Proceedings of First European Conference on Mobile Government 2005, Brighton, UK, pp. 7–16 (2005)

---

[20] http://www.gfk.com (last access 2012-26-03).

2. Bertot, J.C., Jaeger, P.T., Munson, S., Glaisyer, T.: Social Media Technology and Government Transparency. Computer 43(11), 53–59 (2010)
3. Biocca, F., David, P., West, M.: Continuous Response Measurement (CRM). A Computerized Tool for Research on the Cognitive Processing of Communication Messages. In: Lang, A. (ed.) Measuring Psychological Responses to Media, Hillsdale, pp. 15–64 (1994)
4. Brend'amour, P.M.: Generisches Framework für die mobile Kommunikation von anonymisierten Gruppen (generic framework for mobile communication of anonymizated groups). University of Koblenz-Landau, Masterthesis (2013)
5. Charalabidis, Y., Loukis, E.: Participative Public Policy Making Through Multiple Social Media Platforms Utilization. International Journal of Electronic Government Research 8(3), 78–97 (2012)
6. Charalabidis, Y., Koussouris, S. (eds.): Empowering Open and Collaborative Governance. Technologies and Methods for Online Citizen Engagement in Public Policy Making. Springer, Heidelberg (2012)
7. Effing, R., van Hillegersberg, J., Huibers, T.: Social Media and Political Participation: Are Facebook, Twitter and YouTube Democratizing Our Political Systems? In: Tambouris, E., Macintosh, A., de Bruijn, H. (eds.) ePart 2011. LNCS, vol. 6847, pp. 25–35. Springer, Heidelberg (2011)
8. Emmer, M., Wolling, J., Vowe, G.: Changing Political Communication and Participation in Germany. Communications 36(3), 233–252 (2012)
9. Goldberg, I.A.: Pseudonymous communications infrastructure for the internet. University of California, Dissertation (2000)
10. Ergazakis, K., Metaxiotis, K., Tsitsanis, T.: A State-of-The-Art Review of Applied Forms and Areas, Tools and Technologies for e-Participation. International Journal of Electronic Government Research (IJEGR) 7(1), 1–19 (2011)
11. Macintosh, A.: Characterizing e-participation in policy-making. In: Proceedings of 37th Annual Hawaii International Conference on System Sciences (HICSS-37). IEEE Computer Society, Los Alamitos (2004)
12. Macintosh, A.: E-Democracy and E-Participation Research in Europe. In: Chen, H., et al. (eds.) Digital Government. Integrated Series in Information Systems, vol. 17, pp. 85–102. Springer, US (2008)
13. Maier, J.: Web 2.0 - Moderatorenrechte für alle? Gibt es eine E-Partizipation 2.0 im Web 2.0? In: Mitarbeit, S. (ed.) E-Partizipation: Beteiligungsprojekte im Internet, Stiftung Mitarbeit, Bonn. Beiträge zur Demokratieentwicklung, vol. (21), pp. 282–296 (2007)
14. Maier, J., Maier, M., Maurer, M., Reinemann, C., Mayer, V. (eds.): Real-Time Response Measurement in the Social Sciences. Methodological Perspectives and Applications. Frankfurt/Main (2009)
15. Olmstead, P., Peinel, G., Tilsner, D., Abramowicz, W., Bassara, A., Filipowska, A., Wisniewski, M., Żebrowski, P.: TheUSE-ME.GOV (USability-drivEn open platform for MobilE GOVernment). In: Kushchu, I. (ed.) Mobile Government: An Emerging Direction in E-Government, pp. 249–270. IGI Global, Hershey (2007)
16. Panopoulou, E., Tambouris, E., Tarabanis, K.: eParticipation Initiatives in Europe: Learning from Practitioners. In: Tambouris, E., Macintosh, A., Glassey, O. (eds.) ePart 2010. LNCS, vol. 6229, pp. 54–65. Springer, Heidelberg (2010)
17. Payne, B.K., Cheng, C.M., Govorun, O., Stewart, B.D.: An inkblot for attitudes: Affect misattribution as implicit measurement. Journal of Personality and Social Psychology 89(3), 277–293 (2005)

18. Phang, C.W., Kankanhalli, A.: A framework of ICT exploitation for e-participation initiatives. Communications of the ACM 51(12), 128–132 (2008)
19. Reussner, R., Hasselbring, W.: Handbuch der Softwarearchitektur. Dpunkt.Verlag Heidelberg (2009)
20. Scherer, S., Wimmer, M.A.: E-participation and enterprise architecture frameworks: An analysis. Information Polity, Special Issue on Open Government and Public Participation 17(2), 147–161 (2012)
21. Scherer, S., Ventzke, S., Wimmer, M.: Evaluation of Open Source Content Management Systems for E-Participation. In: Janssen, M., et al. (eds.) Electronic Government and Electronic Participation: Joint Proceedings of Ongoing Research and Projects of EGOV and ePart 2011. Schriftenreihe Informatik, vol. 37, pp. 413–421. Linz, Trauner Druck (2011)
22. Sharma, S.K., Gupta, J.N.: Web services architecture for m-government: issues and challenges. An International Journal Electronic Government 1(4), 462–474 (2004)
23. Tambouris, E., Liotas, N., Tarabanis, K.: A Framework for Assessing E-Participation Projects and Tools. In: Proceedings of the 40th Annual Hawaii International Conference on System Sciences. IEEE Computer Society, Washington, DC (2007)
24. Trimi, S., Sheng, H.: Emerging Trends in M-Government. Communications of the ACM 51(5), 53–58 (2008)
25. United Nations, Department of Economic and Social Affairs: United Nations E-Government Survey 2012 - E-Government for the People. Report ID ST/ESA/PAS/SER.E/150, United Nations (2012), http://unpan1.un.org/intradoc/groups/public/documents/un/unpan048065.pdf (last access March 24, 2013)
26. Tambouris, E., Liotas, N., Kaliviotis, D., Tarabanis, K.: A framework for scoping eParticipation. In: Proceedings of the 8th Annual International Conference on Digital Government Research (dg.o 2007). Digital Government Society of North America (2007)
27. Wimmer, M.A.: Ontology for an e-participation virtual resource centre. In: Janowski, T., Pardo, T. (eds.) Proceedings of the 1st International Conference on Theory and Practice of Electronic Governance (ICEGOV), pp. 89–98. ACM Press, New York (2007)
28. Wimmer, M.A., Bicking, M.: Method and Lessons from Evaluating the Impact of E-Participation Projects in MOMENTUM. In: Gil-Garcia, J.R. (ed.) E-Government Success Factors and Measures: Theories, Concepts, and Methodologies, pp. 213–234. IGI (2013)

# Targeted Policy Making by Transforming Social Networks

Efthimios Tambouris

University of Macedonia, Thessaloniki, Greece
tambouris@uom.gr

**Abstract.** Current economic conditions press governments worldwide to develop more efficient policies with significantly lower budgets. A possible way
to achieve this is by exploiting online social networks. The tremendous impact
of social networks in everyday life (e.g. obesity, financial situation, smoking
etc.) is now well established in the literature. However, up to now, the impact of
online social networks in policy making has not been thoroughly investigated.
We claim that policies, in addition to their traditional aims, should also aim to
improve the online connections of target population as this will enable more
targeted thus more efficient and effective policy making. In this paper, we present this idea, relate it to traditional policy making lifecycles, and investigate
relevant technological aspects. We anticipate this work will contribute to the
on-going discussion on the pros and cons of exploiting online social networks
in policy making.

**Keywords:** policy making, online social networks.

## 1    Introduction

Today, a large number of economic, social, health and other policies are not sufficiently successful. In many case, funding and social benefits do not reach those is real
need. Even when they do so, they still fail to assist beneficiaries to permanently overcome their problems. As an example, many policies for promoting entrepreneurship
provide funds for young entrepreneurs taking into account pre-defined criteria e.g.
age, business idea etc. Additional funds may be also provided for supporting entrepreneurs in their first steps in terms of open lectures and workshops. These approaches however are expensive and in many cases have limited only effectiveness in
terms of successful new businesses and economic growth.

At the same time, current conditions and especially the economic crisis press
governments worldwide to develop more efficient policies with significantly lower
budgets [1]. A straightforward way to achieve this is to develop more *targeted policies*, i.e. policies that reach and affect the target population in a cost-effective and
efficient manner. To this end, policy modelling can assist in evaluating different
approaches and forecasting the effect of policies.

Yet, an unexplored idea is to exploit the *full potential of social networks and
particularly online ones* (e.g. those created in social networking sites). The fact that

M.A. Wimmer, E. Tambouris, and A. Macintosh (Eds.): ePart 2013, LNCS 8075, pp. 14–25, 2013.

social networks have tremendous impact in a number of everyday areas (e.g. obesity, financial situation, smoking etc.) is now well established in the literature. The heavily influential book "Connected" in its final pages suggests that in order to reduce social inequalities we should also consider the personal connections of those we wish to assist [2]. As an example it is stated that we could reduce crime by *improving the connections* of potential criminals. But is this actually true? And if so, how social network analysis can be exploited in actual policy making?

During the last few years, an increasing number of research projects are investigating the potential of online social networks in policy making. For example, Padgets (e.g. [3]) developed a central system that publishes various types of policy-related content (e.g., short text long text, images, video) and micro-applications in multiple social media and collects back data on citizens' interactions (e.g., views, comments, ratings, votes, etc.). The platform also offers analytics, opinion mining and forecasting future trends through simulation modelling to support policy making. WeGov project (e.g. [4]) developed an online toolbox for policy makers to engage with citizens on social networking sites (SNS). It provides three broad categories of functions, enabling the policy maker to (i) search for discussions, topics and opinions from different SNS; (iii) analyse and summarize these discussions to determine the themes and important posts; and (iii) inject information into the SNS. The topics and opinions analysis identify groups of words that represent the topics within a discussion. The prediction of user activity shows posts that are going to generate more attention and the modelling of user behaviour analysis classifies users according to their behaviour and interactions within the SNS. The on-going NOMAD project (e.g. [5]) aims to develop a technical platform that enables government agencies to search for content on a public policy under formulation in various social media and other sources (e.g. blogs and micro-blogs, news sharing sites, online forums, etc.). The gathered content is processed to extract arguments, opinions, issues and proposals on the particular policy, identify their sentiments (positive or negative) and finally summarise and visualise them.

In summary, current projects (such as Padgets and NOMAD) mainly aim to facilitate open and transparent discussions between policy makers and citizens through online social networks. WeGov goes further to classify users' behaviour. None however aims to *transform* online social networks.

The main objective of this paper is two-fold: First, to introduce an approach that enables exploiting online social networks in order to improve targeted policy making. Second, to present a high-level technological view of this approach, including how it fits a traditional policy making lifecycle, relevant high-level requirements and architecture, and a usage scenario.

The rest of this paper is structured as followed. In Section 2, the methodology is presented. In Section 3, the main principles of the proposed approach for targeted policy making are outlined while in Section 4 the relevant steps in a policy making lifecycle are provided. In Section 5, high-level requirements and a high-level architecture of a platform to support targeted policy making are presented. In Section 6, a usage scenario is presented on the envisaged use of the approach. Finally, in Section 7, conclusions are drawn and future work is presented.

## 2    Methodology

The overall methodology that is followed in this paper is influenced from the principles of software engineering and systems analysis and design. For example, an
approach to systems analysis and design suggests one should start with a briefly
described idea and then perform a feasibility study including technical, financial and
organizational feasibility [6]. The technical feasibility aims to answer the question
"*can we build it?*", the economic feasibility aims to answer the question "*should we
build it?*" and the organizational feasibility aims to answer the question "*if we build it,
will they come?*" In addition, architectural models, e.g. [7], have been proposed
to describe the architecture of software systems based on the use of different viewpoints, such as logical, development, process, physical, and scenarios. Finally, usage
scenarios have been proposed as a starting point for software development [8].

In this paper, we concentrate on presenting the driving idea as well as a high-level
technological view to support it. In this respect, we follow a four-step approach.

First, we present the overall vision and approach towards targeted policy making
(section 3). This clarifies the main idea proposed in this paper at a conceptual level.

Second, we outline how our idea fits a traditional policy making lifecycle (section
4). This enables putting our ideas in context of policy making but also deriving the
high-level requirements of the necessary technical infrastructure to support targeted
policy making. It should be noted that the ideas presented in this paper rely heavily
on new technological developments and innovations. Hence, we chose to focus on
technical aspects to also facilitate conducting a first technical feasibility study.

Third, we present high-level requirements and architecture (section 5) for the necessary technical infrastructure to support targeted policy making. Once again, these
aim at evaluating the technological feasibility of our approach rather than providing
detailed development guidelines.

Finally, we present a hypothetical usage scenario (section 6). This enables better clari-
fying the vision of targeted policy making and the role of the technical infrastructure in
supporting it.

It should be noted that other equally interesting questions arise from introducing
the idea of exploiting online social networks for targeted policy making. Some of
these include an evaluation of the relevant benefits and pitfalls (e.g. using a SWOT
analysis), the legal and ethical issues that may arise from introducing such
policy interventions, the economic feasibility as well as issues related to acceptance
by stakeholders etc. All these issues however are outside the scope of this paper.
Nevertheless, we will come back to some of these in the last section.

## 3    Towards Targeted Policy Making

The main idea behind this paper is that policy interventions should not only be based
on the characteristics of a person or a group (such as age, income, skin colour etc.) but
also on the position of a person in a relevant social network.

We introduce the term *policy social networks to refer to social networks where nodes and links are important to a particular policy*. We claim that policies should not only try to *understand* and *exploit* but also *transform* policy social networks and we aim to investigate that by doing so, policies will achieve their goals in a more efficient and effective manner. If our hypothesis is true then e.g. an entrepreneurship policy that changes the structure of the relevant policy social network will be more efficient than a traditional policy. In other words, policies enabling to *improve the connections* of potential entrepreneurs will be more successful.

Thus, the main assumption behind this paper is that "*targeted policies that involve understanding, exploiting and transforming policy social networks are potentially more efficient and effective than those that do not do so*".

We believe it is important to scientifically investigate whether the hypothesis is actually true. Indeed, the potential of social network analysis in policy making has not been systematically examined [9] despite the efforts in various relevant but currently disparate scientific areas, e.g. agent-based simulation [10].

If this assumption is proven right, then policy making could become more targeted (even personalised) and thus potentially more efficient and cost-effective. Policy interventions could have maximum impact with less cost as they will no longer be horizontal but rather very much targeted by exploiting and even transforming relevant policy social networks to have desirable characteristics, such as improved connections.

As an example we consider promoting entrepreneurship, a policy particularly important due to the debt crisis [11] [12]. Here, the policy social network may contain nodes such as potential entrepreneurs, successful and unsuccessful entrepreneurs, venture capitalists, angel investors etc. and links may represent connections such as ones in Facebook and LinkedIn but also in real life. We claim relevant policies should aim to improve the connections of potential entrepreneurs and provide incentives for beneficiaries to do the same.

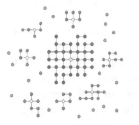    

**Fig. 1.** A. Before policy intervention      B. After policy intervention

Here, policy analysis might show that in *young entrepreneurship*, it is essential for new entrepreneurs to exchange ideas with successful businessmen and venture capitalists. The analysis might also show that currently, the social network of potential entrepreneurs in one region is isolated from such other groups. We therefore need to first of all represent this *policy social network* (see fig. 1A). There is therefore a need to develop and possibly simulate various alternatives aiming to change the structure of the network to facilitate improved communications. A technological platform is needed to exploit social media (such as twitter, LinkedIn and Facebook) trying to propose connections between entrepreneurs in the region with successful businessmen and venture capitalists. As an example, the platform might include software agents in Twitter that will (a) understand that entrepreneurs do not *follow* successful businessmen and venture capitalists, and (b) try to establish such connections e.g. by sending introductory invitation tweets. This will change their social network which will now have the desirable characteristics and measures values e.g. in terms of new connections that will enable ideas on entrepreneurship to flow to new entrepreneurs (see fig. 1B). In fig. 1B the new lines represent new connections (e.g. realised through *follow* in Twitter) that were introduced by the platform to implement the targeted policy interventions. These connections were deemed essential for new entrepreneurs to acquire the needed position in the network in order to succeed.

## 4    Targeted Policy Making Lifecycle

In this section we present the enhancements needed in a traditional policy making lifecycle to incorporate and exploit Policy Social Networks (PSN) for more targeted policy making. These enhancements provide an upper level description of the requirements of a relevant supporting technical infrastructure to assist in targeted policy making.

**Fig. 2.** Traditional policy making lifecycle

The policy-making lifecycle is usually defined as a 5-levels process [13] including:

1. The *agenda-setting* stage, referring to establishing the need for a policy change and defining what the problem to be addressed is.
2. The *analysis* stage, referring to exploring the challenges and opportunities regarding an agenda item, gathering evidence and knowledge on it as well as citizen opinions, understanding the context and developing alternative options.
3. The *creation* stage, referring to drafting of a policy document but also including formal consultations, pilots' studies, etc., if relevant.
4. The *implementation* stage, referring to the development and implementation of the relevant legislation and/or regulations.
5. The *monitoring* stage, referring to closely following policy in action and evaluating its impact.

Actually, the traditional lifecycle is a circle (from monitoring back to agenda setting) but we present it here as a sequence for simplicity. In traditional policy lifecycles, policy modelling is restricted mainly to evaluating alternatives and forecasting policies (or the lack of any policy) impact on the population. Different approaches have been followed for this purpose including, for example, agent-based simulation and mathematical epidemiology modelling.

In this paper, we suggest integrating and exploiting the concept of Policy Social Networks (PSN) in the policy lifecycle. For this purpose, contributions to each of the policy-making stages are required as follows:

- To the analysis stage, a new way to define and explore different policy options by exploiting trends and knowledge gathered from the policy's social network and by simulating different policy alternatives is required.
- To the policy creation and implementation stage, an environment for defining and implementing a policy alternative by performing certain interventions on the PSN and actively transforming its structure and other characteristics is required.
- To the monitoring stage, an environment for closely monitoring policy implementation and its impact on the social interconnections of the targeted subpopulation is required.

**Fig. 3.** Targeted policy making lifecycle

The proposed enhanced targeted policy making lifecycle consists of 5 steps (fig. 3):

*Step 1: Understanding and depicting the policy social network (PSN).* This step initially involves the understanding of the policy area and the definition of all important (influential) parameters and network characteristics relevant to the selected policy area. Furthermore, this step involves the definition of the selected policy's social network (PSN) for a targeted population and its depiction both topologically and numerically by measuring its most important characteristics. Essentially, in this step, the policy maker obtains an overall understanding of the social networks' potential in the selected policy area and gets acquainted with the relevant policy social network (PSN) and its characteristics.

*Step 2: Definition and simulation of alternative policies.* This step initially refers to the definition of different alternative policies by modifying the relevant PSN metrics and connections, thus designing target social networks that will have desirable policy characteristics and network measures' values to achieve the desired policy goal. Then, one or more alternative policies are being simulated providing to the user a depiction of the final PSN after policy alternatives' implementation. Essentially, in this step, the policy maker explores alternative policy options and experiments with their impact by simulating the transformation of PSN for each option. Thus, the policy maker can take an informed decision on which policy alternative(s) to actually implement.

*Step 3: Fine-tuning of the selected PSN.* This step refers to selecting one of the alternative policies and refining its technicalities (e.g. finalise PSN metric changes needed to achieve target PSN) making it thus ready for implementation. Essentially, in this step, the policy maker selects one of the alternative policies explored in the previous steps and decides on suitable PSN interventions to be performed.

*Step 4: Implementation of policies.* This step refers to actual implementation of the selected policy alternative by modifying the relevant PSN connections, according to the decisions made in the previous step. Essentially, in this step, the policy maker applies the decided social network interventions to the current PSN in order to change it towards the target PSN. For example, the policy maker may propose specific, new connections to users so that PSN's density and central nodes are increased.

*Step 5: Monitoring of policies.* This step refers to evaluating the impact of implemented policies through real-time monitoring of PSN's topology and metrics and comparing progress of implemented policy vis-a-vis expected outcomes from prior simulation. Here, the policy maker can monitor PSN's transformation and conclude whether the expected impact of the implemented policy has been achieved. If not, the policy maker may decide to perform additional interventions to the PSN. Alternatively, the policy maker may decide to implement other policy alternatives, in which case the process makes a loop returning to step 2 and continuing from there on.

# 5    Towards a Platform to Support Targeted Policy Making

This section presents two artefacts towards a platform to support targeted policy making: high-level requirements and architecture.

Based on the analysis of the previous section, fig. 4 presents the main functionality expected from a supporting technical platform (i.e. platform). For this purpose, UML use case diagrams notation is employed. In UML use case diagrams, the stickman (called actor) represents a user of a system that can be either a human or another system, while the oval (called use case) represents an essential functionality of a system. A connection between the two suggests a user triggers or is involved in a specific functionality.

A relevant high-level architecture is depicted in fig. 5. This architecture can be used to illustrate the technical feasibility of the requirements presented above but also as a guideline for subsequent detailed architectures and ultimate prototype implementations. Some information on the architecture's main components follows.

The *Social Network Connectors* enable the connection of the platform with existing online social networks (e.g. Facebook, twitter and LinkedIn) thus feeding the platform with up-to-date information regarding the PSN under investigation e.g. connections and contacts of the nodes of interest, etc.

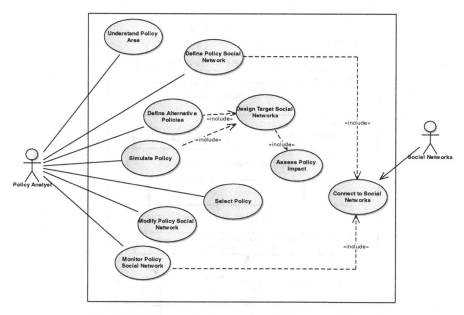

**Fig. 4.** High-level requirements (using UML use case diagram)

The *Social Network Interaction* layer provides the mechanisms and tools for the secure retrieval of data related to the PSN (the policy maker can define the target population and the type of network data that will be retrieved for the scenario under investigation) from the existing online social network and for the alignment, transformation, anonymisation and semantic interconnection of this heterogeneous network data to a common reference format. Finally, this layer provides the mechanisms and tools required for transforming social networks through effective social-computational network interventions.

The *Policy Application and Simulation* layer implements the social network analysis and monitoring mechanism for representing the social network structure and calculating the values of its metrics. This will enable policy makers to understand the current state of the network and identify important metrics that could be improved through network interventions. The platform should also offer a recommendation mechanism to propose the most effective improvements (network interventions) related to the policy. The recommendations are based on identified social network patterns that define the "ideal" structure/characteristics of a social network. Moreover, the system analyses the PSN data and detects the current trends in the network, thus assist the policy maker to select the best policy. The layer should also provide mechanisms for: (i) initiating simulations to derive expected results of different potential policies and (ii) applying various social-computational network interventions to transform the network. Last, the layer should support a mechanism for identifying social network patterns in social relationships and how these may be related to metrics or behaviours.

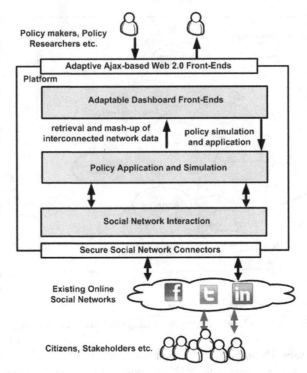

**Fig. 5.** High-level architecture

The *Adaptable Dashboard Front-ends* layer supports the user-centric focus of the platform and enables the easy, personalised access of users to the visualisation, simulation and intervention functionalities.

High-level requirements and architecture are first only steps towards platform development. However, they are sufficient for an initial technical feasibility study. They also provide the basis for further refinement towards platform implementation according to the principles of iterative and incremental software engineering.

## 6     Usage Scenario

In this section, we present a usage scenario to better illustrate the foreseen use of the ideas presented above. It should be noted that this scenario is based on the principles and high-level architecture presented above. Thus, no actual platform has been implemented yet. The scenario aims to facilitate a better understanding of the proposed approach and relevant requirements e.g. within a phase of system analysis.

Maria, a policy maker, wants to apply a policy in order to improve the entrepreneurship among young people. Due to economic constraints she cannot apply horizontal strategies, but she has to apply more targeted and efficient policy interventions.

Initially, Maria launches the platform dashboard (fig. 6) to define the targeted Policy Social Network (PSN) (i.e. the targeted population of the policy). The platform offers tools and mechanisms that help Maria define the basic characteristics of the PSN. When the PSN is defined, Maria can see a visual representation of the social network showing the relations between the individual social entities of the network through the "Current Policy Social Network" tool of the dashboard. In this case, relations can be *follow* relationships in Twitter.

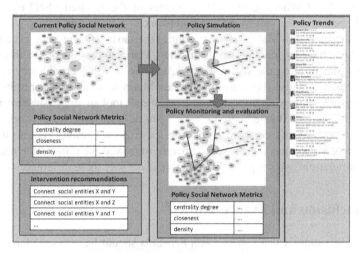

**Fig. 6.** Mockup of platform dashboard

The visualisation allows Maria to observe that a group of potential entrepreneurs in the PSN is probably isolated from other relevant groups, thus information and ideas do not "flow" to this part of the network. Additionally, the platform computes and displays a set of relevant metrics, through the "Current Policy Social Network" tool of the dashboard. This allows Maria to monitor the status of the online social network. These metrics are divided into network-level metrics (e.g. network density, centralization, hierarchy and symmetry, connectivity and complexity) and node-level metrics (e.g. centrality indices and ego-network indices). The former allow Maria to identify e.g. persons in positions of prominence while the latter allow the exploration of the social environment of a given individual.

In order to apply the policy, Maria has to select the most efficient network interventions. Due to the complexity of the social network the number of potential network interventions is large, thus making difficult the selection of the most appropriate and efficient. The platform offers an "Intervention recommendation" mechanism at the dashboard that recommends network interventions based on identified PSN patterns and on the metrics values of the current network. Specifically, the platform recommends the establishment of new connections (by sending introductory invitation tweets in Twitter) between budding entrepreneur of the isolated network and experienced entrepreneurs. Moreover, the platform analyses the PSN data and detects the current trends in the social network, thus assist the policy maker to select the best policy.

Before applying the policy to the social network, Maria wants to see the effects of the intervention to the social network. The platform enables Maria to simulate the policy in the PSN using the "Policy simulation" tool at the dashboard and measure the effects of the policy. This allows her to experiment with different policies and measure the results in a simulation environment (e.g. how did the PSN change after the transformation? What are the metrics values of the resulted PSN? etc.) before applying the policy to the real world social network.

The simulation results assist Maria to identify the most efficient policy strategy i.e. the one that has the best simulation results. Then, Maria applies the policy through the platform by transforming the social network, e.g. by sending introductory tweets to targeted persons. Finally, the platform enables Maria to monitor the results of the policy using the "Policy monitoring and evaluation" tool of the dashboard (e.g. to monitor if the suggested interventions have been adopted and the network metrics have been improved) and compare them with the expected results coming from the simulation process e.g. has the network structure improved the same at the real world and at the simulation? what type of differences exists? why these differences occur?

## 7    Conclusion and Future Work

In this paper we suggest that *online social networks* should be exploited for more targeted policy making. This can potentially increase the efficiency and effectiveness of policy making. For this purpose, we introduce the term *policy social networks to refer to social networks where nodes and links are important to a particular policy*. Therefore, the main assumption behind this paper is that "*targeted policies that involve understanding, exploiting and transforming policy social networks are potentially more efficient and effective than those that do not do so*".

We also present the amendments needed in a traditional policy making lifecycle in order to incorporate these ideas. This analysis reveals that a sophisticated technical infrastructure is essential to support the use of policy social networks within the policy making processes. It also reveals the high-level requirements of such technical infrastructure. We subsequent outline a high-level architecture for such infrastructure that can be used to investigate its technical feasibility and also as a guide for subsequent implementation. This is followed by a usage scenario to illustrate the policy making process and the use of the relevant technical infrastructure.

Although we believe the ideas presented in this paper seem promising we do not claim they have been investigated thoroughly in all their aspects. Indeed, further work is needed in various directions.

First, there is a need to more thoroughly investigate the idea of exploiting online social networks for targeted policy making. Indeed, analysing and using data from online social networks might be undesirable from a legal and/or ethical perspective. This can be due, for example, provisions related to data protection, such as those imposed by Directive 95/46/EC in the European Union. Furthermore, the idea that policy making will be based on data resting within private companies and governed by their access policies might not be appealing. Finally, one might claim that new methods of fraud might emerge if, for example, one develops an artificial social network just to enable him to become beneficiary of a particular public service or benefit. Thus, additional research is needed in these directions. In any case, our position is that these ideas should be used with cause and to supplement rather than replace traditional policy intervention methods.

Second, research is needed in the technical aspects of these ideas. Here, development and evaluation of a prototype is an essential ingredient of future work needed in the area.

**Acknowledgements.** I would like to thank the colleagues at Information Systems laboratory and particularly Eleni Panopoulou and Dimitrios Zeginis for fruitful discussions and feedback on this paper's ideas. I would also like to thank the anonymous referees for their useful comments and insights. Although some comments could not be integrated in this work, mainly due to space limitation, they will certainly influence my future research in the area.

# References

1. United Nations, World Economic Situation and Prospects 2013 Report (2012)
2. Christakis, N.A., Fowler, J.: Connected: The Surprising Power of Our Social Networks and How They Shape Our Lives. Little, Brown and Company, New York (2009)
3. Charalabidis, Y., Loukis, E.: Participative Public Policy Making Through Multiple Social Media Platforms Utilization. International Journal of Electronic Government Research (IJEGR) 8(3), 78–97 (2012)
4. Wandhofer, T., Van Eeckhaute, C., Taylor, S., Fernandez, M.: WeGov analysis tools to connect policy makers with citizens online. In: Proceedings of the tGov Conference, p. 7. Brunel University (May 2012)
5. Karkaletsis, V., Karampiperis, P., Konstantopoulos, S.: Social networks as a resource for policy formulation. In: Intersocial Workshop on Online Social Networks: Challenges and Perspectives, IWOSN 2012 (2012)
6. Tegarden, D., Dennis, A., Wixom, B.H.: Systems Analysis and Design with UML, 4th edn. Wiley (2013)
7. Kruchten, P.: Architectural Blueprints-The "4+1" View Model of Software Architecture. IEEE Software 12(6), 42–50 (1995)
8. Rosenberg, D., Stephens, M.: Use Case Driven Object Modeling with UML. Theory and Practice. Apress (2007)
9. Marin, A., Wellman, B.: Social Network Analysis: An Introduction. In: Carrington, P., Scott, J. (eds.) Handbook of Social Network Analysis. Sage, London (2010)
10. Macal, C., North, M.: Agent-based modelling and simulation. In: Proceedings of the 2009 Winter Simulation Conference (2009)
11. Roudini, A., Osman, M.H.M.: Global Economic Crisis and Entrepreneurship Development. International Journal of Fundamental Psychology and Social Sciences 2(1), 13–18 (2012)
12. Organisation for Economic Co-operation and Development, OECD (2012), Entrepreneurship at a Glance (2012), http://www.oecd.org/ (retrieved online)
13. Macintosh, A.: Characterizing E-Participation in Policy-Making. In: Proceedings of the 37th Hawaii International Conference on System Sciences, pp. 5–8 (2004)

# Crisis, Innovation and e-Participation: Towards a Framework for Comparative Research

Joachim Åström[1], Hille Hinsberg[2], Magnus E. Jonsson[3], and Martin Karlsson[4]

[1] Örebro University, Sweden
joachim.astrom@oru.se
[2] PRAXIS Center for Policy Studies, Tallinn, Estonia
hille.hinsberg@praxis.ee
[3] Research School for Technology Mediated Knowledge Processes, Örebro, Sweden
magnus.jonsson@oru.se
[4] Örebro School of Public Affairs, Sweden
martin.karlsson@oru.se

**Abstract.** Why and how do e-participation policies sometimes flow with politics as usual and sometimes lead to challenging powerful elites and institutions? With the aim of investigating this question, we introduce a framework for comparative research that includes not only systemic but also circumstantial factors. The approach is tested in a comparative case study of three northern European countries--Sweden, Estonia and Iceland--that are all experimenting with e-participation but which are experiencing rather different levels of crisis. The results show that innovation and elite challenging aspirations are very much related to the type and degree of crisis. It is therefore argued that the interplay between institutional constraints and circumstantial catalysts needs further scholarly attention and elaboration.

**Keywords:** Democratic Innovation, Crisis, e-Participation, Comparative Research, ICT.

## 1 Introduction

Regardless of all the differences among European democracies, similar challenges regarding a gap between citizens and their governments seem to work as a starting point for democratic renewal initiatives which show remarkable similarities across countries [1]. One intriguing development is the introduction of "democratic innovations", which refers to institutions that have been specifically designed to increase and deepen citizen participation in the political decision-making process, such as different forms of e-participation [2]. In the scholarly debate on these innovations, much attention has been paid on finding successful recipes of design. By following Archon Fung [3], many scholars have argued that the success of democratic innovations and their consequences for democratic governance depend, to a large extent, on "the details of their institutional construction". Empirical research supports this view by showing that the methods by which participants are selected, the timing of consultations within

M.A. Wimmer, E. Tambouris, and A. Macintosh (Eds.): ePart 2013, LNCS 8075, pp. 26–36, 2013.

the policy cycle, and the mode of communication adopted set a decisive context for participant interaction. Even though not all democratic innovations succeed in engaging citizens, some do, and the odds for success and failure differ considerably according to aspects of design [4].

However, democratic innovations, just as any innovation, are more than ideas and designs; they are ideas in action. Therefore, as Newton aptly points out [5], they depend on implementation, and "good innovations depend on good ideas and designs that can be implemented successfully". But empirical research on the implementation of democratic innovations is still in its infancy, and there is still little knowledge on how similar designs are in fact mediated by various local contexts: how they are translated locally, why they are implemented differently, and what consequences they have on democracy.

Examples of comparative internet political research are growing in numbers, but these have mainly been conducted in the field of electoral politics. Concentrating primarily on European and U.S. case studies, this research has criticized the idea that American innovations in e-campaigning could simply be replicated elsewhere. By accounting for mainly institutional variables such as party structure and funding, electoral regulations, and media systems, research shows how similar instances of e-campaigning are shaped by national contexts [6, 7].

When it comes to e-participation, it is local government that is the laboratory for research and experimentation. In most countries, experimentation in e-participation, if there is any, takes place primarily at this level [4]. This focus on local-level experimentation offers researchers some specific advantages and challenges. The closeness of political actors makes the effects of new processes more readily observable to those who govern localities - and to researchers - than to those at higher levels of governance. Furthermore, the large number of local governments is advantageous when it comes to generalizing results [8]. However, local government vary across countries on multiple dimensions (i.e., its purpose; its autonomy and relationship to other levels of government; its relationship to its residents; its structure, form and setting; and its politics and policy), which is challenging [9]. As a consequence of this complexity, there is a general lack of systematic comparison on local politics across countries. This is not only the case in the field of e-participation. Urbanists in general, Pierre [10, p. 446] states, "have been surprisingly slow in using comparison as a research strategy", and according to Wolman [9, p. 88], the main threshold problem is "the lack of a common framework to conduct such research, to place results, and build upon them".

The general aim of this paper is to help remedy this research gap by exploring what constitutes the "context" that surrounds and influences the implementation of e-participation at the local government level. The specific question we set out to explain is why and how e-participation policies sometimes flow with politics as usual and sometimes lead to challenging powerful elites and institutions. While "elite-challenging" or "citizen-centric" forms of participation reflect a critical citizenry whose members want to put incumbent authorities under pressure to respond to their demands [11], and while they tend to have a positive impact on democracy [12], they are still rare exceptions [13,14].

To grasp a better understanding of why, when and how these rare exceptions occur, we will start by proposing a new approach to comparative research, based on a wider, more flexible understanding of "context" that accounts for the interplay between institutional constraints and circumstantial catalysts [6]. This framework is subsequently used in order to compare e-participation implementation in Sweden, Estonia and Iceland, three northern European countries that are all experimenting with e-participation but are experiencing rather different levels of crises. While different "systemic elements" come to the fore in the implementation of e-participation depending on the political system, circumstantial factors--or different degrees of crises--transcend boundaries and thus provide an interesting starting point for empirical analysis. Information about the three cases is based on a series of personal interviews conducted with local politicians and civil servants in Sweden, Estonia and Iceland during the spring 2012, as well as a joint workshop with participants from all three countries in the autumn 2012. Additionally, we have used evaluations and case-reports from respective countries (our own and others) as well as public data.

## 2      What Context Matters for e-Participation?

Encouraged by Trevisian and Oates [6], this study will thus introduce a broader framework that accounts for the interplay between institutional constraints and circumstantial catalysts in the implementation of e-participation. Following the footsteps of previous comparative local government research, we will particularly analyze *the local government system*, or central-local relations, as well as *the character of local democracy*. When it comes to circumstantial factors, we will separate between *the nature of policy-problems* on the one hand and the *political climate* on the other. In combination, these elements are expected to be key factors influencing the degree of innovation in the implementation of e-participation. Innovation is usually seen as offering an opportunity to change the rules of the game, which is more motivating in situations characterized by crises. However, this is seldom recognized in theoretical frameworks in comparative digital research. Instead, "context" is usually narrowed down to different institutional constraints.

### 2.1      Sweden

**Systemic Factors.** The Swedish political system is first and foremost characterized by a strong position of political parties. Every elected politician represents a political party, and Swedish elections are centered on parties rather than individual candidates. Also, political participation in Sweden has traditionally been channeled through political parties and popular mass movements, fostering a collectivist ideal for citizen participation and democratic citizenship. In a recent comparative analysis of sixteen European countries, investigating the extent to which local democratic institutions and political cultures are "party democratic" or "citizen democratic", Sweden is found to be the most "party democratic" political system [15, p. 9].

The Swedish system is also based on strong local government with far-reaching autonomy [16, p. 233]. Local governments raise the majority of the income taxes from the population and have gained the responsibility for a growing number of welfare services (from national as well as county governments) during the last fifty years [16, p. 236]. The local government sector is also a large employer that occupies around 20% of the Swedish workforce.

Swedish citizens are usually considered relatively informed about politics [17], and turnout in elections is comparatively high (approximately 80% of the electorate vote in local authority, county council and national elections) [18].

**Circumstantial Factors.** During the last decades, there has been a growing debate over the state of democracy in Sweden. As in many other European countries, the Swedish public is becoming more dissatisfied with the traditional institutions of representative democracy and with conventional forms of participation [19, 20]. A notable strengthening of the socio-economic status in the country has resulted in a change towards individualization among its citizens. In recent comparative studies, Swedes are found among the most individualized citizens in the world [12]. As a result of this transformation, the strong collectivistic tradition of political engagement in the country has been questioned. The formerly strong mass popular movements, including the political parties, have lost a large share of their members. A widespread decline in political trust and party membership as well as party identification has caused some scholars to claim that political parties are losing their legitimacy [21, 20].

However, the contemporary political situation is still one of stability. Sweden has not been directly involved in a war since 1809 and is, along with Canada, the only state rewriting its constitution despite the absence of a political crisis [22]. The country has managed through the current economic crises better than most other European countries, and the parliamentary situation is still characterized by pragmatism, coalition-building and striving for consensus. While turnout and levels of trust are going down, they are still at a relative high from a comparative perspective.

**e-Participation Implementation.** In attempts to mend the apparent challenges of Swedish representative democracy, a trend of introducing new forms of citizen participation (e.g., e-participation initiatives) has nonetheless emerged [23]. In line with the Swedish tradition of strong local governments, the vast majority of these participatory initiatives have been implemented at the local level, championed by local governments. However, local e-participation initiatives are still rather few and unevenly diffused among Swedish local governments. The local governments that have implemented e-participation initiatives are often characterized by relatively low electoral participation as well as relatively weak political trust among citizens. Case studies report that local politicians often view e-participation initiatives as a potential remedy for these challenges [24]; [25], which indicates a link between circumstantial factors and e-participation initiatives. However, it soon becomes evident that the catalyst for change is not very strong. First, the initiatives are implemented as potential remedies for a declining trust in political parties and institutions, but not as a process for solving specific policy problems. One illustrative example is the online referendums in the municipality of Sigtuna. The local government decided to implement a large number of local referendums in order to spire greater political participation and foster political trust, but the policy issues for these referendums were chosen at a later stage and were not the main focus of the participatory process. Second, the new arenas of engagement have often been detached from the traditional party arena of representative democracy. Local governments are locked into old structures and ways of working, only with islands of participatory practice [cf. 26, 27].

## 2.2   Estonia

**Systemic Factors.** Since the restoration of independence in 1991, Estonia has built and developed a democratic structure. Practically starting from scratch after the occupation of the Soviet Union, all the functions and apparatus of a modern state, including a legal code, a civil service, and national and sub-national institutions have been built up. Today, Estonia is a Parliamentary Republic. The political parties are the main instrument of channeling power from the citizens, and the general elections are the central mechanisms that give the people influence over policy-making. Another important trait of the Estonian political system is central authority. This is partly due to the fact that the "cornerstone of Estonian local governance—the municipality—was abolished by the Soviet regime" [28, p. 168]. The local authorities are thus formally autonomous in acting within the framework on fiscal and normative matters, but the framework has "not been conducive to actual autonomy and, hence, the development of local democracy" [28, p. 190]. Due to the regulations of tax collection and private enterprise in social services, the revenues for local governments are low. Therefore, the possibility for local governmental maneuvers is low.

**Circumstantial Factors.** The political parties dominate Estonian political life, yet they do not enjoy high public trust, with around 40% of the citizens claiming they would not vote for any of the competing parties in an election [29]. The public distrust was recently manifested in a much-publicized debate article in November 2012, in which the *Charter 12* was presented. The article was published in connection with a political scandal concerning party financing, with the explicit message that "Estonia's democracy is crumbling before our eyes", and "democratic legitimation [sic] has ceased" [30]. *The Charter* did catch both the public (17,000 supported *The Charter* in an online process) and the President's interest (who supported the call). *The Charter* then became the platform for an online political process, leading to the creation of the site *The Peoples Assemble,* 'Rahvakogu', was ended with a "Deliberation Day" in April 2013. The political climate can thus be said to be characterized by instability and low trust towards the political establishment. The policy problems facing Estonia are, despite the current *Charter 12* events, of a *resource* character. The political parties are currently under pressure and scrutiny and do, in general, receive low trust.

**e-Participation Implementation.** With a diffusion of approximately 75% of the population, Estonia is among the top 30 states in the world when it comes to internet access. Already early on in the process of democratization, the Estonian government turned to ICT solutions to enhance citizen participation. The earliest and most notable actions were the introduction of the TOM (Today I Decide) system in 2001, the introduction of e-voting in 2005 and the osale.ee platform in 2007. Due to the national-level crisis and the creation of the "People's Assembly" platform in 2013, Estonia gained its first elite-challenging e-participation process. The process was initiated by the President and shaped in co-operation with the civil society. Aimed to invite lay citizens to discuss and propose fundamental changes in the party structure, the initiative must be viewed as rather radical.

On the local level, however, e-participation tools have been developing at a considerably slower pace than those created by the central government or citizen initiatives. For example, the VOLIS system is an online decision-making system for local councils, and the application aims to integrate e-governance, participatory democracy, and records management. It is in some sense similar to the TOM system, offering possibilities for citizens to propose issues to the council for discussion or adoption and to collect supporting signatures. However, the system has not been widely adopted. The basic reason for this is the centralized institutional framework and the additional costs brought on the municipalities and regions interested in the system.

### 2.3    Iceland

**Systemic Factors.** Despite Iceland's long tradition of democracy with the first parliament, the Althing (Alþingi), established as early as 930 CE, the modern democratic state took shape after its independence from Denmark in 1944, when Iceland constituted itself as a semi-presidential republic with parliamentary rule. Iceland is a decentralized state with strong local democratic traditions. Municipalities as a political unit date back to the first "free men" that conquered Iceland in 800 CE. Iceland consists of 75 municipalities, which, with a total population of 320,000 citizens, makes a "great number of small, sparsely populated municipalities" [31, p. 21].

With its structure as a unitary state, the national government of Iceland rules the state, while the local authorities, with restrictions from the national level, rule the municipalities. Tax revenue is collected by the municipalities, and thus a huge part of the welfare services is provided by the municipality. The municipalities are, therefore, under the law, entitled to maneuver within the frames of their budgets.

**Circumstantial Factors.** The contemporary Icelandic political context can be characterized as being in a stable post-crisis condition, after the economic and political crisis that began in the wake of the global financial crisis in 2008. In the aftermath of the financial and political crisis, the sitting government was toppled in 2009. A public discussion on the fundamentals of the Icelandic political system took form. One of the main issues was the drafting of a new constitution. The constitution was drafted online in a crowd-sourcing process, which is unique in its kind.

Iceland has traditionally been considered of good democratic health, with high turnout levels in parliamentary elections (e.g., 85.1% in 2009) and relatively high turnouts in presidential elections (e.g., 69.3% in 2012). Parallel to this high level of participation, Icelanders are dissatisfied with the political establishment, a visible trend in that political parties attract fewer members. Some scholars argue that the "political parties in Iceland have become almost empty shells" [32].

The recent developments (i.e., the financial and political crisis), in combination with a notion that the political parties resemble "empty shells", have affected the levels of general trust in politics in Iceland. In a poll conducted in 2011, only one in ten

Icelanders expressed "great trust" in parliament [33]. The political climate is thus characterized by low trust. The policy problems in Iceland concern fundamental political issues. The crisis did affect all political and societal institutions, and it must therefore be considered of fundamental character.

**e-Participation Implementation.** Early on, Iceland's government was positive to ICT solutions. Already in 1996, the prime minister announced, "The chief objective is that Iceland shall be in the forefront of the world's nations in the utilization of information technology in the service of improved human existence and increased prosperity" [3]. But despite the infrastructure and governmental rhetoric, the rate of democratic innovation and e-participation was low in Iceland until 2008, both on local and national levels. Only a few examples of e-participation innovations could be found on the local level, as, for example, the e-voting referendum in 2001 on whether or not to move the national airport located in Reykjavik as well as a deliberative online project concerning the "Local Agenda 21" policy in 2004 [35].

After the crisis in 2008, the rate of e-participatory innovation rose and became ever more elite-challenging. The first and most prominent example on the national level was the process of drafting the new constitution, while the most prominent example on the local level was the launch and implementation of the Better Reykjavik system. The process of drafting the new constitution began with the National Forum in 2010 in which a decision was taken that a citizen assembly, the "Constitutional Council", should be elected by popular vote. The Constitutional Council then chose to put the process online, and the drafting of the constitution soon metamorphosed into an online process that invited every citizen of Iceland to participate in the writing of the new constitution [36]. Social media platforms used were YouTube, Twitter, Facebook and Flickr. A first draft of the new constitution was handed over to parliament in July 2011, and an advisory referendum was held in October 2012. The drafting is thus still in progress. On a local level, the *Better Reykjavik* system was implemented by the new local party, the *Best Party,* in co-operation with the non-profit organization *Citizen Foundation.* The system allows citizens of Reykjavik to participate by posting, discussing and voting upon citizen initiatives.

# 3    Comparative Analysis

At first glance, Sweden, Estonia and Iceland share many similarities in relation to e-participation. All three countries are characterized by strong ICT-infrastructure and high levels of ICT-modernization among its populations. However, the e-participation initiatives implemented in these countries differ widely in terms of innovation and elite challenging aspirations. How can these differences be understood in relation to the interplay between circumstantial and systemic factors?

In the Swedish case, e-participation initiatives are primarily implemented at the local level and are seldom initiated to handle specific policy problems. Rather, these initiatives are used as a tool among many to foster citizen participation and political trust in the light of a declining trend in electoral participation and political trust (although from comparably high levels). The degree of pervasiveness and innovation is low in comparison to the other cases, which might be understood in relation to systemic (party-centric) as well as circumstantial (stability) factors. In a comparably stable political climate, without any imminent policy problems, e-participation initiatives have not been implemented so as to challenge the party-centric style of policy making. Despite the use of some interesting tools such as e-referendums, online discussion forums, e-panels and e-petitioning, implementation pretty much speaks in favour of "politics as usual".

By comparison, the Estonian case is interesting, since the country is beginning to move beyond the elites' comfort zone. While the Estonian local governments do not have the capacity for innovative e-participation implementation, the country was early in developing a national e-participation platform. The government thus "paved the way" for innovation by constructing a physical and cultural infrastructure for e-participation early on. However, it was not until the emergence of a legitimacy crisis that a more elite-challenging practice developed with the creation of the "Rahvakogu" and "Deliberation Day". With its roots in an instable political climate, this crisis was also related to a specific policy problem: how to regulate party finance.

However, the Icelandic case is a *sui generis* due to the extent of the economic crisis as well as the degree of elite-challenging democratic innovations in its wake. The financial crisis facing Iceland in 2008 brought with it not only policy problems related to financial issues but also a substantial challenge to the political climate in terms of governmental and local government institutions lacking legitimacy. These developments spired innovative and pervasive forms of e-participation processes at the national level as well as in the city of Reykjavik. In contrast to the elements of crisis described in Sweden and Estonia, the situation in Iceland could be described as a more fundamental crisis affecting several sectors and functions in society.

**Table 1.** Key contexts influencing e-participation implementation

|  | Circumstantial factors | | Systemic factors | | |
|---|---|---|---|---|---|
|  | Policy problems | Political climate | Local government | Local democracy | E-participation implementation |
| **Sweden** | Everyday | Slow decline in trust | Decentralized system | Strong democratic tradition | Local government only |
|  |  | Stability | High local capacity | Party centric | Politics as usual |
| **Estonia** | Resource | Low trust | Centralized system | Weak democratic tradition | Central government only |
|  |  | Instability | Low local capacity | Citizen centric | Beyond comfort zone |
| **Iceland** | Fundamental | Low trust | Decentralized system | Strong democratic tradition | Local and central government |
|  |  | Crisis | High local capacity | Party centric | Innovative and Challenging |

Table 1 summarizes the main differences and similarities among the cases. As has been argued above, both systemic and circumstantial factors seem to influence e-participation implementation. When it comes to circumstantial factors, which are of particular interest in this paper, the results suggest that the lower the trust and the deeper the policy problems are, the higher the chances are for an elite-challenging implementation. An interesting common feature of the more innovative and elite-challenging initiatives are their lack of sole management by state bodies from the top-down. Instead, they have come into being from outside the state, with civil society participating in deciding the rules of the game. It would thus seem that crisis makes e-participation more innovative by making it less government-organised and interpreted more in terms of citizen or civil-society concerns, reflecting the tension in democratic theory between models of participation promoted by incumbent power-holders and autonomous initiatives driven by self-actualizing citizens [37].

# 4     Conclusions

The crisis of representative democracy may work as a starting point for democratic re-newal initiatives in many cities around the world, but these initiatives vary considerably in terms of their elite-challenging aspirations. In this article, we have argued that circum-stantial factors are as important as systemic factors in order to understand why. Within this framework, it becomes just as important to distinguish between crises as to distinguish between institutions. Without both these sets of factors, the results of the comparative case study would be more difficult to understand, but empirical work on less-straightforward case studies would help to achieve a more sophisticated understand-ing between crisis and e-participation.

Earlier studies of e-participation have focused foremost on the influence of institu-tional and systemic factors on e-participation implementation while largely ignoring or overlooking *crisis*, a concept that has had a central position in other related fields of social scientific research interested in innovations in government and society (i.e., organizational studies and economics). The findings of this analysis encourage more research on the interplay between crisis and institutions in shaping the e-participation processes and on how different kinds, or degrees, of crisis affect e-participation im-plementation. [38]

# References

1. Daemen, H., Schaap, L.: Renewal of Local Democracies: Puzzles, Dilemmas and Options. Springer VS, Wiesbaden (2012)
2. Smith, G.: Democratic Innovations – Designing Institutions for Citizen Participation. University Press, Cambridge (2009)
3. Fung, A.: Recipes for Public Spheres: Eight Institutional Design Choices and Their Consequences. Journal of Political Philosophy 11(3), 338–367 (2003)

4. Åström, J., Grönlund, Å.: Online Consultations in Local Government: What works, When and Why? In: Coleman, S., Shane, P.M. (eds.) Connecting Democracy: Online Consultation and the Flow of Political Communication. MIT Press, Cambridge (2011)
5. Newton, K.: Curing the democratic malaise with democratic innovations. In: Geissel, B., Newton, K. (eds.) Evaluating Democratic Innovations: Curing the Democratic Malaise? Routledge, Oxon (2012)
6. Trevisan, F., Oates, S.: Same Recipe but different Ingredients? Challenges and Methodologies of Comparative Internet/Politics Research. Paper presented at the 2012 American Political Science Association Annual Meeting, New Orleans, LA, August 30-September 2 (2012)
7. Åström, J., Karlsson, M.: 2011. Blogging in the shadow of parties: Collectivism and individualism in the Swedish 2010 election. Paper präsentiert bei den ECPR JointSessions, 12–17. St. Gallen (April 2011)
8. John, P.: Methodologies and Research Methods in Urban Political Science. In: Baldersheim, H., Wollman, H. (eds.) The Comparative Study of Local Government and Politics: Overview and Synthesis, pp. 67–82. Budrich, Opladen (2006)
9. Wolman, H.: Comparing local government systems across countries: conceptual and methodological challenges to building a field of comparative local government studies. Environment and Planning C, Government and Policy 26, 87–103 (2008)
10. Pierre, J.: Comparative Urban Governance: Uncovering Complex Causalities. Urban Affairs Review 40(4), 446–462 (2005)
11. Dalton, R.J.: Citizenship Norms and the Expansion of Political Participation. Political Studies 56, 76–98 (2008)
12. Inglehart, R., Welzel, C.: Modernization, cultural change, and democracy: the human development sequence. Cambridge University Press, Cambridge (2005)
13. Blaug, R.: Engineering Democracy. Political Studies 50(1), 102–116 (2002)
14. Coleman, S., Blumler, J.G.: The Internet and democratic citizenship: theory, practice and policy. Cambridge University Press, Cambridge (2009)
15. Denters, B., Klok, P.-J.: Citizen Democracy and the Responsiveness of Councillors: The Effects of Democratic Institutionalisation on the Role Orientations and Role Behaviour of Councillors. Local Government Studies (2012) (Online first)
16. Bäck, H., Larsson, T.: Den Svenska politiken: Struktur, processer och resultat. Liber, Malmö (2006)
17. Fraile, M.: A comparative study of Political Knowledge in the, European Elections. Paper presented at the PIREDEU Final Conference, November 18-20, Brussels (2010)
18. Swedens Elections Authority (SEA), Electoral results 2010 (2010).
    http://www.val.se
19. Goul Andersen, J.: Udviklingen i den politiske deltagelse i de nordiske lande. In: Esaiasson, P., Westholm, A. (eds.) Deltagandets Mekanismer: Det Politiska Engagemangets Orsaker och Konsekvenser. Liber, Malmö (2006)
20. Holmberg, S.: Down and down we go: political trust in Sweden. In: Norris, P. (ed.) Critical Citizens: Global Support for Democratic Governance. Oxford University Press, Oxford (1999)
21. Montin, S.: Mobilizing for participatory democracy? The case of democracy policy in Sweden. In: Zittel, T., Fuchs, D. (eds.) Participatory Democracy and Political Participation–Can Participatory Engineering Bring Citizens Back in? Routledge, Oxon (2007)
22. Elster, J.: Forces and mechanisms in the constitution-making process. Duke Law Journal 45, 364 (1995-1996) (retrieved: HeinOnline)

23. Karlsson, M.: Participatory initiatives and political representation: The case of local councillors in Sweden. Local Government Studies 38(6), 795–815 (2012)

24. Åström, J.: Mot en digital demokrati? Teknik, politik och institutionell förändring. Örebro Univ., Örebro (2004)

25. Granberg, M., Åström, J.: Civic Participation and Interactive Decision-making: A Case Study. In: Amnå, E. (ed.) New Forms of Citizen Participation. Normative Implications. Nomos, Baden-Baden (2010)

26. Amnå, E.: Playing with fire? A Swedish mobilization for deliberative democracy. Journal of European Public Policy 13(4) (2006)

27. Åström, J., Granberg, M., Khakee, A.: Apple Pie-Spinach Metaphor: Shall e-Democracy make Participatory Planning More Wholesome? Planning Practice and Research 26(5), 571–586 (2011)

28. Sootla, G., Toots, A.: Report on the State of Local Democracy in Estonia. In: Soós, G. (ed.) Local Democracy in Central Europe - Reports from Bulgaria, Estonia, and Slovakia. Local Government and Public Service Reform Initiative. Open Society Institute, Budapest (2006)

29. Madise, Ü.: Elections, Political Parties, and Legislative Performance in Estonia: Institutional Choices from the Return to Independence to the Rise of E-Democracy. Tallinn University of Technology Press, Tallinn (2007)

30. Charter 12 (2012), http://www.harta12.ee/eng/

31. Hovgaard, G., Eythórsson, G.T., Fellman, K.: Future Challenges to Small Municipalities - The Cases of Iceland, Faroe Islands and Åland Islands, Nordregio, Stockholm, Sweden, p. 21 (2004)

32. Kristjánsson, S.: Iceland: A Parliamentary Democracy with a Semi-Presidential Constitution. In: Strøm, K., Müller, W.C., Bergman, T. (eds.) Delegation and Accountability in Parliamentary Democracies, p. 399. Oxford University Press, New York (2003)

33. Gylfason, T.: From Collapse to Constitution: The Case of Iceland. Cesifo Working Paper No. 3770 (2012b)

34. Vision of the Information Society, The Icelandic Government (October 1, 1996), http://eng.forsaetisraduneyti.is/information-society/English/nr/890 (retrieved August 23, 2012)

35. Guðmundsson, H.J.: The role of public participation in creating a sustainable development policy at the local level. An example from the City of Reykjavík, Iceland. Report (For publication in: Local Environment. The International Journal of Justice and Sustainability), The City of Reykjavik, Department of Environment (2007)

36. Gylfason, T.: Constitutions: Send in the Crowds (2012a), http://notendur.hi.is

37. Bennet, W.L.: Changing Citizenship in the Digital Age. In: Bennet, W.L. (ed.) Civic Life Online: Learning How Digital Media Can Engage Youth. MIT Press, Cambridge (2007)

38. We gratefully acknowledge financial support from Vinnova, Nordforsk, the Icelandic Centre for Research (Rannis) and Estonian Ministry for Economic Affairs and Communication. The research presented in this article has received funding from Citizen-Centric eGovernment Services Programme

# E-Participation among American Local Governments

Donald F. Norris[1] and Christopher G. Reddick[2]

[1] Department of Public Policy
University of Maryland, Baltimore County
Baltimore, Maryland USA
norris@umbc.edu
[2] Department of Public Administration
University of Texas-San Antonio
San Antonio, Texas USA
chris.reddick@utsa.edu

**Abstract.** Using data from national surveys conducted in 2006 and 2011, we examine whether local governments in the United States have adopted e-participation (a.k.a. e-democracy). The results show that few American local governments have done so. These results are highly inconsistent with the claims of e-democracy advocates. Two important factors account for the lack of e-democracy at the American grassroots: lack of funding and lack of perceived demand. Another reason may be that early predictions were incorrect. Based on these findings, we would expect that e-democracy among US local governments will not be substantially different in the foreseeable future than it is now.

**Keywords:** E-participation, e-democracy, e-government.

## 1   Introduction[1]

In this paper, we examine empirically whether American local governments have adopted electronic participation (e-participation), also known as e-democracy (herein, we use these terms synonymously). For years, scholars and advocates have argued that e-government has the potential not simply both to deliver governmental information and services online and to produce e-democracy (e.g., Nugent, 2001; Garson, 2004: and Ward and Vedel 2006). Proponents' claims about the potential of e-democracy suggest that it will produce primarily positive results in such areas as democratic engagement and deliberation, citizen participation in government and politics, and voter turnout in elections (e.g., Meeks, 1997; Baum and DiMaio, 2000; Becker, 2001; Gronlund, 2001; Hiller and Belanger, 2001; and Westcott, 2001; OECD, 2003; King, 2006; Ward and Vedel, 2006; Amoretti, 2007).

---

[1] This is a revised and expanded version of a paper that we presented at the ECEG 2013 Conference in Como, Italy in June of 2013.

M.A. Wimmer, E. Tambouris, and A. Macintosh (Eds.): ePart 2013, LNCS 8075, pp. 37–48, 2013.

## 2    Defining E-democracy

Currently, there is little agreement in the literature about what e-democracy means in theory or constitutes in practice, which should not be surprising because the same can be said of democratic theory in general.  According to Dahl (1956), "One of the difficulties one must face at the outset is that there is no democratic theory – there are only democratic theories (1)."  The term e-democracy is often conflated with constructs labeled e-participation, virtual democracy, teledemocracy, digital democracy, cyber democracy and e-democracy.

Several authors have offered definitions of e-democracy (e.g., Hacker and van Dijk, 2000; Gronlund, 2001; Kakabadse, et al., 2003; European Commission, 2005; Pratchett, et al., 2005; Tambouris , et al., 2008; and Spirakis, et al., 2010, among many others). Most commonly, definitions of e-democracy are involve the use of ICTs for citizen participation.  Additional elements common to such definitions are normative in nature and suggest purposes for e-democracy, such as improving or enhancing democracy, involving citizens in decision-making, fomenting organizational (that is, governmental) change and transforming governments.

For the purposes of this paper, we define e-democracy descriptively as: *The use of electronic means, principally although not solely through government websites and the Internet, to promote and enhance citizen engagement with and participation in governmental activities, programs and decision-making. (This is the same definition that we used in our survey.)*

## 3    Literature Review

For this research, we conducted an extensive review of the e-democracy literature. The great majority of the works we found were speculative or theoretical in nature or addressed e-government applications. Very few were empirical. We reviewed the empirical works to find those that sought hard evidence (e.g., through case studies, surveys, website analyses, etc.) of the existence of e-democracy anywhere around the world. We discuss findings from this review in the following paragraphs.

Gibson, et al., in 2008, reported that there was little citizen uptake of e-participation efforts in Australia.  They also suggested that "...widespread mobilization is unlikely to occur in the near future (111)." Medaglia (2007) found that very few Italian municipal websites provided opportunities for active citizen participation (93 percent did not).  In an examination of Korean government websites, Lyu, et al. (2007), discovered low citizen uptake of and demand for e-participation efforts.

Astrom (2004) found that although the elected heads of Swedish municipalities favored aspects of e-democracy, there was little evidence of these initiatives on municipal websites. "As the analysis shows, most local governments "...use the Internet for modernization rather than radical regeneration (111)." Astrom, et al. (2011), found little evidence of e-participation in municipal planning in Sweden, despite the fact that a large fraction of local planning directors said that they favored it.

In a paper about e-government in Istanbul, Turkey, Akdogan (2010) was unable to identify any significant amount of e-democracy via governmental websites in that metropolis. Similarly, Sobaci (2010) found that the Turkish parliament website offered very little in terms of e-participation. In a web based survey of civil servants in six New Zealand government departments, Baldwin, et al. (2012), found that while civil servants generally had favorable views of e-government (though not of e-transformation), the actual extent of e-participation efforts among those agencies was limited. This, the authors argued, "...suggests that 'e-participation' largely remains a method of informing, keeping happy and convincing the public (116)."

After conducting an analysis for the *Local e-Democracy National Project* in the UK, Pratchett, et al. (2005), found that "Despite the existence of a range of e-democracy tools and some significant experience of using them in different contests, the penetration and take-up of e-democracy in the UK, as elsewhere, remains limited (4)." Writing about the effect of the Internet on citizen participation in politics in the UK, Ward and Vedel (2006) reported only a limited impact. Indeed, they cautioned that, based on the extant evidence, "the Internet per se is unlikely to stimulate wide-spread mobilization or participation... (215)." Polat and Pratchett (2009) reviewed the UK's local e-government program that operated between 2000 and 2006, which they argued was "...arguably one of the biggest initiatives of its kind in the world (20)," and found that it largely ignored what the authors called online practices of citizenship and instead favored themes of modernization and efficiency.

Studies in the US have similarly failed to find evidence of the adoption of e-democracy by governments there. Using data from a survey of residents of the state of Georgia, Thomas and Streib (2005) categorized citizen visits to government websites as e-commerce, e-research or e-democracy. E-democracy visits were the least frequent. Norris (2006) conducted focus groups with local officials and found that e-democracy was not a consideration when these governments initiated their e-government efforts nor a part of their future planning for e-government.

After examining planning-related websites among US municipalities with populations of 50,000 and greater, Conroy and Evans-Crowley (2006) found little evidence of the use of e-participation tools. Scott (2006) reviewed the websites of the 100 largest US cities and found little evidence that these websites supported "...significant public involvement in accordance with direct democracy theory (349)." Finally, D'Agostino, et al. (2011), reviewed the websites of the 20 largest American cities for their practices of e-government (information and services) and e-governance (participation) and found that information and service delivery predominated and that "...governance applications are only marginally practiced via the Internet. (4)"

A number of scholars have conducted comparative studies, mostly concerning e-government and e-democracy initiatives in the US, the UK, European nations, and by the European Union (EU) and the European Commission (EC). These works, like those reviewed above, have also failed to find evidence that governments in those nations have adopted or are practicing e-democracy (see, for example: Anttiroiko (2001); Chadwick and May (2003); Needham (2004); Zittel (2004); and, Chadwick (2009). The principal conclusion that we draw from these empirical studies is that, despite much early enthusiasm, there is little evidence that governments anywhere around the world have not adopted or are practicing e-democracy.

# 4     Research Methods

We study e-democracy at the American grassroots for two important reasons. First, the US has a large number of general purpose local governments – about 39,000 -- 19,429 municipalities; 16,504 towns and townships; 3,034 counties (Census, 2002). Second, local governments are the closest governments to the people and have the greatest direct impacts on people's lives.

To produce the data needed for this study, we contracted with the International City/County Management Association (ICMA) to conduct a survey of e-democracy among American local governments.[2] (For readers from outside of the US, the ICMA is a major and highly respected local government association that, among other things, conducts and publishes considerable research for its members.) The questionnaire that we used for this study is based in part on an e-democracy survey conducted by ICMA in 2006 (Norris, 2006b). Because we wanted to be able to compare the results from our 2011 survey with data from the 2006 survey, we based the 2011 instrument on the instrument from 2006. However, recognizing that much has changed in the world of e-government and e-democracy in the five years between the surveys, we needed to update the 2006 instrument at least somewhat to capture recent e-democracy issues and trends.

Therefore, prior to developing the 2011 instrument, we asked a convenience sample of local Information Technology (IT) directors and Chief Information Officers (CIOs) to review the 2006 instrument and make recommendations to us based on their expert knowledge of local e-democracy developments since then (see Appendix A). Armed with these expert practitioners' suggestions, we worked cooperatively with the ICMA survey research staff to write the 2011 questionnaire. While many of the questions are identical to those in the 2006 survey, we added a number of new questions. In order to keep the length of the survey manageable, as we added new questions to the 2011 instrument, we deleted a nearly equal number from the 2006 instrument. Note that we told survey respondents that, for our purposes, the terms e-participation and e-democracy were synonymous and, that to simplify things for the questionnaire, we used the term e-participation to mean both.

Of 2,287 surveys mailed in 2011, 684 local governments responded, for a response rate of 29.9 percent. This response rate is consistent with other recent surveys recently conducted by the ICMA at around 30 percent, although lower than the response rate of 36.8 percent 2006 survey. ICMA has noticed a decline in responses to its surveys in recent years and attributes this, in part, to the impact of the "Great Recession" on local staff cutbacks. As a result, local governments understandably have fewer resources to devote to completing surveys (Moulder, 2011).

When we examined the responses for representativeness (that is, of the responding governments to US local governments as a whole), we found that local governments with over 1 million in population were underrepresented. Local governments in the Northeast were underrepresented, while those in other regions of the nation were about evenly represented. Among municipalities, the council manager form of government was substantially overrepresented, while among counties the council-administrator form of government was also overrepresented when compared with governments with elected executives.

---

[2] We wish to thank UMBC's Research Venture Fund and the College of Public Policy research grant at UTSA that enabled us to conduct the survey that produced the data on which this paper is based.

## 5    Findings

We begin by examining whether responding governments had implemented one or more of several possible e-participation activities (Table 1). The first and most important finding from these data is that very few local governments had undertaken any of these e-participation activities. Second, most of the e-participation activities that the governments had undertaken did not provide much, if any, opportunity for meaningful citizen participation, at least by our definition (that is, activities that promote and enhance citizen engagement with and participation in governmental activities, programs and decision-making).

**Table 1.** Has your local government has done any of the following electronically within the past 12 months?

| | 2006 | | 2011 | |
|---|---|---|---|---|
| | N | % | N | % |
| **One-way** | | | | |
| Enabled citizens to view a hearing or meeting | - | - | 447 | 68.3 |
| Enabled citizens to post comments | - | - | 322 | 49.9 |
| Enabled citizens to participate in a poll or survey | - | - | 315 | 47.9 |
| Straw polls | 61 | 8.7 | - | - |
| Web surveys | 180 | 25.2 | - | - |
| **Two-way** | | | | |
| Enabled citizens to participate in a hearing or meeting | - | - | 128 | 19.8 |
| Formal public hearings | 76 | 10.7 | - | - |
| Informal public hearings | 60 | 8.5 | - | - |
| Public consultations | 47 | 6.7 | 204 | 31.8 |
| Non-narrated or guided discussion forums | 49 | 7.0 | 104 | 16.0 |
| Narrated or guided discussion forums | 45 | 6.3 | 96 | 14.7 |
| Enabled citizens to vote in election or referendum | - | - | 51 | 7.9 |
| Referenda | 17 | 2.4 | - | - |
| Conducted electronic town halls | - | - | 33 | 6.1 |
| Citizen petitions | 17 | 2.4 | 35 | 5.4 |
| Voting for local elected officials | 14 | 2.0 | - | - |
| Chat rooms | 9 | 1.3 | 33 | 5.1 |

Note: Blank spaces indicate that the question was not asked in that year.

Only one e-participation activity had been implemented by more than half of the governments responding to the 2011 survey (enabling citizens to view a hearing or meeting, 68.3 percent – not asked in 2006). While an adoption rate of this magnitude might appear impressive, merely viewing a hearing or meeting hardly constitutes meaningful citizen participation. Far fewer governments (only one in five, 19.8 percent) enabled active citizen participation in meetings or hearings. This does, however, represent a substantial increase over 2006.

Two activities approached half of local governments reporting. The first, enabling citizens to post comments (49.9 percent), was not asked in 2006. The second, enabling citizens to participate in a poll or survey (47.9 percent), was asked in 2006, when a quarter of governments (25.2 percent) said that they had conducted web surveys. Posting comments and responding to surveys or polls represents a type of active citizen participation, but it is one-way communication (citizen to government).

Next we inquired about why local governments engage in e-participation projects and activities (Table 2). We did not ask this question in 2006. The great majority (82.5 percent) responded that it was "the right thing to do." Although the survey instrument did not delve into the meaning, we suspect that doing the right thing is driven by both professional norms and a public service motivation.

Slightly more than four in ten governments said that both top local administrators (43.8 percent) and local elected officials (43.3 percent) demanded e-participation. About one third (32.3 percent) said demand by local citizen.

**Table 2.** Why does your local government engage in e-participation? (2011)

|  | N | % |
|---|---|---|
| Demanded or required by local elected officials | 236 | 43.3 |
| Demanded or required by top administrators | 238 | 43.8 |
| Demanded by citizens | 176 | 32.3 |
| Demanded by important local interest groups | 54 | 9.9 |
| It is the right thing to do | 449 | 82.5 |
| To keep up with other local governments | 179 | 32.9 |
| Other | 80 | 14.7 |

Next we asked (2011only) whether these governments' e-participation projects were mostly one-way from governments to citizens or mostly citizen to government (Table 3). The great majority of governments (71.0 percent) said mostly one-way. Only 2.9 percent said mostly citizen to government, while about one-quarter (26.0 percent) said a combination of one- and two-way.

**Table 3.** Are your local government's e-participation projects and activities today mostly communication from the government to citizens or mostly from citizens to government? (2011)

|  | N | % |
|---|---|---|
| Mostly government to citizen | 183 | 33.3 |
| Somewhat government to citizen | 207 | 37.7 |
| A mix of both, about half and half | 143 | 26.0 |
| Somewhat citizen to government | 7 | 1.3 |
| Mostly citizen to government | 9 | 1.6 |

**Table 4.** Barriers

|  | 2006 | | 2011 | |
|---|---|---|---|---|
|  | N | % | N | % |
| Lack of funding | 504 | 75.7 | 515 | 83.5 |
| Need to upgrade technology infrastructure | 408 | 62.2 | 403 | 69.6 |
| Lack of technology staff | 419 | 63.3 | 359 | 60.7 |
| Concerns that the digital divide would prevent participations by some citizens | 290 | 47.2 | 299 | 55.7 |
| Concerns that unrepresentative groups would dominate e-participation channels | 188 | 31.4 | 263 | 49.3 |
| Difficulty justifying the cost of e-participation applications | - | - | 259 | 48.2 |
| When we have provided opportunities or mechanisms for e-participation, few citizens participated | 173 | 30.9 | 247 | 47.8 |
| Issues around security | 335 | 53.9 | 262 | 47.1 |
| Lack of demand by citizens | 396 | 60.3 | 257 | 45.8 |
| Lack of technology expertise | 265 | 41.7 | 240 | 42.9 |
| Issues around privacy | 267 | 44.1 | 227 | 42.5 |
| Lack of demand by elected officials | 377 | 57.7 | 233 | 42.1 |
| Lack of demand from elected officials | 169 | 27.7 | 190 | 36.5 |
| Lack of information about e-participation applications | - | - | 169 | 32.9 |
| Inadequate bandwidth | - | - | 142 | 27.0 |
| Lack of support from top administrators | - | - | 68 | 13.0 |

Note: Blank spaces indicate that the question was not asked in that year

To help understand why so few local governments had adopted e-democracy, we asked about barriers to adoption (Table 4). The top four barriers, all of which were reported by greater than a majority of governments, were lack of funding (83.5 percent – up eight percent from 2006); need to upgrade technology (69.6 percent – up seven percent); lack of technology staff (60.7 percent – down nearly three percent); and concerns about the digital divide (55.7 percent – up nine percent). The second and third of these barriers are directly related to the first, funding.

The survey also asked about whether local elected officials and local administrators promoted e-participation (Tables 6 and 7). Answers here could also be important to understanding why so few local governments have adopted e-participation.

**Table 5.** Elected officials promote e-participation?

|  | 2006 | | 2011 | |
|---|---|---|---|---|
|  | N | % | N | % |
| Don't promote | 363 | 49.5 | 243 | 38.0 |
| Promote some | 207 | 28.2 | 199 | 31.1 |
| Actively promote | 163 | 22.2 | 198 | 30.9 |

**Table 6.** Top appointed officials promote e-participation?

|  | 2006 | | 2011 | |
|---|---|---|---|---|
|  | N | % | N | % |
| Don't promote | 260 | 35.9 | 152 | 24.1 |
| Promote some | 210 | 29.0 | 203 | 32.2 |
| Actively promote | 253 | 35.0 | 275 | 43.6 |

Three in 10 respondents (30.9 percent) to the 2011 survey said elected officials actively promoted e-participation (up 8.7 percent over 2006); a similar fraction (31.1 percent) said that elected officials promoted it some (up 2.9 percent); and 38.0 percent said these officials did not support e-participation (down 11.5 percent). More than four in 10 respondents (43.6 percent, up 8.6 percent over 2006) said that appointed officials actively supported e-participation; one-third (32.2 percent) promoted it some (up 3.2 percent); and one-quarter (24.1 percent) did not promote it (down 11.6 percent).

Finally, we wanted to know whether these local governments perceived any citizen demand for e-participation (Table 8). This, too, could be important to an understanding of why so few local governments had adopted e-participation. Here we asked whether citizens or grassroots organizations actively pushed for e-participation opportunities. We asked the respondents to answer based on a scale of 1 to 5, with 1 meaning no citizen demand and 5 meaning significant citizen demand. For ease of analysis, we collapsed responses 1 and 2 to mean little or no citizen demand, 3 to mean some citizen demand, and 4 and 5 to mean significant citizen demand.

**Table 7.** Are citizen groups actively pushing for e-participation

|  | 2006 | | 2011 | |
|---|---|---|---|---|
|  | N | % | N | % |
| No citizen demand | 583 | 79.8 | 464 | 72.5 |
| Some citizen demand | 115 | 15.8 | 124 | 19.4 |
| Significant citizen demand | 32 | 4.4 | 52 | 8.2 |

The data suggest a slight trend in the direction of greater citizen demand, but the trend is so small that it could be an artifact of the survey, rather than an indication of anything substantive. The percentage of governments indicating the existence of significant citizen demand nearly doubled between 2006 and 2011, but only from 4.4 percent to 8.2 percent (still miniscule). Those indicating no citizen demand diminished slightly (from 79.8 percent to 72.5 percent). "Some" citizen demand remained at around three in 10 respondents (29.0 percent in 2006 and 32.2 percent in 2011).

## 6     Findings and Conclusion

The most striking finding from this study is that few American local governments have adopted e-participation and those that have been adopted, for the most, have not implemented what we would consider meaningful citizen participation. Data from the 2011 survey strongly suggest two explanatory factors: lack of funding and lack of demand. The responding governments cited lack of funding as the most frequently barrier to their adopting e-participation in both 2006 and 2011. Respondents also cited the need to upgrade technology, lack of technology staff, difficulty justifying costs, and lack of technology expertise as barriers – all of which are directly related to lack of funding. This finding is also consistent with surveys of local e-government in the US, where lack of funding nearly always tops the list of barriers to adoption (e.g., Coursey and Norris, 2008).

A second important reason for the lack of local e-democracy in the US may well be lack of demand – from local officials and citizens. When asked about barriers to e-participation, 46 percent of local governments cited lack of demand by citizens and 42 percent said lack of demand by elected officials. Moreover, only three in ten felt that elected officials actively promoted e-participation and about 4 in 10 appointed officials did so. And, only about a quarter of governments perceived any citizen demand at all.

Finally, the literature on e-government increasingly points to the probability that early predictions for e-government were simply wrong. In part, they were technologically deterministic (Coursey and Norris, 2008) and they also were based on a lack or an incomplete understanding of the prior relevant literature (Coursey and Norris, 2008; Kraemer and King, 2006; and Danziger and Andersen, 2002).

Whatever the causes, the reality is that there is very little e-democracy among US local governments. Based on the available evidence, we suspect that the state of e-democracy at the American grassroots it is not likely to change much in the foreseeable future (see also, Norris 2010). Moreover, based on our reading of the empirical studies of e-democracy, we strongly suspect that the state of local e-democracy in the US is more similar to than it is different from that of local e-democracy elsewhere in the world. Of course, only further study will allow us to support or reject these suspicions.

# References

1. Akdogan, I.: Evaluating and improving e-participation in Istanbul. Journal of E-Governance 33, 168–175 (2010)
2. Amoretti, F.: International Organizations ICTs Policies: E-Democracy and E-Government for Political Development. Review of Policy Research 24(4), 331–344 (2007)
3. Annttiroiko, A.-V.: Toward the European information society. Commuincations of the ACM 44(1), 31–35 (2001)
4. Astrom, J.: Digital Democracy: Ideas, intentions and initiatives in Swedish local governments. In: Gibson, R.K., Rommele, A., Ward, S.J. (eds.) Electronic Democracy: Mobilisation, Organization and Participation Via New ICTs. Routledge, London (2004)
5. Astrom, J., Granberg, M., Khakee, A.: Apple pie-spinach metaphor: Shall e-democracy make participatory planning more wholesome? Planning Practice and Research 26(5), 571–586 (2011)
6. Baldwin, J.N., Gauld, R., Goldfinch, S.: What public servants really think of e-government. Public Management Review 14, 105–127 (2012)
7. Becker, T.: Rating the impact of new technologies on democracy. Communications of the ACM 44(1), 39–43 (2001)
8. Baum, C.H., Di Maio, A.: Gartner's Four Phases of E-government Model (2000), http://www.gartner.com (accessed October 15, 2003)
9. Chadwick, A.: Web 2.0: New challenges for the study of e-democracy in an era of informational exuberance. I/S: A Journal of Law and Policy for the Information Society 5(1), 9–42 (2009)
10. Chadwick, A., May, C.: Interaction between states and citizens in the age of the Internet: "E-government" in the United States, Britain and the European Union. Governance: In International Journal of Policy, Administration and Institutions 16(2), 271–300 (2003)
11. Conroy, M.M., Evans-Cowley, J.: E-participation in planning: an analysis of cities adopting on-line citizen participation tools. Environment & Planning C: Government & Policy 24(3), 371–384 (2006)
12. Coursey, D., Norris, D.F.: Models of E-Government: Are They Correct? An Empirical Assessment. Public Administration Review 68(3), 523–536 (2008)
13. Dahl, R.: A Preface to Democratic Theory. University of Chicago Press, Chicago (1956)
14. D'Agostino, M., Schwester, R., Carrizales, T., Melitski, J.: A study of g-government and e-governance: An empirical examination of municipal websites. Public Administration Quarterly 35(1), 4–26 (2011)
15. Danziger, J.N., Andersen, K.V.: The Impacts of Information Technology on Public Administration: An Analysis of Empirical Research from the Golden Age of Transformation. International Journal of Public Administration 25(5), 591–627 (2002)
16. European Commission, Factsheet 10: Transforming Government. European Commission, Brussels (2005)
17. Garson, G.D.: The Promise of Digital Government. In: Pavlichev, A., David Garson, G. (eds.) Digital Government Principles and Best Practices, pp. 2–15. Idea Group Publishing, Hershey (2004)

18. Gibson, R., Lusoli, W., Ward, S.: The Australian public and politics on-line: Reinforcing or reinventing representation? Australian Journal of Political Science 43(1), 111–131 (2008)
19. Gronlund, A.: Democracy in an IT-framed society. Communications of the ACM 44(1), 23–26 (2001)
20. Hacker, K.L., van Dijk, J.: Digital Democracy. Sage Publications, London (2001)
21. Hiller, J.S., Belanger, F.: Privacy Strategies for Electronic Government. In: Abramson, M.A., Means, G.E. (eds.) E-Government 2001. Rowman and Littlefield, Boulder, CO (2001)
22. King, J.: Democracy in the Information Age. Australian Journal of Public Administration 65(2), 16–32 (2006)
23. Kraemer, K.L., King, J.L.: Information Technology and Administrative Reform: Will E-Government be different? International Journal of Electronic Government Research 2(1), 1–20 (2006)
24. Kakabadse, A., Kakabadse, N.K., et al.: Reinventing the Democratic Governance Project through Information Technology? A Growing Agenda for Debate. Public Administration Review 63(1), 44–60 (2003)
25. Lyu, H.-S.: The public's e-participation capacity and motivation in Korea: A web analysis from a new institutionalist perspective. Journal of Information Technology and Politics 4(4), 65–79 (2007)
26. Medaglia, R.: Measuring the diffusion of eParticipation: A survey on Italian local government. Information Polity: The International Journal of Government & Democracy in the Information Age 12(4), 265–280 (2007)
27. Meeks, B.: Better Democracy through technology. Communications of the ACM 40(2), 75–78 (1997)
28. Moulder, E.: Personal Communication. International City/County Management Association, Washington, DC (2011)
29. Needham, C.: The citizen as consumer: e-government in the United Kingdom and the United States. In: Gibson, R.K., Rommele, A., Ward, S.J. (eds.) Electronic Democracy: Mobilisation, Organization and Participation Via New ICTs. Routledge, London (2004)
30. Norris, D.F.: E-government 2020: Plus ca change, plus c'est la meme chose. Public Administration Review 70 (2010)
31. Norris, D.F.: Electronic Democracy at the American Grassroots. International Journal of Electronic Government Research 1(3), 1–14 (2006)
32. Nugent, J.D.: If e-democracy is the answer, what's the question? National Civic Review 90(3), 221–233 (2001)
33. Organization for Economic Cooperation and Development (OECD), Promise and Problems of e-democracy: Challenges of online citizen engagement. OECD, Paris (2003)
34. Polat, R.K., Lawrence, P.: E-citizenship: Reconstructing the public online. In: Durose, C., Greasley, S. (eds.) Changing Local Governance, Changing Citizens? Policy Press, Bristol (2009)
35. Pratchett, L., Wingfield, M., Polat, R.K.: Barriers to e-democracy: Local government experiences and responses. In: A Report Prepared for the Local e-Democracy National Project in the UK, Local Government Research Unit, De Montfort University, Leicester (2005)
36. Scott, J.K.: 'E' the People: Do U. S Municipal Government Web Sites Support Public Involvement? (2006)
37. Sobaci, Z.: What the Turkish parliamentary web site offers to citizens in terms of e-participation: A content analysis. Information Polity 15, 227–241 (2010)

38. Spirakis, G., et al.: The impact of electronic government on democracy: e-democracy through e-participation. Electronic Government: An International Journal 7(1), 75–88 (2010)
39. Tambouris, E., Kalampokis, E.: A survey of e-participation research projects in the European Union. International Journal of Electronic Business 6(6), 554–571 (2008)
40. Thomas, J.C., Streib, G.: E-democracy, e-commerce and e-research: Examining the electronic ties between citizens and governments. Administration and Society 37(3), 259–280 (2005)
41. Ward, S., Vedel, T.: Introduction: The potential of the Internet revisited. Parliamentary Affairs 59(2), 210–225 (2006)
42. Wescott, C.: E-government in the Asia-Pacific Region. Asian Journal of Political Science 9(2), 1–24 (2001)
43. Zittel, T.: Digital parliaments and electronic democracy: A comparison between the US House, the Swedish Riksdag and the German Bundestag. In: Gibson, R.K., Rommele, A., Ward, S.J. (eds.) Electronic Democracy: Mobilisation, Organization and Participation Via New ICTs. Routledge, London (2004)

# Appendix A

## Expert Practitioners

We wish to acknowledge and express our appreciation to the following local government officials who reviewed the 2006 survey instrument and provided comments and suggestions that we then used in developing the 2011 instrument. Any errors or omissions are those of the authors and in no way reflect on these officials or their advice.

Michael Cannon, Chief Information Officer, City of Rockville, Maryland, USA
Ira Levy, Director of Technology and Communication Services, Howard County, Maryland, USA
David Molchany, Deputy County Executive Fairfax County, VA, USA
Elliot Schlanger, Chief Information Officer, State of Maryland
Paul Thorn, IT Manager, City of Annapolis, Maryland

# Modeling the German Legal Latitude Principles

Stephan Neumann[1], Anna Kahlert[2], Maria Henning[2], Philipp Richter[2],
Hugo Jonker[3], and Melanie Volkamer[1]

[1] CASED / Technical University Darmstadt
Hochschulstraße 10
64289 Darmstadt, Germany
{stephan.neumann,melanie.volkamer}@cased.de
[2] University of Kassel
Pfannkuchstraße 1
34109 Kassel, Germany
{a.kahlert,maria.henning,prichter}@uni-kassel.de
[3] University of Luxembourg
rue Richard Coudenhove-Kalergi 6
1359 Luxembourg, Luxembourg
hugo.jonker@uni.lu

**Abstract.** Postal voting was established in Germany in 1956. Based on
the legal latitude of the national legislator, the Federal Constitutional
Court confirmed the constitutionality of postal voting several times. In
contrast, the constitutionality of electronic voting machines, which were
used for federal elections from 2002 to 2005, was rejected as the possibility to control the essential steps in the election was not provided to all
citizens. These two cases emphasize that the legal system allows to limit
realization of election principles to the advantage of other election principles, but that there are limits. In order to introduce new voting systems,
in particular Internet voting systems, it is essential to have guidelines on
what is and what is not acceptable. This work provides such guidelines.
It identifies the principles of the legal latitude in the German constitution, and captures this latitude in a model. This model enables a review
of the constitutionality of new voting systems.

## 1   Introduction

Holding regular parliamentary elections is essential for the exercise of popular
sovereignty and an expression of the democratic form of government. The fundamental decision for democracy is established in Article 20.1 and 2 of the German
Constitution. According to this, the authority of the state originates with the
people and is exercised in elections and votes. The Federal Electoral Act was
enacted in 1956. At this time, the legislator considered traditional paper-based
polling station voting as the main voting channel. Postal voting was only allowed
in exceptional cases. However, the number of absentee voters constantly rose in
the following years as society became more and more mobile (in the 2009 federal elections 21.4% of the cast votes were postal votes). De facto, postal voting
became an alternative to the conventional voting process.

M.A. Wimmer, E. Tambouris, and A. Macintosh (Eds.): ePart 2013, LNCS 8075, pp. 49–56, 2013.

In 1967, the Federal Constitutional Court decided on the constitutionality of postal voting for the first time. In these proceedings, the Constitutional Court declared that the principles of the free and secret elections were not violated [3, Decision: 21, 200:1967]: the increase in election participation offered by postal voting, which translates to an improvement of the principle of the universal elections, is strong enough to offset the impairment of the secret elections, and thus can be accepted. This means, the legislature is entitled to broaden latitude when lending concrete shape to the principles of electoral law within which it must decide whether and to what degree deviations from individual principles of electoral law are justified in the interest of the uniformity of the entire voting system and to ensure the state policy goals which they pursue [3, Decision: 59, 119 (124 f):1981]. However, this latitude has its limitations as the Constitutional Court's "Election Computers Judgment" [3, Decision: 123, 39, (75):2009] illustrates: Hereafter, the use of the Nedap electronic voting machines in the 2005 federal elections was unconstitutional. This judgment was justified by the lack of any possibility to verify the essential steps in the elections. The Constitutional Court argued [3, Decision: 123, 39, (75):2009]:

> "Where the deployment of computer-controlled voting machines aims to rule out inadvertent incorrect markings on voting slips, unwanted invalid ballots, unintentional counting errors or incorrect interpretations of the voter's intention when votes are counted which repeatedly occur in classical elections with voting slips, this serves the interest of the implementation of the equality of elections under Article 38.1 sentence 1 [...] It certainly does not justify by itself foregoing any type of verifiability of the election act."

In order to avoid such a debacle with future new voting systems, it is necessary to have clear guidelines on what is and what is not acceptable when balancing legal provisions. Then the compliance of proposed voting systems can be properly analyzed with the legal latitude *before* their use. This is especially pertinent in the case of Internet voting systems – Internet voting systems are already used in various European countries, and the possibility of voting in such a manner seems to enjoy support amongst German constituents [1].

*Contribution.* This work supports an interdisciplinary dialog by constructing a model for comparing newly proposed voting systems, e.g. an Internet voting system, with established voting systems, e.g. postal voting in the German federal election. We therefore identify and model the principles of the legal latitude. The developed model allows to compare voting systems based on the legal latitude. As such, the model helps developers of new voting systems in identifying and mitigating constitutional shortcomings of their systems which ultimately should lead to the identification or construction of a constitutionally compliant (electronic) voting system. The model is meant as a guideline, which allows conceptual design to be carried out in the right direction, but results will still need legal review in case of planned application of voting systems in political environments. While the model is specifically tailored to the German constitution, we believe the election principles therein to be of a generic nature. As such, adapting the model to another constitution should be straightforward.

## 2    Explanation of Legal Latitude

The election of the representatives is regulated in Article 38 of the German constitution. Correspondingly, the principles of the universal, direct, free, equal, and secret elections established in Article 38.1 sentence 1 are of particular relevance. While the principle of universal elections concerns the eligibility to vote without applying to personal qualities or political, financial or social aspects [3, Decision: 15, 165 (166f):1962. Decision: 36, 139 (141):1973], the principle of equal elections addresses the impact of every valid vote on the election result. That is, every voter needs to have the same number of votes and must be able to cast his or her vote in the same way as any other one [7, § 1, Rn. 43]. Furthermore, all candidates need to be presented equally, so all of them have the same chance to win the election [7, § 1, Rn. 48f]. The principle of direct elections forbids the integration of electoral delegates [3, Decision: 7, 63 (68):1957. Decision: 47, 253 (279):1978] and requires that the representatives get elected through voters only by casting their vote personally [2, Art. 38, Rn. 75] [5, Art. 38, Rn. 101]. The principle of secret elections claims that the voting decision remains secret during and after the election process [9, Art. 38, Rn. 67]. It needs to remain secret whether voters split their votes or cast them based on a single preferred party, whether they spoiled their vote or abstained from voting at all [7, § 1, Rn. 95]. The secrecy of the vote guarantees the principle of free elections which covers the process of opinion making prior to the election as well as the process of vote casting within the election. In formal aspects it ensures the right to choose whether one wants to casts a vote or not. In material regards it provides the freedom to cast a vote for the preferred candidate or party [7, § 1, Rn. 21]. In addition to these principles, another election principle emerging from Article 20.1, 20.2 and 38.1 of the German constitution has been emphasized by the Federal Constitutional Court in 2009 [3, Decision: 123, 39:2009]: The so called public nature of elections requires that all essential steps in the elections are subject to public examinability unless other constitutional interests justify an exception. However, the German constitution only gives the election principles but does not purport a specific voting system. The legislator needs to provide a system that fulfills the illustrated principles as best as possible. This follows from Article 38.3 of the German constitution. After this, a federal act needs to define full particulars regarding the federal elections. Note that this article contains no legal proviso but authorizes and obligates the federal legislator to enact an execution law [8], [2, Art. 38, Rn. 61]. In essence, this article constitutes a regulation that assigns the exclusive law authority to the Federation in order to shape the German electoral law [2, Art. 38, Rn. 125]. Even though all election principles are of equal importance in the context of parliamentary elections [3, Decision: 99, 1 (13):1998], they cannot be fulfilled simultaneously [3, Decision: 59, 119 (124):1981]. Due to the necessity to balance all principles, a legal latitude is open for the legislator [2, Art. 38, Rn. 62]. Colliding election principles need to be assigned to one another to such an extent that each of them is fulfilled in the best possible way [3, Decision: 59, 119 (124):1981]. Insofar, the legislature is entitled to broad latitude when lending concrete shape to the principles of electoral law within which it must decide if deviations from individual principles of electoral law are justified in the interest of the uniformity of the entire election system and to ensure the state policy goals which they pursue [3, Decision: 123, 39 (71):2009]. Furthermore, while weighing the election principles the convention of the unity of the constitution needs to be respected [2, Art. 38, Rn. 166]. According to this, restrictions of constitutionally required positions are possible only in case a collision with other principles of constitutional status is given and "practical accordance" [4] regarding the restricted principle can be made [2, Art. 38, Rn. 61]. During the necessary consideration, the basic principle of commensurability is of great importance, i.e., a relation of two mutable values that comes as close as possible to the particular optimization, not a relation between a constant purpose and one or more variable instruments [4]. Since all election principles have equal potential [3, Decision: 99, 1 (13):1998], it needs to be decided in each individual case which election principle can be restricted in favor of another one. In case the legislator decides to realize one election principle in the best possible way as it happened with the implementation of postal voting in view of the principle of the universal elections, it is not objectionable from a constitutional point of view as long as this decision does not go along with an exceeding restriction or hazard of other election principles [3, Decision: 59, 119 (125):1981]. The Federal Constitutional Court only reviews whether the legislature has remained within the boundaries of the latitude or whether it has violated a valid constitutional election principle by overstepping these boundaries [3, Decision: 123, 39 (71):2009].

From the legal latitude discussed in this section, three principles can be derived: the principle of *minimum degree of fulfillment*, the principle of *necessity*, and the principle of *overall degree of fulfillment*. The general view is that the current voting system fulfills the election principles in an acceptable way, allowing it to be used as the reference system: any new voting system must therefore simultaneously fulfill all three principles with reference to the current voting system.

## 3    Modeling the Legal Latitude Principles

In this section, the three principles of the legal latitude are modeled. Before diving into the modeling process, we shall first provide the reader with conventions used throughout this work.

### 3.1    Foundations of the Model

The degree to which individual election principles are fulfilled by a specific voting system can be charted by a network diagram, having one axis for each considered principle (see Figure 1 for a reference system and Figure 2 for a proposed new voting system). On each axis is marked to which degree the election principle is fulfilled by the system under consideration. Higher degrees of fulfillment are plotted further out from the center than lower ones.

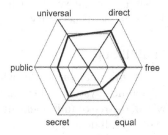 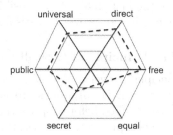

**Fig. 1.** Reference voting system        **Fig. 2.** Proposed new voting system

## 3.2   The Principle of Minimum Degree of Fulfillment

The principle of *minimum degree of fulfillment* requires that a minimum degree of fulfillment has to be achieved for all election principles. That means that a voting system is tied to the minimum degree of fulfillment of all election principles. For a given minimum degree of fulfillment $deg_{min}$, the correlation is modeled as follows:

$$\min_{a \in SEP} (degree_a^{system_{new}}) \geq deg_{min} \tag{1}$$

For an election principle $a$ from the set of election principles $SEP$, the mathematical term $degree_a^S$ denotes the degree of fulfillment of $a$ in system $S$.

Figure 3 shows the proposed voting system in reference to a potentially prescribed minimum degree of fulfillment. It can be seen that the hypothetical voting system complies with the principle of minimum degree of fulfillment.

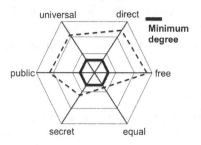

**Fig. 3.** Minimum degree of fulfillment in new voting system

### 3.3    The Principle of Necessity

An election principle may be fulfilled to a lesser degree in a proposed voting system than in a reference system if and as far as this is necessary to fulfill another election principle to a higher degree than in the reference system, thus enhancing the reference system with respect to that principle.

Due to the fact that not all possible voting system alternatives are available, it is not possible to prove the satisfaction of the principle of necessity.

### 3.4    The Principle of Overall Degree of Fulfillment

The principle of overall degree of fulfillment is an optional principle, when a proposed system is only meant to enhance a reference system. Then the two principles described before apply strictly and overall degree of fulfillment may be viewed as good practice. However, the principle of overall degree of fulfillment is obligatory, when a proposed voting system is meant to replace a reference system or to be applied equally with a reference system. Compliance with the principle of overall degree of fulfillment is achieved when all election principles are fulfilled at least to an equal degree as in the reference system (refer to Formula (2a)) or when more are fulfilled to a higher degree than to a lesser (refer to Formula (2b)). These alternate correlations are modeled as follows:

$$\forall a \in SEP : (degree_a^{system_{new}} - degree_a^{system_{old}}) \geq 0 \tag{2a}$$

$$\exists SEP' \text{ s.t. } |SEP'| > \frac{|SEP|}{2}, \forall a \in SEP' :$$
$$(degree_a^{system_{new}} - degree_a^{system_{old}}) > 0 \tag{2b}$$

There may also be cases where one election principle is fulfilled to a very high degree in the proposed system and may balance more than one lesser fulfillment, but these cases may not be appropriately expressed in abstract rules but depend very much on the individual case and must be reviewed legally in any case from the beginning.

Figure 4 shows a comparison of two voting systems (the voting systems depicted by the solid line in Figure 1 and the system depicted by the broken line in Figure 2), where moving from the reference system to the new system adheres to the principle of overall degree of fulfillment as modeled by Formula (2b). This is shown by the fact that four election principles are improved in the new system (public, universal, direct, free), while only two principles are weakened (equal, secret).

### 3.5    Model Compliance

If a system fulfills the two (optionally three) legal latitude principles (where the reference system acts as a baseline for comparison), it can most likely be seen as legally acceptable. If not all principles are fulfilled, this entails an ad hoc decision and it requires an additional interdisciplinary evaluation.

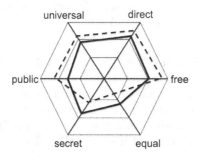

**Fig. 4.** Overall degree of fulfillment in both voting systems

# 4 Conclusion and Future Work

In the development and usage of voting systems for federal elections, not all constitutional election principles can be deployed in purity and impairments of these principles among each other must be accepted. From the legal point of view the legal latitude enables the legislator to constrain the fulfillment of certain constitutional principles in favor of others. Based on an analysis of the legal latitude, we developed a model capable of comparing voting systems with regard to fulfillment of election principles. To build our model, we decomposed the legal latitude into its basic principles and modeled these principles. The developed model will support technical developers in the creation of new voting systems on a legal basis.

The focus of this work is on the evaluation of voting systems based on election principles. In the context of Internet voting and electronic authentication in the polling station certain additional constitutional rights play an important role: the Right to Informational Self-Determination and Secrecy of Telecommunications. How these two basic rights have to be considered in the procedure described in here is a topic for future research.

In its current state, the model does not specify measures to assess the degree of fulfillment of specific election principles. In order to estimate the degree for abstract election principles, these principles must be refined into more precise requirements. Consequently, in the future, the herein developed reference model will be refined by integrating measures to assess the degree of fulfillment of election principles built upon fine-grained requirements.

To date, the model serves as a reference model for parliamentary elections in Germany. In the future, we plan to apply the developed model to a concrete election scenario and a concrete newly proposed voting system. At this point in time, the authors do not consider any Internet voting system an adequate substitute for postal voting for German federal elections. The most promising scenario in which to consider Internet voting seems the upcoming German social election[1] in 2017. As outlined by Richter [6], social elections do not demand the public nature principle of elections in its full strength.

**Acknowledgment.** This paper has been partially developed within the projects "ModIWa2" - Juristisch-informatische Modellierung von Internetwahlen, "VerKonWa" - Verfassungskonforme Umsetzung von elektronischen Wahlen, which are funded by the German Science Foundation (DFG), and partially within the project "BoRoVo" - Board Room Voting - which is funded by the German Federal Ministry of Education and Research (BMBF).

# References

1. Forsa survey: Jeder zweite würde online wählen (2013),
   http://www.microsoft.com/germany/newsroom/
   pressemitteilung.mspx?id=533684 (accessed May 31, 2013)
2. Dreier, H.: Grundgesetz-Kommentar. Morlok Siebeck Verlag (2006)
3. Federal Constitutional Court. Decisions of the Federal Constitutional Court (BVer-fGE) referred to in this work
4. Hesse, K.: Grundzüge des Verfassungsrechts der Bundesrepublik Deutschland, §2, Rn. 72. C.F. Müller (1995)
5. Maunz, T., Dürig, G.: Grundgesetz-Kommentare (2013)
6. Richter, P.: Wahlen im Internet rechtsgemäß gestalten. Nomos (2012)
7. Schreiber, W.: Bundeswahlgesetz-Kommentar. Carl Heymanns (2009)
8. Mangoldt, H.V.: Kommentar zum Grundgesetz (Art. 38 GG, Rn. 157). Franz Vahlen (2010)
9. von Münch, I., Kunig, P.: Grundgesetz-Kommentar. C.H. Beck (2012)

---

[1] The social election is conducted via postal voting every six years to elect bodies of the social insurances. There are over 40 millions eligible voters.

# Social Media Participation and Local Politics: A Case Study of the Enschede Council in the Netherlands

Robin Effing[1], Jos van Hillegersberg[1], and Theo W.C. Huibers[2]

[1] University of Twente, School of Management and Governance,
P.O. Box 217, 7500 AE, Enschede, The Netherlands
[2] University of Twente, Human Media Interaction, Enschede, The Netherlands
{r.effing,j.vanhillegersberg,t.w.c.huibers}@utwente.nl

**Abstract.** Social media such as Facebook, Twitter and YouTube are often seen as political game changers. Yet little is known of the effects of social media on local politics. In this paper the Social Media Participation Model (SMPM) is introduced for studying the effects of social media on local political communities. The SMPM aims to explore the relationship between Social Media Participation and Community Participation. The model comprises four constructs: Social Media Choice, Social Media Use, Sense of Community and Community Engagement. The design of the case study was based on the SMPM and took place among the members and parties of the Enschede council, from a large municipality in the Netherlands. Social media participation levels were measured and compared with the Social Media Indicator (SMI). A negative correlation between Social Media Use and Sense of Community has been discovered. However, we could not find a causal effect that explains this correlation. To analyze the effects in more detail, we show directions for further improvement of the model.

**Keywords:** social media, council, politics, participation, web 2.0.

## 1 Introduction

Social media change the game of politics both on a national and local scale. Politicians increasingly use social media such as Facebook, Twitter, Blogs, YouTube and LinkedIn. Recent political events showed that social media influence the rules of political participation today.

During the "Arab spring" in 2011, social media allowed social movements to reach once-unachievable goals eventually leading to the fall of oppressing regimes [1]. In presidential elections, the cases of Barack Obama (US) and Ségolène Royal (France) show that effective social media campaigns can make a difference in politics [2-9]. A US Congress Facebook message increased the voting outcome with 340,000 voters [10].

Yet we know little about which social media strategies contribute to political party communities and which do not. The Twitter campaign from the CDU (Germany), for instance, did not result in high numbers of reach and engagement [11].

M.A. Wimmer, E. Tambouris, and A. Macintosh (Eds.): ePart 2013, LNCS 8075, pp. 57–68, 2013.
© IFIP International Federation for Information Processing 2013

Furthermore, more research should be carried out to understand how social media affects local politics. Local politicians may think that integrating social media in their political work is easy. However, an effective social media strategy requires more than just creating profiles to have a presence on social media. "Considering the novel culture of social media and the shift in power relations, the internalization of social media expertise within an organization may prove to be a much harder task than expected" [12]. Next to the national elections cases, more attention should be paid to the effects of social media on a local scale as well. Local concerns should be an explicit part of the social media strategy in order to be effective [13-14].

In order to maximize the impact of time and effort spent on social media, members of local councils would like to understand the effects of these tools on their work and political communities. Municipalities and their councils are relatively near to the citizens. Social media can potentially help people to establish and foster authentic relations with each other [13]. However, little is known about the effects of social media participation by politicians on such local political communities. Political party communities are relational communities for a professional cause and are not necessarily territorially bounded [15]. The members of political parties are engaged in their communities because of shared beliefs, goals or interests. Does social media participation by members of the party contribute to a stronger party-community? Or is the opposite true? Some parties make social media participation too much of a goal in itself, without any underlying strategy. Such initiatives seem destined to fail.

The aim of this paper is to investigate social media effects within local politics and to learn from local practices. To achieve our goal, we conducted a case study based on the Social Media Participation Model. This model can be used for exploring causal effects of social media participation on communities. The model is still in an early stage of development. By applying this model as the theoretical lens for a case study we can both validate the model and increase understanding of the effects of social media.

Only few models and methods are aimed at understanding the effects of social media participation. The Unified Theory of Acceptance and Use of Technology (UTAUT) from Venkatesh et al. [16],[17] is known to be used to study social media acceptance. However, this theory, and related ones such as the Technology Acceptance Model (TAM), focus merely on adoption of technology and do not capture the effects of use. Other theoretical frameworks from the field of e-participation, such as the participation ladder from Macintosh [18-21], do help to place social media use against a theoretical background, but are too abstract to investigate effects in detail. Therefore, we designed the Social Media Participation Model (Figure 1), aimed at capturing the effects of Social Media Participation on Community Participation. We conducted a case study within the Enschede council and its members based on this model. The municipality of Enschede is located in the eastern part of the Netherlands and has more than 150,000 citizens.

The remainder of this paper is structured as follows. First, we will introduce the Social Media Participation Model. Second, we will clarify our methodology. Third, we will share results from the case of the local government in Enschede. Finally, we will discuss our observations and we will present our future research agenda.

## 2    Introducing the Social Media Participation Model

Since models to study the effects of social media within the non-profit sector are still scarce [22], we decided to design the Social Media Participation Model for this purpose. This is a model that is aimed to explore the relationship between Social Media Participation on the one hand and Community Participation on the other hand (Figure 1).

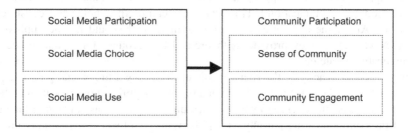

**Fig. 1.** The Social Media Participation Model

The model takes a high-level approach to a complex reality of social behavior of politicians in both the online and offline world. This means that there can be many (causal) relationships between the included concepts. However, the model concentrates on the assumed causal relation between Social Media Participation by politicians and their Community Participation. We assume that being active on social media affects to some extent the community participation of a politician.

We have three grounds to assume the causality. First, the number of relationships between people tends to increase when people use social network sites, because these sites reveal relationships by making them transparant [23]. As a result, users of social media tend to make more connections with each other, bridging relationship networks [24]. Second, social media do not completely replace offline communication, but augment them, reducing the transaction costs of communication [8],[25]. Third, by taking part in online communities, people become more aware of their connections to others in the community which leads to a stronger bonding to the community in general [24].

After a literature review [22] regarding social media, participation and communities, we decided to derive four more specific constructs from the two concepts in the model.

### 2.1    Social Media Choice

According to Kaplan and Haenlein social media: "is a group of Internet-based applications that build on the ideological and technological foundations of Web 2.0, and that allow the creation and exchange of User Generated Content" [26]. While some politicians start using social media just because they feel they cannot stay behind, others approach them as being part of underlying communication strategies. The choice for certain social media out of the vast amount of available social media channels can be dependent of multiple factors but: "Nothing impacts the success of a Social Media effort more than the choice of its purpose" [27]. However, not all communication by social media is appropriate for all communication strategies. Therefore, we have to take the choice and appropriateness of Social Media into account when determining variations in impact on the dependent concept of Community Participation.

After a literature review [22], we selected the theories of Social Presence [28], Media Appropriateness [29],[30] and the Theory of Cognitive and Affective Organizational Communication [31] to warrant Social Media Choice as a construct in the model. All of these theories have shortcomings and should not be applied too rigidly. Nevertheless, they provide us theoretical backgrounds for media choice and communication strategies.

The expected capacity of the social media channels regarding social presence [28] and interaction [29] can influence the choice made by a political party or its members. Social presence is "the degree to which a medium is perceived as conveying the presence of the communicating participants" [28]. While the theory was initially created for telecommunications, it is currently used for social media as well [26]. For different forms of media, differences exist in their capacity to transmit immediate feedback, the interaction capacity [29]. Different communication strategies (for example Exchanging information, Problem solving and Generating Ideas [28], or Contextualization, Affectivity or Control [31]) can require different choices in social media channels (e.g. Twitter for higher level of interaction, YouTube for higher level of social presence). There can be differences in effectiveness of social media use for different purposes. The choice can even be inappropriate for certain communication tasks [26],[30]. Therefore, the strategy and choice determine for a large part the effectiveness of social media for communication goals. Decisions can be made on both the individual and the group level. Sometimes decisons are based on a strategy-plan considering goals, media-channel choice, target audiences and local concerns [12-14].

To explore to what extent politicians use these social media channels, we introduce the next construct of the model: Social Media Use, which is a more quantitative approach.

## 2.2   Social Media Use

We decided to create an instrument, the Social Media Indicator, with metrics based on the participation ladder of Macintosh, including a distinction between e-Enabling and e-Engaging. Macintosh [18-21] created a three-step participation ladder, which can be applied to the Social Media phenomenon from a high-level perspective. The first step on the ladder is e-Enabling. At this step, party members provide access and information to citizens. The second step is e-Engaging. At this step, politicians react, have conversations and interact with citizens based on dialogue. The third step is e-Empowering. At this step, citizens are being invited to take part in the political activities. Politicians start working together with citizens, empowering them with responsibilities, tasks and opportunities to collaborate with the party's community. Previous efforts at trying to empower citizens often failed because of low levels of citizen engagement in electronic tools and other technological and democratic shortcomings [32-34]. As Social Media mature, the question remains if social media eventually will lead to the step of e-Empowering. This step is left out of the instrument because it is too difficult to recognize by direct metrics without additional content analysis. In the section of methods, we show our instrument for the measurements. We now continue with the dependent side of the causal model: community participation.

### 2.3    Sense of Community

Community participation has both a tacit and an apparent construct. We address the tacit construct as Sense of Community (SOC), which is: "a feeling that members have of belonging, a feeling that members matter to one another and to the group and a shared faith that members' needs will be met through their commitment to be together" [15]. The Sense of Community can be further divided in four elements [15]: membership, influence, reinforcement and shared emotional connection. The importance of these four elements can vary depending of the type of the community [15]. The theory can be used for studying and comparing different kinds of communities, including political parties and council communities.

### 2.4    Community Engagement

Community engagement is the more apparent construct of community participation. The construct reflects the actual behavior of community members, such as time spent in the community and existing communication ties between members. Since communities are networks of people, the communication ties between politicians can also reflect their actual engagement levels. Christakis and Fowler [2] found out for instance that being connected to each other in a social network influences political party campaigns, voting and co-sponsorship within politics. The social network is more of a group characteristic and makes sense on a higher level: the community level instead of the individual level. Community engagement can be approached from various abstraction levels. In our case we distinguish the individual level and the network level. All four constructs have been explained and we can continue with the methodology that underpinned our case study.

## 3    Methodology

The proposed design we present here is based on comparative case study research [7], including both quantitative and qualitative data collection techniques.

We propose a multi-level approach for studies incorporating both the individual level (e.g. the politician) and the group level (e.g. the political faction). The level of inquiry is the individual level. To recognize effects, it is required to conduct more measurements with time intervals in between.

## 3.1    Social Media Choice: Qualitative Interviews

A selection of members from all parties in the Enschede council were invited for face-to-face semi-structured open interviews. Specific members were selected for interviews in collaboration with the municipality of Enschede. The questions were partly exploratory for getting to know their existing strategy plans. Another part of the interviews was based on the theories of Short et al. [28], Rice [30] and Te'eni [31] and were more directly aimed at understanding their choices for their social media practices. Eight parties accepted the invitation. All interviews were recorded, transcribed and analyzed.

## 3.2    Social Media Use: Quantitative Metrics of the Social Media Indicator

The Social Media Indicator (SMI) has been developed to compare how active community members use social media [22]. This instrument was used in five prior studies, mostly regarding social media use by political candidates and elections outcome. The division between e-Enabling and e-Engagement is based on the e-Participation ladder from Macintosh [18-21]. Due to privacy settings and application programming interface (API) limitations some potentially valuable metrics are excluded from the Social Media Indicator, such as Wall Posts on Facebook. Nevertheless, the SMI provides us with indicative scores. The metrics of the SMI are presented in Table 1 and are based on social media-reach numbers from market researchers ComScore and NewCom. Other social media with high reach can be added for specific studies. The symbol # means: the number of. Scores can be calculated with the metrics of the SMI to indicate the use of members. We calculated scores for all members of the Enschede council based on the profile information they provided us with an online questionnaire.

Table 1. The Social Media Indicator

| Social media: | e-Enabling: | e-Engagement: |
|---|---|---|
| **Facebook profile** | # friends | # likes |
| **Twitter account** | # tweets | # following |
|  | # followers | # retweets* |
|  |  | # replies and mentions* |
| **YouTube channel** | # videos | # comments |
| **LinkedIn** | # connections | # recommendations |
| **Blog** | # posts | # replies |
| **Total:** | **Sub score Contribution** | **Sub score Interaction** |
| **TOTAL SMI = SUB SCORE CONTRIBUTION + SUB SCORE INTERACTION** | | |
| *of the last 200 Tweets (to limit contribution to total score). | | |

## 3.3    Sense of Community: Questionnaire with 24 Statements

To measure the Sense of Community we make use of the SCI-2 instrument [36]. It consists of 24 statements that respondents can respond to on a Likert scale and provides a standardized scoring instruction to evaluate belonging, influence, reinforcement and shared emotional connection. We sent this questionnaire to all members of the Enschede council. The total SCI-2 score gives an assessment of the individual sense of community of a member. We asked them for both the overall council community and their own party community as a part of the Enschede council. Because the scale is 24 * 3 points, there is a maximum of 72 points for the SCI-2.

### 3.4    Commmunity Engagement: Questionnaire and Social Network Analysis

In the questionnaire we inquired about the average time members spent per week on their council-affiliation. While such a question does not lead to very reliable information, since members can exaggerate or have different ways of counting, it does help to understand how actively the politicians perceive their own engagement. If there are more reliable ways to obtain the engagement, these should be preferred. Additionally, we created social network diagrams of the primary communication relationships within the community. These network diagrams can be made after asking the member for a top five list of other members of the council, with which they communicate the most. This helps to understand how communication, power and influence within a community are distributed [2].

### 3.5    Data Analysis, Statistics and Social Networking Analysis

We analyzed our four constructs and relationships as follows. For the quantitative constructs we applied regular forms of statistical analysis (means, graphs and Std. Dev.). For the qualitative interviews we took an exploratory approach to capture motivations, and underlying reasons for social media choices. Social networking analysis software, such as Gephi, was used to create network diagrams of the existing ties between members. Furthermore, to discover effects, we applied various statistical methods with SPSS to explore possible relationships between the constructs.

## 4    Case Study Results from the Enschede Council

The municipality of Enschede, located in the eastern part of the Netherlands with more than 150,000 citizens, was interested in how social media affected the work of politicians within their council. In April 2011 the initiative was taken to start this research project. The case study was conducted between June 2011 and March 2013. The 39 members of the Enschede council were elected in March 2010. The members represent nine different parties (political factions).

The design of the case study was based on the Social Media Participation Model. The researchers took the role of observers and did not interfere with any social media planning or helping the candidates. Two measurements were carried out regarding the entire population of the council (n=39). The first measurement (T1) was from November 2011 until April 2012 (n = 29 response 74%). The second measurement (T2) was from October 2012 until December 2012 (n= 26 response 67%). We will now present results from this study.

## 4.1    Social Media Choice

Twitter is the preferred social platform of the interviewees of the council. The members believe Twitter can contribute the most towards increasing political participation of citizens. However, members argue the importance of "the physical side of communication … it is important to keep having conversations" (Interviewee). And, based on their experiences, the members do not think that social media is revolutionary for local politics: "Twitter did not deliver the miracle we hoped for in advance". Only one of the nine political parties prepared a social media strategy. Some parties had a few loosely defined agreements about what they do with social media. Generally, the parties did not approach social media strategically: "we are in the end amateurs, we just do something, in our free time … we would like social media strategies, but we need external help for that" (Interviewee).

One interviewee, one of the most active social media users of the council, mentioned difficulties with interaction: "during the past months where I have been spokesman on Facebook, I have created links to the documents we discuss so that people can read them and you would like to see interaction as a result, but that does not happen."

## 4.2    Social Media Use

Based on the Social Media Indicator we discovered that 93% of the members of the Enschede council use social media (n=28). 93% of all members use LinkedIn. 82% uses Twitter. Figure 2 shows a chart of the social media use by all members of the council sorted from high to low (Entire history use until April 2012). The lighter areas in the bars indicate the part of the communication that is interaction (e-Engagement) while the darker areas indicate contribution (e-Enabling). The highest SMI score of a member in this measurement was 19,141.

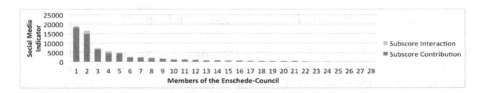

**Fig. 2.** Social Media Use (Sorted high to low) of members on until April 2012

The second measurement captures a shorter period of time (April – November) and shows increased levels of interaction (e-Engagement) and fewer differences between members in comparison with measurement one in figure 3. The highest score in the second measurement was 7,598 from the same member as in the first measurement.

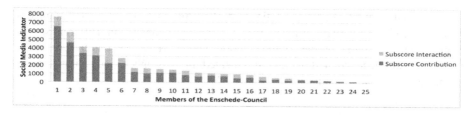

**Fig. 3.** Social Media Use (Sorted high to low) of members from April 2012 – November 2012

## 4.3    Sense of Community

96% (n=23) of the members of the council have a positive score (37-72) for the Sense of Community (SCI-2) within their parties. The second measurement showed an increase of positive scores to 100% (n=21). A SCI-2 score above 36 is positive. Values between 0 and 36 in the figure below are negative scores.

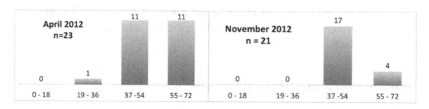

**Fig. 4.** Measurement of SCI of members in April (left) and November (right) 2012

One of the four factors of the Sense of Community was relatively low for all members, the shared emotional connection. This makes sense since the parties (fractions) are primarily professional communities and offer fewer incentives for emotional bonding.

## 4.4    Community Engagement

The average member of the Enschede council spends 23.8 hour per week (n=20) (Std. Dev. 7,9) on his or her job.

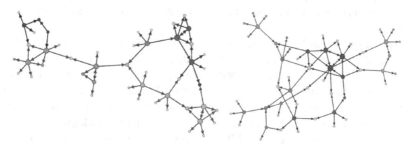

**Fig. 5.** Social network diagrams April (left) and November (right) 2012

The social network diagrams in figure 5 show the primary communication ties between members. Every dot is a person and every line a connection. Different shades of grey refer to different parties. In the diagrams above, we can see that the community of the Enschede council is less fragmented in November, indicating a more connected council community.

### 4.5    Analysis of Relationships between Concepts

We found a statistically significant negative correlation between Social Media Use and Sense of Community of members. The Spearman's rho correlation is - .454* (*significant at the 0.05 level, n=23). This means that, on average, members who are relatively more active users of social media have relatively lower scores on sense of community. This correlation remained present in the second measurement. We also analyzed effects from SMI on SCI. We checked for variance (with a SPLIT-PLOT ANOVA Repeated Measures) based on splitting the council in two groups. One group of frequent social media users (SMI above 1,000) and a control group. No variance could be proven to signal a causal effect in the Enschede council. Also this analysis showed that the group of frequent social media users had a lower sense of community than the controlgroup of infrequent users.

## 5    Discussion and Future Research

In the case of the Enschede council we see that social media participation by political parties and their members did not make much of a difference for the political game yet. The parties seem to struggle with finding ways to use social media for their own benefits. In Enschede, the parties have not yet professionalized their social media campaigns. Furthermore, strategic approaches considering social media choice, goals, target audience selection and local concerns are still to be defined.

We found a negative correlation (-.454) between social media use and sense of community. However, during the period of the research, the sense of community of members was not influenced by the social media use. This leaves us with a paradox. What does cause the negative correlation? Do members that already have lower levels of sense of community tend to use social media more? This may be the case if there is less bonding with colleagues. Or is it valuable to be connected to others outside the party-fraction, bridging with citizens and organizations? These questions still remain unanswered.

The model can be further refined to recognize more precisely how social media affects political communities such as the Enschede council and its parties. By working with the Social Media Participation model and the specific design of the case-study we encountered four limitations. First, monitoring the use of social media with this instrument has limitations for presenting the real-world behavior of members. Members could have use-scores that actually represent a different background or a large offline network size influences the SMI score. Second, the Sense of Community cannot be separated for online or offline behavior and it can consist of various echelons (such as local versus national communities). Third, the decision for members whether or not to participate in social media is sometimes dependent from a higher authority level in the political party, exceeding the communication strategies as provided in our model. Fourth, the SMPM is based on a linear causal view, while in reality the constructs also influence each other in cycles and maybe Community Participation influences the Social Media Participation.

In the near future we will finish measuring two other types of non-profit communities: church-communities and charities. Additionally, we will develop a tool to automatically retrieve SMI scores for social media use. We have also planned to integrate more social media strategy theory in our work. We encourage other scholars to contribute to more refined models and methods to investigate how social media affects local politics and their communities.

**Acknowledgements.** The case study was initiated in collaboration with the Municipality of Enschede and the broader research project is supported and funded by Saxion University of Applied Sciences, Enschede, The Netherlands.

# References

1. Howard, P.N., Hussain, M.M.: The role of digital media. Journal of Democracy 22, 35–48 (2011)
2. Christakis, N.A., Fowler, J.H.: Connected: The Surprising Power of Our Social Networks and How They Shape Our Lives. Little, Brown and Company (2009)
3. Citron, D.K.: Fulfilling Government 2.0's Promise with Robust Privacy Protections. Arguendo, The George Washington Law Review 78, 822–845 (2010)
4. Greengard, S.: The First Internet President. Comm. of the ACM 52, 16–18 (2009)
5. Lilleker, D.G., Pack, M., Jackson, N.: Political Parties and Web 2. 0: The Liberal Democrat Perspective. Political Studies 30, 105–112 (2010)
6. Montero, M.D.: Political e-mobilisation and participation in the election campaigns of Ségolène Royal (2007) and Barack Obama (2008). Quaderns Del. Cac. 33, 27–34 (2007)
7. Talbot, D.: How Obama Really Did It: The Social-networking Strategy that took an Obscure Senator to the Doors of the White House. Technology Review (2008)
8. Ren, J., Meister, H.-P.: Drawing Lessons from Obama for the European Context. The Internetional Journal of Public Participation 4, 12–30 (2010)
9. Zhang, W., Johnson, T.J., Seltzer, T., Bichard, S.L.: The Revolution Will be Networked. Social Science Computer Review 28, 75–92 (2010)
10. Kiderra, I.: Facebook Boosts Voter Turnout. UCSan Diego News Centre (2012), http://ucsdnews.ucsd.edu/pressreleases/facebook_fuels_the_friend_vote
11. Jungherr, A.: Online Campaigning in Germany: The CDU Online Campaign for the General Election 2009 in Germany. German Politics 21(3), 317–340 (2012)
12. Munar, A.M.: Destination Management Social Media Strategies and Destination Management. Scandinavian Journal of Hospitality and Tourism 12(2), 101-120, 37–41 (2012)
13. Bottles, K., Sherlock, T.: Who should manage your social media strategy? Physician Executive 37, 68–72 (2011)

14. Berthon, P.R., Pitt, L.F., Plangger, K., Shapiro, D.: Marketing meets Web 2.0, social media, and creative consumers. Business Horizons 55, 261–271 (2012)
15. McMillan, D.W., Chavis, D.M.: Sense of community: A definition and theory. Journal of Community Psychology 14, 6–23 (1986)
16. Venkatesh, V., Morris, M., Davis, G., Davis, F.: User Acceptance of Information Technology: Toward a Unified View. MIS Quarterly 27, 425–478 (2003)
17. Curtis, L., et al.: Adoption of social media for public relations by nonprofit organizations. Public Relations Review 36, 90–92 (2010)
18. Macintosh, A., Smith, E.: Citizen Participation in Public Affairs. In: Traunmüller, R., Lenk, K. (eds.) EGOV 2002. LNCS, vol. 2456, pp. 256–263. Springer, Heidelberg (2002)
19. Grönlund, Å.: ICT Is Not Participation Is Not Democracy – eParticipation Development Models Revisited. In: ePart 2009, pp. 12–23 (2009)
20. Medaglia, R.: Measuring the diffusion of eParticipation: A survey on Italian local government. Information Polity 12, 265–280 (2007)
21. Sommer, L., Cullen, R.: Participation 2.0: A Case Study of e-Participation. In: 42nd Hawaii International Conference on System Sciences (2009)
22. Effing, R., Van Hillegersberg, J., Huibers, T.W.C.: Measuring the Effects of Social Media Participation on Political Party Communities. In: Reddick, C.G., Aikins, S.K. (eds.) Web 2.0 Technologies and Democratic Governance (2012)
23. Boyd, D.M., Ellison, N.B.: Social Network Sites: Definition, History, and Scholarship. Journal of Computer-Mediated Communication 13, 210–230 (2008)
24. Tomai, M., et al.: Virtual communities in schools as tools to promote social capital with high schools students. Computers & Education 54, 265–274 (2010)
25. Vergeer, M., Pelzer, B.: Consequences of media and Internet use for offline and online network capital and well-being. A causal model approach. Journal of Computer-Mediated Communication 15, 189–210 (2009)
26. Kaplan, A.M., Haenlein, M.: Users of the world, unite! The challenges and opportunities of Social Media. Business Horizons, 59–68 (2010)
27. Bradley, A., McDonald, M.P.: Social Media Success Is About Purpose. Harvard Business Review Blog (2011), http://blogs.hbr.org/cs/2011/11/
28. Short, J., Williams, E., Christie, B.: Social Psychology of Telecommunications. Wiley, London (1976)
29. Daft, R.L., Lengel, R.H.: Organizational Information Requirements, Media Richness and Structural Design. Management Science 32, 554–571 (1986)
30. Rice, R.E.: Media appropriateness: using social presence theory to compare traditional and new organizational media. Human Communication Research 19, 451–484 (1993)
31. Te'eni, D.: Review: A Cognitive-Affective Model of Organizational Communication for Designing IT. MIS Quarterly 25, 251 (2001)
32. Phang, C.W., Kankanhalli, A.: A Framework of ICT Exploitation for E-Participation Initiatives. Communications of the ACM 51, 128–132 (2008)
33. Roeder, S., Poppenborg, A., Michaelis, S., Märker, O., Salz, S.R.: "Public Budget Dialogue" – An Innovative Approach to E-Participation. In: Böhlen, M.H., Gamper, J., Polasek, W., Wimmer, M.A. (eds.) TCGOV 2005. LNCS (LNAI), vol. 3416, pp. 48–56. Springer, Heidelberg (2005)
34. Stern, E., Gudes, O., Svoray, T.: Web-based and traditional public participation in comprehensive planning. Environment and Planning 36, 1067–1085 (2009)
35. Yin, R.K.: Case Study Research: Design and Methods. Sage Publications (2009)
36. Chavis, D.M., Lee, K.S., Acosta, J.: The Sense of Community (SCI) Revised: The reliability and Validity. In: Community Psychology Conference, Lisboa, vol. 2 (2008)

# How, Why and with Whom Do Local Politicians Engage on Facebook?

Eirik Rustad and Øystein Sæbø

Center for eGovernment, Department of Information Systems University of Agder,
4604 Kristiansand, Norway
{eirik.rustad,oystein.sabo}@uia.no

**Abstract.** This article focuses on how, why and with whom local politicians engage on Facebook. Based on a literature review of the public sphere, eParticipation and research related to social media, we propose a theoretical framework that identifies thematic areas integral to understanding the nature of political participation. The explanatory potential of our 'ENGAGE' model (Exchange, Narcissist, Gather, Accented, General and Expense) is exemplified by conducting a qualitative case study focusing on politicians in a local municipality in southern Norway. The findings indicate various uses of Facebook among the respondents, and a dissonance between what the politicians state as being important (engaging in dialogue with citizens) and what they really do (posting statements). We conclude our paper by discussing the use and usefulness of our proposed model, and by summarising how, why and with whom local politicians use social media.

**Keywords:** eParticipation, political engagement, social media, Facebook, case study.

## 1 Introduction

Despite a growing research interest in the use of social media in the area of eParticipation [1, 2], more work is needed to understand the role of politicians in this capacity. Most studies within the field of eParticipation focus on citizens' roles, whereas the role of politicians is emphasised to lesser degree [3]. This paper focuses on the politicians, by exploring how, why and with whom local politicians engage on Facebook. Based on current literature and empirical findings from an exploratory case study, we introduce an explanatory framework entitled "ENGAGE". Understanding politicians' use of social media is essential to understanding how political discourse among citizens, politicians and other external stakeholders may influence and impact decision-making processes. Facebook is currently the most common social media platform, with most age groups now well represented and with more than one billion members globally. Thus, we choose to focus on politicians' use of Facebook for our research purpose. By doing so, we attempt to understand how and why politicians and citizens alike engage on a technical platform that upholds many of the characteristics normally associated with formal eParticipation efforts.

M.A. Wimmer, E. Tambouris, and A. Macintosh (Eds.): ePart 2013, LNCS 8075, pp. 69–79, 2013.
© IFIP International Federation for Information Processing 2013

Habermas' ideas represent our point of departure to understand how communication between politicians and citizens enhances democracy. Although Habermas has been criticised for leaving organisations and politicians out of the mix [4], many recent eParticipation efforts are based on norms and theoretical backdrop strongly influenced by Habermasian ideas. We argue that the theory of 'the public sphere' [5] is a valuable point of departure to understand eParticipation initiatives. The public sphere is a separate common ground where ordinary citizens can enlighten each other through discussions and find common causes that transform into real politics through the intervention of traditional media, which set the agenda to which politicians must adhere and respond. Our framework aims to apply Habermas' normative concept to a modern-day view of society, where social media plays a major role. Social media provide users the ability to interact, collaborate, contribute and share online contents [6], and to communicate and maintain their networks [7]; the rapid growth in use and number of members increases the importance of understanding its effects on society and people.

We propose a theoretical framework that identifies thematic areas integral to understanding the nature of political participation. By doing so, we aim to identify different attitudes and motivations which are important to understanding various forms of engagement. We illustrate the explanatory potential of the framework by conducting a qualitative case study analysing local politicians' use of Facebook in a Norwegian municipality.

## 2      Theoretical Approaches

Our 'ENGAGE' framework, introduced below, is mainly based upon Habermas' theory of 'the public sphere' [5], the discourse on how technology influences democracy (see ([8]) for a more detailed discussion), and research focusing on the use of social media in the eParticipation area [1, 2, 6]. ENGAGE is an acronym that helps identifying important thematic characteristics in order to gain knowledge of politicians' motivations for using social media. The framework focuses on thematic areas that are related to the theory of the public sphere and eParticipation by finding answers to certain key questions: Who is engaging with each other? What are the outcomes for citizen input? Why is the politician participating?

ENGAGE borrows its structure from 'SLATES' (Search, Links. Authoring, Tags, Extensions and Signals) [9]. McAfee (2006) calls attention to components that should be included in an understanding of 'Enterprise 2.0'. By emphasising which new technologies could enhance effective knowledge sharing within enterprises, this framework helps simplify the thematic areas that are critical to successful operation in a new world. Hence, even though the two schemes do not share a focus on the use of social media in the eParticipation area, the structure of McAfee's (2006) work nevertheless proved important for our purpose.

The framework for our study is presented below, followed by a summary model demonstrating connections between the framework and current streams of research. The individual categories of the ENGAGE model were devised by reviewing literature discussing dimensions of the public sphere theory and literature discussing eParticipation, and introduce a conceptual representation of important aspects related to «Web 2.0» technologies, eParticipation and public sphere The scope and length of this paper limits the possibility to discuss in detail the theories upon which the framework is based.

## 2.1   ENGAGE

The framework focuses on thematic areas necessary to understand politicians' behaviour on social media. Building on major themes of the public sphere within an eParticipation context, 'ENGAGE' aims to improve our understanding of the nature of politicians' participation.

**E - Exchange.** Communication is the core of a thriving democracy [5]. Whether the politician wears his or her private 'hat' or engages in political activity is essential to understanding his or her activity online. In this regard, we do not value exchanges of, for example, cake recipes as equal to an exchange of opinions in a political debate. Thus, centring on exchange involves focusing on the content and context of the online communication exchange.

**N - Narcissist.** Politicians may or may not consider Facebook to be an isolated arena where 'what happens on Facebook stays on Facebook'. It is important to consider the extent to which politicians change their own opinion, or bring forward prevalent views, into formal political decision-making processes [4]. Politicians may very well be on Facebook solely for the exposure and visibility that it can provide.

**G - Gather.** Politicians may use social media to engage with citizens either by broadcasting political victories, or by asking for their input on topical issues; both strategies represent important aspects of politics. By preferring the broadcasting strategy with limited gathering of input from other stakeholders, their use of social media becomes more of a one-way dialogue than a deliberative discourse. The distribution of questions asked or statements posed may indicate the type of participation that the politician prefers.

**A - Accented.** Language is a form of capital that can translate to power, but is also a differentiating factor that can either create distance or 'close the gap' between a political power elite and public participants [5]. An indicator for exclusion or inclusion is the extent to which politicians post detailed or general questions or statements, and how they inform the public and discuss the political process.

**G - General.** Many groups are marginalised and underrepresented, and eParticipation studies have long warned about the digital divide [3]. Thus, an important area of interest is who the politician receives 'friend requests' from, and who they befriend. Journalists, old classmates, friends, family and other acquaintances are part of politician's networks. It is of common interest to investigate the potential predominance of particular groups in their network, and the potential targeting of specific groups in explaining politicians' participation.

**E - Expense.** Available resources limit politicians' engagement on social media. Time, competence and perceived gains are all important factors to consider when we look at the quality of engagement. If a politician does not answer enquiries, or does not actively follow up on discussions and comments, this may diminish citizens' willingness to engage with the politician in question. Expense can therefore be used as a tool to determine whether the participation is meaningful in a comprehensive way, or if it merely resembles a casual pastime without direction.

### 2.2    Relationship between 'ENGAGE' and Current Research

Figure 1 illustrates the relationship between the theoretical backdrop of the public sphere, eParticipation literature and the proposed ENGAGE framework.

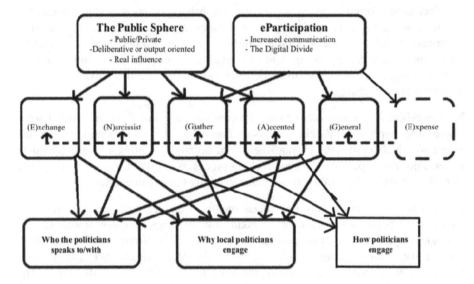

**Fig. 1.** Relational model for 'ENGAGE'

The theory of public sphere relates to:

- **(E)xchange** by focusing on engagement of a public or private nature, and prevelant two-way communication. This is a fundamental principle at the core of deliberation in a public sphere.
- **(N)arcissist** by discussing whether communication has practical implications on policy or political process, or if politicians' communication on social media is isolated from decision-making processes.
- **(G)ather** by exploring potential prioritising from politicians concerning input and output.
- **(A)ccented** by discussing how engangement might be influenced by specific goals, and identifying potential target groups.

eParticipation theory relates to:

- **(G)ather** by exploring the socio-technical characteristics of social media, and how such systems influence the amount of discourse with external stakeholders.
- **(G)eneral** by discussing the digital divide by asking who is left out and who is included.
- **(E)xpense** by discussing resources needed in relation to time spent utilising social media, in comparison to competing communication platforms.

## 3  Introducing the Case, Data Collection and Analysis Strategy

To illustrate the explanatory potential of ENGAGE, we designed a qualitative study to explore politicians' use of Facebook in the Norwegian city of Kristiansand (approximately 75,000 inhabitants). The politicians were selected using a snowball method [10] among city council members with a Facebook account. The politicians were contacted on Facebook and everyone asked agreed to participate. Ages ranged from 20 to 41 years with four female politicians and one male politician interviewed.

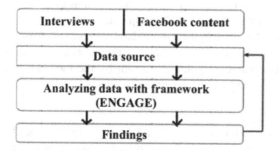

**Fig. 2.** Data analysis strategy

Given the emphasis on understanding phenomena within their real-life context through a rich description of particular instances [10], it is appropriate to adopt a case study approach [11]. The study is exploratory by nature, aiming to define questions, proposing new constructs and eventually identifying new theoretical propositions, additional constructs and the relationships between constructs [12] that may complement the original framework.

Data came from two sources. The primary source of data was semi-structured interviews covering the thematic areas introduced above (the ARENA framework). Since we limited our case study to interviews with five politicians, we also had a secondary data source, which consisted of a content analysis [13] of data from the five politicians' Facebook pages. Interviews were transcribed and analysed based on a pattern-matching logic, in which themes were identified and put in context within the framework presented. The data from the politicians' Facebook pages were analysed by placing 20 status updates from each politician in a spreadsheet. The spreadsheet categorised the status updates according to their different thematic areas of focus.

# 4     Findings

Below we introduce our findings related to the ENGAGE framework, illustrated by quotations from interviews.

### E - Exchange

> *'I'm very concious about what I post because I know that my profile is in fact public.'* (Respondent #4).

The politicians are very much aware that what they post on Facebook can turn into news stories. However, they have several concerns on the use of Facebook as a public arena, including a lack of confidence with the technical use of Facebook, as well as how to use the systems in place to develop and maintain their networks. The politicians have limited resources available to really exploit the potential uses of Facebook and social media. Politicians may be wary of becoming tiresome, boring their audience with political discourses that do not necessarily interest everyone.

During the interviews, most politicians expressed believe in using Facebook for two-way dialogue, but the content analyses of their Facebook accounts provided contradictory indicators. The limited number of questions asked to their followers and the number of times the original poster responded to subsequent comments do not uniformly support the claims that politicians engage in two-way dialogues on Facebook. Further questioning as to what constitutes 'two-way dialogue' could have clarified what each individual politician meant by the term. Is 'liking' a statement tantamount to commenting in the eyes of the politician?

### N - Narcissist

> *'I may have strenghtened my belief in an opinion or had second thoughts because of input or the like. But I have not changed my opininon'.*(Respondent 5)

The politicians do not alter their opinions based on inputs and dialogue on social media, but might be open to minor adjustments. This might relate to the fact that politicians post 'status updates' with opinions expressing their strong beliefs, rather than in the form of open questions welcoming inputs to the decision-making processes. Two of the interviewees argued that by mediating wishes expressed by citizens, Facebook might actually influence the political process.

> *'I have absolutely done that* (changed opinions based on inputs on Facebook). *Both in political meetings as well in letters or op-eds in the newspaper.'* (Respondent 3).

The above statement is an example from one politician stating that she uses Facebook actively as a tool for gathering citizens' opinions on political issues.

> *'In theory it* (Facebook) *must be a good arena for discussion, especially for youth, since we are always online and the smartphone is always on the table with Facebook present. Me, I don't discuss much on Facebook because it is*

*tiring. The discussion quickly gets out of hand and I have a perception that people discuss just for discussion's sake on Facebook. I discuss so much every day that I can't manage. But in theory it is a good arena.'* (Respondent 2).

The statement above echoes other politicians' points of view, while another politician argues that Facebook is a good arena for deliberation because the quality of argumentation is preferable to alternative sources, such as the comment section below online newspaper articles, and since 'everyone' is using Facebook.

## G - Gather

*'It is probably input because I scroll and browse more on Facebook than I write myself.'*

Most of the 'status updates' analysed in the content analysis are not questions, but opinions or links to online content. Among the five politicians included in our study and out of twenty 'status updates', the highest number of questions was three. Politicians, whenever interviewed, stated that they gather information by browsing Facebook, which takes up a lot of the time that they are 'on' Facebook. Politicians are aware of journalists seizing material posted on their Facebook pages, potentially presenting part of the communication outside its natural context. One politician reported fearing 'flame wars' when posting political 'status updates', thus reducing their willingness to participate in the online discussions, and limiting the potential for improved political deliberation. The content analysis revealed mixed results on how commenting and 'liking' posts related to their own 'status updates' proliferate. The most active politician commented on 13 out of 16 possible 'status updates' that generated comments by external stakeholders, down to a low of three status updates commented out of 15 by the least active politician.

## A - Accented

*'[...]if there is something I want to put out there, a purpose may be that one of the journalists I have on Facebook will pick up the story. But that is also why I need to be sure that I want to post it, because then I know it is something I can defend, something that may be printed.'* (Respondent 1)

The politicians consider themselves to be very conscious of what they are posting. They know that journalists are watching and, as one politician commented, this represents a double-edged situation in which politicians strive for exposure in traditional media, but at the same time are reluctant to make certain comments or statements out of fear of negative exposure in the same media channels. Most of the 'status updates' indicate that the more general statements dominate. Few of the 'status updates' seem to have specific target groups in mind.

## G - General

*'I have made a choice that Facebook is a public arena for me, a politician's arena, not my personal playground.'* (Respondent 3)

Some of the politicians view Facebook as a private arena where they do not accept 'friend requests' from unknown individuals, unlike the view expressed by the quotation above. One respondent commented on who the 'friends' are:

*'There are probably many, except those that are my friends and people I know
personally, involved in societal matters of some sort. I think that if you took a
few hundred people in there that I don't know, but are from Kristiansand, or
the southern part of Norway... I would think almost everyone is either
politicians, youth politicians, media people, business people or people from the
arts. There are probably some people I don't know that "add me" because
they are involved in societal matters of some sort.'* (Respondent 3).

The politicians' networks of 'friends' do not really indicate any expansion of the
public sphere. Their networks are mainly made up of family, friends, colleagues,
other politicians and journalists. People in the network that the politicians do not
personally know consist mainly of people being active (and visible) in their local
society by belonging to elite groups. However, there is a shortcoming in our research
approach concerning the network effects. If a 'friend' of the politician comments on
something, this might be visible to friends of the friend, depending on the personal
settings chosen by the politicians. Hence, a broader audience may possibly be
informed by politicians' online activities, compared to those actually able to
participate in the discussions.

### E - Expense

*'Many will say too much time* (is spent on Facebook)*! And that is probably
true as well. I can say this: generally, independently of if I'm in front of the
computer or cell phone, Facebook is always on in the background. As TV is
always on in the background for some, Facebook is always on for me.'*
(Respondent 3).

All the politicians use Facebook on a daily basis, some for several hours a day.
Time spent on Facebook does not easily translate to an activity identified within the
framework of this case study, since politicians most probably read more than they
write. Moreover, one of our interviewees explained that personal messages are often
used to answer comments on the politicians' wall, which are not publicly visible. One
politician argues that to successfully use Facebook as a political tool, you need to
invest time and presence when engaging your audience; if you don't follow up your
initial statement when comments are made, you may lose out on what could have
been an interesting discussion.

## 5     Discussion and Conclusion

The findings from our case study concerning the thematic areas identified in the
current literature are summarised in Table 1.

**Table 1.** Case findings summarised

| Thematic area | Main findings |
|---|---|
| Exchange | Politicians differ in their views on what two-way communication is. Politicians believe they engage in two-way dialogue, while the secondary data source points to differences in what politicians consider to be two-way dialogue. |
| Narcissist | The politicians rarely change their minds on political issues. With one exception they mainly post opinions that they strongly believe in. |
| Gather | Politicians mostly post statements, not questions. Questions regarding political issues are not prevalent. Politicians engage on Facebook through activity that is not necessarily easily monitored. Some use private messages in an extensive way; others centre their activity on their 'wall'. Much of the time spent on Facebook is not spent actively posting or commenting, but browsing profiles, an activity that may influence politicians but is difficult to measure. |
| Accented | The politicians emphasise that they will use different means in different parts of the political process, but the main finding is that politicians are more likely to use Facebook to broadcast outputs than to gather opinion early in the political processes. The politicians vary the level of detail in their posts. |
| General | Politicians' friends are mostly made up of already engaged citizens and cultural, political or civic elites. There is no active strategy for 'adding' ordinary citizens into the mix. This suggests a strengthening of bonds between established elites, even though the platform has the potential to provide more democratic influence, as politicians don't differentiate among authors of opinions. |
| Expense | The politicians allocate a great deal of time to maintaining a presence on Facebook. The activity that results from this presence is highly diverse. One of the politicians stated that while she checks Facebook four to five times a day, she has posted less than 20 'status updates' in over a year. Others are extremely active in posting status updates or commenting. Facebook represents a channel in addition to present communication channels. |

**How** politicians engage on Facebook varies greatly, with different modes of operation. Most politicians in our study believe in the use of Facebook primarily for collecting opinions from citizens and other stakeholders. However, content analysis of the politicians' Facebook accounts suggest otherwise.

**Why** politicians engage also varies within our sample. Some view Facebook as a personal and private arena where politicians enter only as private persons, while others view Facebook as a tool for gathering relevant information vital to their role as a politician.

**With whom** the politicians engage is more uniform. Friends, family, colleagues and journalists are well represented in all respondents' Facebook networks. The remaining 'friends' of the politicians consist mostly of already established elites within cultural or political sectors, or civic society in general.

Politicians with an explicit strategy for how to engage citizens through the use of Facebook are more likely than others to make sense of comments, discussions and other forms of feedback in a meaningful way. Even though most of our respondents do not find their online presence and the input they may receive through their use of Facebook to be especially valuable, with the one exception aiming to use her Facebook presence effectively as valuable resource, social media remains a potentially useful tool if used in a systematic manner.

The general characteristics of social media, and particularly that relevant information can be distributed, gathered and discussed within minutes of posting, may potentially represent a shift in how politicians interact. We argue that politicians may benefit from viewing Facebook as a democratic arena by gathering valuable and relevant information that can influence decisions in political processes. However, our empirical results indicate that politicians, in a local Norwegian context, still have some work to do to strategically harness their use, or non-use, of social media in political discourse.

For now, Facebook as an arena for deliberation may not live up to the strict ideals of public sphere theorists. Habermas' critique of internet as an arena for public deliberation is centred on the fear of echo chamber effects, and the fragmentation that leads to many separate public spheres [14]. Habermas still believes traditional news media is key to setting the agenda. A common criticism when applying public sphere theory to social media is the lack of face-to-face interaction that is an essential aspect of how deliberation should ideally entail [15]. Although there is a gap between a face-to-face meeting between peers, and the nature of Facebook as an arena for engagement, we strongly believe that the use of such media it is a step in the right direction concerning public deliberation. As one of the respondents comment, the «friend» relationship on Facebook is likely to increase incentive to engage by removing barriers. Habermas' critique of «new media» is based mainly on web-forums and the like [16]. A non-anonymous arena such as Facebook has arguably different qualities and characteristics than face-to-face encounters, but is still relevant to counter some of Habermas' concerns about an online public sphere.

An interesting observation is the role Facebook and other social media can play in the agenda-setting phase of public decision-making. News-stories published in traditional news media often originate from Facebook. Hence, social media is not only a valuable direct source for news, but plays a mayor role in aggregating news stories, where an increasing number of referrals to news stories originate from social media channels. Facebook may influence the transformation of power from news editors towards a more democratic form of involvement by the public themselves.

The strength of our proposed model is its potential to encompass a range of important dimensions within different fields of study that are needed in order to obtain a more comprehensive understanding of the phenomena of engagement. The ENGAGE model could easily be confirmed and/or elaborated by further research. Further research is also needed to answer questions regarding how the size of the community influences the quality of the participation. Moreover, the role of the technology could be further investigated, to explore whether the difference in participation (e.g. inability to maintain a dialogue) could be caused by specific technicalities (interface) of the Facebook platform itself rather than politicians' competencies or desire to deepen engagement and participation.

# References

1. Hong, S., Nadler, D.: Which candidates do the public discuss online in an election campaign?: The use of social media by 2012 presidential candidates and its impact on candidate salience. Government Information Quarterly (2012)
2. Linders, D.: From e-government to we-government: Defining a typology for citizen coproduction in the age of social media. Government Information Quarterly (2012)
3. Sæbø, Ø., Rose, J., Skiftenes Flak, L.: The shape of eParticipation: Characterizing an emerging research area. Government Information Quarterly 25, 400–428 (2008)
4. Westling, M.: Expanding the public sphere: The impact of Facebook on political communication. The New Vernacular (2007)
5. Habermas, J.: The Structural Transformation of the Public Sphere. MIT press, Cambridge (1991)
6. McGrath, K., Elbanna, A., Hercheui, M., Panagiotopoulos, P., Saad, E.: Exploring the Democratic Potential of Online Social Networking: The Scope and Limitations of E-Participation. Communications of the Association for Information Systems 30, 16 (2012)
7. Medaglia, R., Rose, J., Nyvang, T., Sæbø, Ø.: Characteristics of social networking services (2009)
8. Päivärinta, T., Sæbø, Ø.: Models of e-democracy (2006)
9. McAfee, A.P.: Enterprise 2.0: The dawn of emergent collaboration. Management of Technology and Innovation 47 (2006)
10. Yin, R.K.: Case study research: design and methods, 4th edn. Sage Publications, Newbury Park (2009)
11. Kirsch, L.J., Beath, C.M.: The enactments and consequences of token, shared, and compliant participation in information systems development. Accounting, Management and Information Technologies 6, 221–254 (1996)
12. Cavaye, A.L.M.: Case study research: a multi-faceted research approach for IS. Information Systems Journal 6, 227–242 (1996)
13. Silverman, D.: Interpreting qualitative data. Sage Publications Limited (2011)
14. Gentikow, B.: Habermas, medienes rolle for den offentlige meningsdannelsen, og en fotnote om Internettet i fire versjoner. Norsk Medietidskrift 1, 55–63 (2009)
15. Habermas, J.: Political communication in media society: Does democracy still enjoy an epistemic dimension? the impact of normative theory on empirical research1. Communication Theory 16, 411–426 (2006)
16. Geiger, R.S.: Does Habermas understand the Internet? The algorithmic construction of the blogo/public sphere. Gnovis: A Journal of Communication, Culture, and Technology 1, 1–29 (2009)

# "Let Us Talk to People, Not to Computers": Obstacles for Establishing Relationships and Trust in Social Workers' Online Communities of Practice

Azi Lev-On[1] and Odelia Adler[2]

[1] School of Communication, Ariel University, Ariel, Israel
azilevon@gmail.com
[2] Department of Communication, Ben-Gurion University, Beer Sheva, Israel
odeliadler@gmail.com

**Abstract.** The paper studies social workers' online communities of practice and presents the perceptions of their members about such online communities' potential for establishing relationships and trust. The interviewees expressed three main clusters of reasons for why relationships and trust cannot be properly established and sustained through online communities of practice. These reasons involve general hostility to computer-mediated communication as an arena for relationship development, the non-computerized professional environment of social workers, and particular features of the communities that were studied.

**Keywords:** communication, online communities, communities of practice, trust, relationships.

## 1 Theoretical Background

This paper investigates the following questions: how do social workers use online communities of practice, and do they perceive of these communities as venues for establishing relationships with peers, mutual accord and trust?

A number of theories have addressed the potential to establish relationships and trust through computer-mediated environments. The 'first wave' of such theories found that Computer-Mediated Communication (CMC) could not sustain elaborate forms of relational development and support as Face to Face (FtF) communication does. For example, the Reduced Cues (or 'cues-filtered-out') theory implies that communication media possess sets of characteristics that correspond to distinct levels of richness. Richer communication media support more cues and help yield higher levels of social presence. Arguably, higher levels of social presence result in greater attention to the presence of others and greater awareness of, and conformity to, social norms [1-3]. The relative absence of cues in CMC leads to reduced awareness of the social environment, reduced opportunities for social control and regulation, reduced concerns for social approbation and decreased adherence to social norms.

M.A. Wimmer, E. Tambouris, and A. Macintosh (Eds.): ePart 2013, LNCS 8075, pp. 80–94, 2013.

Later theories, such as Social Information Processing (SIP) theory [4,5] recognize that continuing communication enables the development of the normative conditions for cooperation in CMC, even if cooperation is established slower than in face-to-face communicative environments. Repeated interaction involves continuous and mutual reception and verification of cues, and people find ways to adapt to the limitations of the medium and reduce uncertainty [5,6]. Consequently, cooperation increases over time, and converges to rates observed in FtF communication [5,7]. Indeed, it may take longer for accord and trust to be established and sustained in computer mediated environments, but time and richness of the environment can assist in achieving accord and trust in a smoother fashion.

The SIDE theory (Social Identity Model of Depersonalization Effects; see [8-10]) manifests a third theoretical sphere. Along with SIP theory, SIDE theory emphasizes the social context of CMC. However, SIDE theory shows, perhaps counter-intuitively, that the social context of communication may be especially salient, and the influence of social norms particularly effective, with the relative absence of information about people. When a CMC environment is characterized by a salient sense of group membership, the lack of other cues leads to a stronger influence of social norms on behavior and to compliance with situational norms. While CMC indeed blocks a range of interpersonal cues, it often leaves some group-level social cues intact. Research demonstrates that in such circumstances, group membership becomes situationally relevant and people are more likely to adapt to the situational norms.

While the earlier literature surveyed above suggests a uniform effect of technology over behavior, later literature demonstrates a differential effect of online interactions on trust and relationships, according to different personality types. For example, the work of Amichai-Hamburger [11,12] demonstrates that introverted character types may benefit more from using the Internet than extroverted types. The Internet also yields great potential in assisting those who suffer from social anxieties and are afraid of exposing themselves to others. Such people can encounter protected environment online, in which they have better control over the communication processes and are more comfortable to expose their "true selves" [13,14]. Thus, in addition to environmental variables that affect the ability to establish accord and trust online, personal characteristics matter as well.

Arguably, the uses and effects of online communities of practice may also vary across practices. For example, it is likely that workers in the hi-tech industry will be more open towards developing relationships and trust online than members of other professions who do not use computers regularly; similarly, older professionals who worked most of their lives in non-digital environments may find it harder to navigate through online relationships than younger, "digitally native" professionals. In reference to social workers' communities in particular, in the only published case study that we could locate, Leung et al. describe one social workers' online community of practice as a source of empowerment and solidarity for its members, which enables them not only to acquire information and knowledge but also to frame a collective identity [15]. Still, Eaglestein et al., in writing about the informational needs of social workers, argue that many potential obstacles exist for social workers to enjoy the benefits of online communities of practice, due to concerns such as breaching patients' confidentiality online, damage to the therapeutic connection, and even lack of technological knowledge and misuse fears that may hinder social workers' optimal utilization of such online environments [16].

Lastly, in addition to the variables concerning personality and profession, the design of the forum can also make a difference in terms of its success in developing trust. For example, anonymity may promote a more open discussion and thus yield a greater quantity of contributions. At the same time, anonymity is also the primary factor that undermines the deliberative potential of the platform. Other key design factors involve synchronisity or lack thereof, rules, and moderation style [17,18].

## 1.1    Research Setting: Social Workers' Online Communities of Practice

The current study takes a fresh look at the potential that online communities of practice yield to establish relationships and trust, by analyzing the case of social workers' online communities of practice that were established by the Israeli Ministry of Social Affairs and Social Services.

The communities of practice studied represent a unique case in Israel, whereby a governmental ministry established online forums to enable interaction between its workers and the broader community of practitioners. Such communities may have many advantages in terms of exposing local knowledge, improving knowledge circulation and even supporting professional acquaintance and solidarity between workers [19]. At the same time, they can disseminate employees' open criticism of their supervisors and damage working relations within the office, as well as generate criticism of the employing agency's work and routines, among other risks. As a result, governmental ministries tend to avoid providing platforms for such interaction among workers [20]. Nonetheless, with the rise of social networking platforms, an increasing number of Israeli governmental bodies are offering more opportunities for direct online interactions amongst workers, as well as between employees and citizens. The communities of practice that are studied here, which were established already in 2006, can be seen as pioneers of this phenomenon.

In establishing these professional networking communities, the Ministry intended to provide a new platform for knowledge exchange and circulation, mainly for social workers who did not have similar arenas. Unlike many other professions whose work is computer-based, many of the social workers who take part in the communities spend their days in the field, dealing with people from low socioeconomic strata who often live under harsh circumstances. In this sense, many of the social workers, including the people who were interviewed for this study, refer to themselves as "people persons" – as opposed to those who spend much of their work-day in front of a computer screen. Hence, the provision of Internet-based communities of practice for such "people persons" yields some interesting research questions.

The Ministry employees who initiated and supervised these online communities of practice were aware of the importance of face-to-face meetings, in addition to the virtual encounters between community members. When the communities were established, a dilemma surfaced regarding whether face-to-face meetings should be carried out. Such meetings would clearly facilitate social and professional links between community members and provide opportunities to form new relationships and strengthen trust. On the other hand, physical meetings may not be accessible to community members who are unable to participate for reasons of distance, cost, disabilities or other barriers. Hence, it was ultimately decided to limit the interaction to the online realm, without a face-to-face component [21].

Since 2006 when the communities were established, 9,000 members have enrolled into one or more of the 31 communities concerning topics such as Domestic Violence, Adoption, Juvenile Delinquency, Mental Disabilities, and other administrative forums in which regulation and ethics are discussed. All communication in the forums is identified, using members' real names. The forum is based on a standard web platform (see Fig. 1 below), where discussion is threaded and latest comments appear first, pushing down earlier comments. The discussion in Figure 1 focuses on legalizing the use of Marijuana for patients with post-traumatic stress disorders.

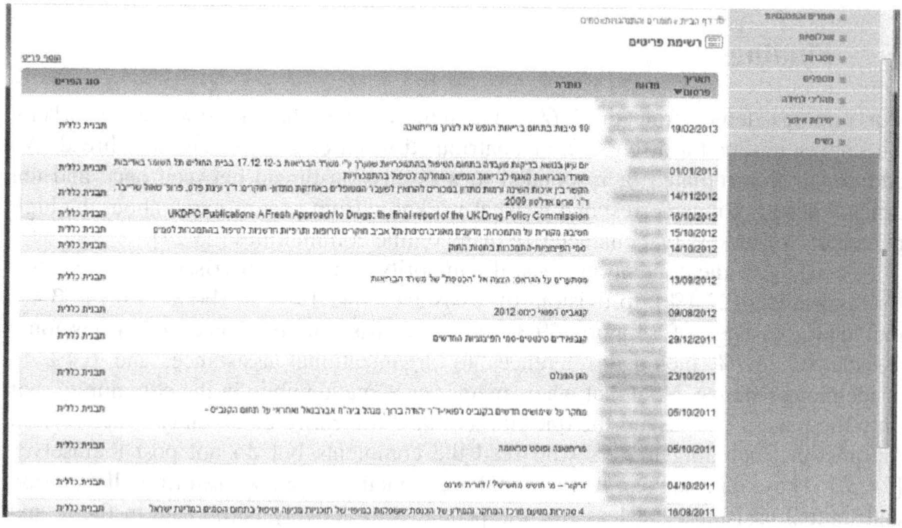

**Fig. 1.** A screenshot of the Addictions community portal

In the current study, we investigate whether online community members perceive the communities as places where they can establish relationships and trust. We hypothesize that community members perceive their computerized interactions as a sphere in which relationships and trust can be created and sustained. The online professional communities studied conform well to the environments in which the SIP and even SIDE model works best, in that they are composed of people who handle the same issues and are familiar with one another over time to a certain degree – online and even offline.

## 2 Methodology

The paper is a part of a larger project that analyzes the content of the online communities of practice of the Israeli Ministry of Social Affairs and Social Services, as well as their perceived effects on their members.

For this purpose, a twofold research methodology was applied. First, we undertook a content analysis of all the available materials – 7,248 posts altogether from the establishment of the communities through mid 2012. Second, 71 semi-structured interviews were conducted with community members. Based on data received from the Ministry of Social Affairs and Social Services, members were sampled according to their levels of engagement – number of logins to the community, as well as number of times that they contributed content. Interviews were conducted by five interviewers across Israel, and the average length of an Interview was some 45 minutes. Interviews were transcribed and analyzed using a thematic-interpretive method [22]. The findings in the paper below are largely based on these interviews.

## 3 Findings

Our findings demonstrate that 76% of community members enrolled were lurkers, who never initiated a discussion or contributed to an existing discussion thread. An additional 21% initiated or responded to a discussion thread between once and ten times. These findings correspond to what we know from past research about the high percentage of lurkers that characterize many online communities [23,24].

According to the content analysis, the majority of posts comprised either requests for assistance (22.1%), provision of assistance (42.1%), or both (2.6%). 3.4% included messages of support. 39.3% of the posts had references to professional assistance, 25.7% included references to organizational assistance, and 6.4% to academic assistance. Note that when an answer is made public in the community, not only the person who asked the question but also the entire community benefits from the answer, including lurkers who read the comments but do not post themselves [24,25]. These data suggest that communities function as a platform for collaboration and mutual assistance, at least for the people who actively participate in them, and possibly for a large chunk of lurkers as well.

Hence, it seems that while not many members actively participate in creating content for the communities, those who do provide a high degree of mutual assistance and support that both benefits the contributors and may also spill over to benefit the lurkers as well. So do community members indeed perceive their online communities as a realm for establishing relationships and trust, and more generally, do they perceive of the Internet – the technical platform of their communities – as hospitable for creating relationships and trust?

### 3.1 Hostility to CMC Arenas as Relationship-Supporting Environments

Contrary to our hypothesis, most the people interviewed expressed the view that Internet forums and the Internet in general are not useful for and actually hinder the establishment of relationships and trust, for a variety of reasons. Social workers interviewed very frequently stated that it was difficult for them to "connect" to the virtual community platforms because face-to-face meetings were irreplaceable and computer-mediation generates a "cold" and "alienated" environment.

Interviewee 1 is a passive participant in the community Juvenile Delinquency, does not read the posts and does post herself. She states that ʹ

[g]enerally, I am not a technological person, I don't do chats or post comments. I am a person who needs to speak [with the others party]. Being in front of a computer is very difficult for me…I keep saying I am a social worker! Let me talk to people, not to computers.

Interviewee 2, a member of the Addictions community, says,

maybe this is because of my advanced age, but I really don't understand how one can have a sense of belonging to something on the Internet…let's talk about work issues, why do we need the forum for that? Why do we need the Internet to get closer to one another as human beings…why those emails? Pick up the phone – let's talk as humans.

Interviewee 3, a member of a community concerning Mental Disabilities, notes the need for an unmediated human connection: "I am interested in some response, some verbal interaction. I am not able to fully connect to the electronic world…" Interviewee 4 argues that "[online interaction does] not replace friendship. It's not instead of acquaintance. It cannot replace a peer discourse that we sometimes generate amongst ourselves."

This latter interviewee expresses the dichotomy between the perceived functioning of a typical social worker and the computerized world. She implies that technology can harm the connection created throughout a long process of relating to her patients. In reference to this issue, Interviewee 5, a member of the Domestic Violence community, notes that while she occasionally posts a comment concerning a dilemma she might have, but she always prefers to ask people face-to-face, as "even a phone call is better than a forum…I like [a] personal touch with people much more." Yet, even the phone is not an ideal communication device for a social worker, in this interviewee's opinion.

Interviewee 6, from the Family Courts community, states that, "I handle myself much better in a human, not text-based environment… [online contact is] not like sitting with people and carrying out a dialogue, getting support and feeling the 'softness.'" Interviewees complained that the online connection hinders their ability to express emotions, grant and receive support – essential elements in this profession. For example, Interviewee 3 notes: "I think that in our world, most people don't get support through this media…we are people persons, and I don't think that the Internet can do the job…" The online forum seems to provide an inferior arena in particular for expressing emotions than face-to-face conversations do. One of the highlights of the community is the support that it provides to its members, but according to members' perceptions, it seems that an emotional message is difficult to convey in text when the physical dimension is absent.

Interviewee 7, a member of the Juvenile Delinquency and Addictions communities who posts frequently, expresses similar concerns. "Generally, I would not go to some Internet forum to ask a question even if I get an immediate online response…this is not my medium." Interviewee 8, from the Addictions community, says that

> This medium has many features that are inferior to face-to-face conversation. A little more of the personal contact, the intonation that allows you to fully understand what was said and reduce misunderstandings […] I prefer to get my support from someone I am personally acquainted with. It's much better to talk to people that I know than [to those that] I don't know.

Interviewee 9, from the Addictions community: "I feel uneasy to address a crowd that I don't see. I need to look at people in the eyes." Interviewee 10, from the Developmental Cognitive Disabilities community, echoes a similar concern, "I am not of the Facebook era, I don't like it, it's not the same. I mean I don't like all this publicity…I personally like…arenas in which people sit and talk, and meet."

Cues that are manifest in gestures, body language and tone in face-to-face communication are generally missing from computer-mediated communication and jeopardize the process of asking for and receiving support, according to the interviewees. These cues reflect what is being said "between the lines," the subtext of the conversation that is necessary to understand the wider context of the written words.

Interviewee 11, a member of Juvenile Delinquency and Social Resilience, was asked about the forum as a source of support. She answered:

> Recently, we had very complex issues here, and needed to support some workers… only when we sat together in a closed room, just us talking, only then could we truly ventilate. We can ventilate in writing, but it's not for real. Because [the situation that we need to address] is very emotional. I think it gets lost when it's on the computer, including what you can express and what others can give you. The emotional support you can get one-on-one, or even in a group, is much greater than in a text-based forum… addressing the cases we run into is very difficult, and our emotional needs cannot be fully fulfilled, in my opinion, in the forum. In any forum. It's not that this particular forum does not fit, no forum would.

### 3.2 The Professional Environment of Social Workers and the Use of Online Forums

Many of the interviewees noted not only a general preference for FtF over CMC, but also stressed that additional factors related to the social work profession lead to a perception of the Internet as an arena ill-suited for social workers. Factors mentioned involve the way in which the profession is taught in universities and practiced in workplaces (this factor was expressed by a small number of interviewees but was in the subtext of quite a few other interviews), as well as the types of relationships formed with clients. Some interviewees said that they initially chose to become social workers despite the low wages that are typical of this profession because they felt that they needed a "human touch" and the opportunity to develop interpersonal relations through their work. They felt more comfortable interacting with a person facing them, whereby his or her gestures can be seen and tone of voice can be heard. Many perceive computer-mediated environments to produce obstacles in the professional discourse.

Interviewee 12, from the Community Work community, argues that social workers usually do not use the Internet while at work. She notes:

We are still a bit technophobic…we are social workers…we don't do communication, computer science… although I am a forum member for five years, I still feel like I am in the dark. I don't always know how to use it, and where to look for what I need to find.

She also says that "the connection to the Internet is very new to social workers, first of all because in many municipalities, there even isn't an Internet connection in the department of social services."

Another practical concern involves the fears of breaches of patients' privacy and confidentiality. Interviewee 13, who belongs to the Youth at Risk and Addictions communities, argues that "I consult many groups, but not this group. This group is too large for me and there are too many holes through which things can 'leak.'"

Interviewee 14, of the Community Work community, says, "it sounds a bit strange to me to write such things on the Internet…this is awkward, because its open and everyone can see [the posts]."A, a member of the Youth Law community states that, "I don't feel the need, and I also don't feel comfortable in terms of privacy and secrecy. …it seems to me too much…I prefer consulting someone face-to-face…although these are colleagues, it is open on the Internet." Interviewee 3, a member of the community concerning the Mental Disabilities, argues, "I don't think that people can really bring up real hardships and dilemmas in such a large-scale forum with many people. This contradicts everything we studied in the university." Critically, she notes that it is not only how the profession is practiced, but also how it is studied in the universities, that increases the tension with technology.

Interviewee 15, a director of a mental institution, describes her concerns regarding technology and hints at the fact that the Internet does not forget: "it's all there until eternity, just stays there. I think people who don't understand that [they are] are irresponsible…there is no delete [button]…you wrote it, it stays there…that's why I don't like this thing…this Internet."

Seemingly, one dominant factor in determining access to and use of communities was age. Most of the interviewees who associated their age with suspicions from and dislike towards technology, were classified as lurkers. According to a survey from 2009 [26], the average age of community members is 43, and ages range between 21 and 77. The largest age group is 30-39 (33%), a quarter of members are between ages 40-49, and another full quarter at the ages 50-59. Among the interviewees in the current study, the average age was 44.

Most likely, the older social workers found it more difficult to think of the communities of practice as a site for bonding. But even a 45-years old interviewee, who has been a member since the communities were established but writes very little, describes herself as highly suspicious of the online realm, and thinks of the Internet as "dangerous". Throughout the interview, she emphasized that her online behavior is cautious and driven by concerns. She herself associates this behavior with her age.

Interviewee 16, from the Families in Judicial Disputes community, who is 62 years old, only replied to messages she read in the communities twice in her three years of membership, although she entered the forum during this time period 170 times. She describes the linkage between her age and level of involvement as follows:

I am not one of the people who open their eyes in the morning and go straight to the computer, I don't have, for example, Internet on my cell phone, I am not subscribed to Facebook…I think this is due to my age and…I just did not grow up with this tool, and with all the need and the joy and the progress…if I have alternatives, I'll use them.

Interviewee 17, a 57-year-old member of the Domestic Violence community, argues that people in her age group do not use the computer frequently, and use other tools to get updates. "I forgot the password…I am not a computer junkie," she says.

### 3.3   Features of the Particular Forums

So far, we addressed obstacles for establishing relationships and trust that are either related to general hostility towards the Internet and preference for FtF as a medium for forming relationships and trust, or else involve social workers' professional environment, which is perceived as "inhospitable" to new technology. The third cluster of reasons for perceiving the online communities as unreceptive for forming relationships and trust has to do with the specific character of the online forums that host these communities.

One complaint by a relatively small number of interviewees, addressed the asynchronous character of the forums. Interviewee 3, from the community concerning the Mental Disabilities, noted: "I don't have the patience to wait for people's replies. If I am interested in something, I will call someone and ask [her]." Interviewee 18, from the Juvenile Delinquency and Domestic Violence communities, concurs: "I don't like the fact that I need to wait until I get a reply. I prefer to chat."

Other complaints involved the forums' text-based nature and the need for a more graphical and interactive user interface. Interviewee 19 argues that "we are not all 'Shakespeares' in writing… When one is not eloquent and may have spelling mistakes, this may deter her from participating."

A number of interviewees raised the need for a more graphical and interactive user interface. Interestingly, the number of interviewees who complained about the lack a more "Facebook-like" interface, and the number of people who expressed fears from technology, was similar.

When asked what was missing in the forums, Interviewee 4 replied: "mostly, the ability to see each others' faces." Interviewee 20 describes the communities as "very schematic, dark, not vivid… something must be done with the graphical interface!" Interviewee 21 agrees: "I think that other forums are conducted in a friendlier, clearer, novel fashion…This seems like something that was created ten years ago and not upgraded since." Interviewee 22 argues that

A 'Facebook-like' interface would have made the forums much nicer… even at the level of professional attachment… suppose that each [member] had his name, profession, where he works, and additional details… like in Facebook, when you suddenly see a picture in some chat.

Another interviewee says:

If a technology like Skype were used, it may have been different because you could see faces, or consult like an online supervision – I know such things exist.

But right now, it's pure textual discussion, you write 5, 6, 10 sentences, it's not like… it's not enough.

## 3.4    Trust and Mistrust

We have discussed above the clusters of factors that explain why community members feel that online forums fail to enable them to develop relationships and trust. Nearly all social workers interviewed argued that for a variety of reasons – general mistrust and recoil from technology, factors associated with social workers' professional environment and training, and even the particular designs of the online communities' interfaces – they felt that the forums were not a good tool for developing relationships and contributing information. How do these circumstances affect the creation of trust?

In online communities, trust is a crucial factor. Each participant must believe that the information in the community is reliable and that he or she can trust the person who provided this information. Mistrust can result in abstaining from participation. Also, community members must believe that other members act for the interests of the entire community and that they have the knowledge and capability to do so [27-29]. Yet despite the theoretical significance of such trust, in line with the issues described above, users argue that it is very difficult to establish such trust in a system that is built on virtual connections.

Interviewee 23, from the Youth Law community, notes that

[Even when] I appreciate people based on their reactions in the forum, when I don't know them in person, I can still never fully trust them. In spite of everything, you don't know them…there are people I know personally in the forum, in which cases I'll take what they say.

According to this interviewee and others, face-to-face familiarity increases the level of trust even as the discussion moves online. The interviewees expressed their concerns regarding "not knowing who the writer really is." In the Ministry of Social Affairs and Social Services' online communities, anonymity is not an option, and any post is accompanied by the first and last name of the writer; yet according to members' perceptions, such identification does not equate actual acquaintance and generates insecurity. Interviewee 24, from Community Work, explains why she makes little use of the communities: "it's more difficult for me, this whole Internet 'thing', talking to people that I know who they are but don't really know them…I prefer direct contact." She also notes that a stronger social presence is needed to generate trust.

One possible way to overcome the obstacle of lack of physical contact is to organize face-to-face meetings and conventions [30]. Indeed, interviewees expressed a need to "at least know who is sitting on the other end". Interviewee 25, in the Youth Law and Community Work communities, says that "it may be a good idea to organize once in a while a conference about the communities of practice, to expose me to the personalities who use the communities…so I can see them in person, and not only through the computer."

Interviewee 24 says that "it seems very important to me to implement common study groups or peer groups so we know who the partners are [for the online discussions] … Because the messages includes the name [of the person who posted them], but we don't know who this person is." Interviewee 25 gives an example of how face-to-face familiarity can contribute to future communication:

One of my positive memories is of a course that was for all the social workers who work with people under arrest…we work a lot with each other over the phone, and this interpersonal contact made a lot [of impact after the course ended]. It also made our contacts better and generated more trust.

Only a few interviewees expressed the opposite notion, i.e. that the interactions in the online communities support and enable trust more easily than other forms of communication do. Yet all interviewees viewe the key building blocks of trust as relationships that continue from the online communities to the professional realm outside them. For example, Interviewee 26, from the Youth Law community, says,

When we need to [transfer files] from town to town, we pick up the phone and you hear, it's X, and it's someone name you already saw in the community and maybe you've even corresponded with…it breaks obstacles and make conducting a dialogue much easier. Because…it's like we know each other.

Interviewee 27, from the Autism, Developmental Cognitive Disabilities and Toddlers with Special Needs communities, explains that

There is a mother of an autistic child who regularly posts a diary like a personal column. I read it all the time…we met in real life when she came to consult with me…it was very funny to learn that I know her and learn from her.

But just as building trust can be prolonged and difficult, breaking it online can be immediate and disastrous for community members. Two examples demonstrate this. A veteran social worker and member of the Children at Risk community, relates an incident in which a divorced social worker was allowed to join the community:

Once there was a discussion in which a father who did not have custody of his children started to intervene and cursed the professionals…if there is a client in there, than it's not a professional community anymore, and then even in this place where I can feely express myself in front of my colleagues, I cannot do it anymore…it's always going to be like that. I can never know who really watches the discussions, there is no way for me to know…for me it was a sort of intrusion…they'll have to rebuild the trust that was compromised.

Hence, it seems that the communities' designation as closed membership by invitation only does not contribute adequately to the sense of intimacy, and although entrance is granted to professionals only, the concern that transgressors might enter always exists. Monitoring for such cases is much more difficult online than offline.

Thinking of these communities as arenas of assistance and support can demonstrate why a breach of trust can be devastating. Interviewee 28, of the Youth Law community, notes:, writes:

We had a crisis in the forum, one of the social workers was arrested… on misdemeanor charges regarding a boy that he acted as the caregiver for… This guy was very, very active in the forum and everyone was shocked.

The manager of the community to which this social worker belonged describes the same case from her perspective:

> We experienced a betrayal...the guy was very, very active in the discussions, and also uploaded a lot of materials to the community... it's like, you know, we are in a closed community, the closed discussion of professionals, we act like protectors and suddenly the offender comes from among us; he came from inside our house.

In referring to this incident as no less than a betrayal, the interviewees demonstrate the high expectations they had regarding mutual sincerity and the ability to trust one another. When the bonds are so strong, the damage may be severe, and the restoration of broken trust may be very difficult. Of course, such cases occur in offline-based communities as well. But in absence of contextual cues, with a better control of the communication and an enhanced ability to expose only very particular sides of one's personality that the Internet offers, such betrayals of trust can be, arguably, more difficult to trace.

## 4 Discussion and Conclusions

Online communities of practice utilized by government ministries are a rare species. The communities of the Ministry of Welfare Services have been established to improve information disclosure and dissemination, as well as to enhance the familiarity of professionals with one another and the sense of solidarity between them. Based on existing theories such as SIP and SIDE, we had initially hypothesized that community members would perceive their computerized interactions as a place where relationships and trust are generated and sustained. The embeddedness in a common professional background and the acquaintance over time, might arguably have made these communities of practice a hotbed for developing relationships and trust.

Yet, contrary to our hypothesis, the predictions of the "Reduced Cues" theory seem to provide a much better fit to the picture portrayed by this study's interviews. With few exceptions, interviewees argued that the communities do not serve as a fertile ground for cooperation, but rather fail to produce accord and trust. Indeed, in their perspective, the physical dimension is necessary to support the trust that forms online, and in absence of the physical dimension there would be very little chance of developing relationships online.

Subjects provided three clusters of explanations regarding why online communities do not generate relationships and trust. One cluster involved general mistrust and dislike of technology and the Internet in particular. It seems that the character of people who use those communities, some of whom declare themselves to be "people persons" who feel much more comfortable in face-to-face settings than in computer-mediated environments, may provide context for the prevalence of such negative attitudes towards technology. Moreover, age may be a factor as well, as such attitudes seem to be more prevalent among older social workers.

Another cluster of reasons involves the professional environment of the social workers. Aside from the seeing predisposition people who choose to be social workers have against technology (especially among older social workers), their education, socialization to the profession and daily dealing with patients and workplaces all hinder the sense that online forums are a hospitable environment for developing relationships and trust.

The third cluster involves characteristics of the particular forums that were studied – for example, the absence of options for a synchronous and more immediate communication, and the graphical environment that seems too basic to some who dislike technology in general, but prefer environments such as Skype and Facebook, which offer richer and more immediate interactions.

Note that these findings are surprising, given the vast literature that argues that online environments similar to the one found in our study can gradually become no inferior to FtF environments in terms of forming relationships and trust; notably, see Rheingold's early study [31] of the rich relationships formed online through the WELL community, which was purely text-based. This is also surprising in light of the rich discussions that do take place in the communities, as well as the significant layers of assistance and support that were located using content analysis.

It seems that a lot of the difference between our findings and earlier findings may be a result of the character traits of social workers, many of whom declare themselves eager to have "human touch" and perceive computer-mediated discussion to disable the development of emotions, support, sense of belonging and trust. At present, the environment in which social workers are trained and work also does not seem to support familiarity with the Internet and Internet-based forums as professional tools.

Still, younger "digitally native" social workers seem better able to adapt to the online communities of practice. Future studies should look at the transformation of the profession to a more technological realm, which seem to many to be unavoidable. Moving online communities to richer environments such as Facebook may assist this process, and Facebook groups of social workers may be an interesting arena for additional future studies. It would also be interesting to compare the social media usage patterns of social workers and other therapeutic professions with those found in online communities generated for other professions.

At minimum, it seems that the conclusion derived from our study is that research about relationship formation and maintenance, participation, collaboration and trust in online communities of practice should be sensitive to the practice of the professionals who use them. Scholars should be hesitant to generalize their findings from one particular online community of practice to all such communities. Researchers should keep in mind that people who practice different professions can behave very differently in the communities of practice that they use and have very different expectations from these professional forums.

# References

1. Kiesler, S., Siegel, J., McGuire, T.W.: Social Psychological Aspects of Computer-Mediated Communication. American Psychologist 39, 1123–1134 (1984)
2. Sproull, L., Kiesler, S.: Reducing Social Context Cues: Electronic Mail in Organizational Communication. Management Science 32, 1492–1512 (1986)

3. Kiesler, S., Sproull, L.: Group Decision Making and Communication Technology. Organizational Behavior and Human Decision Processes 52, 96–123 (1992)

4. Walther, J.B., Anderson, J.F., Park, D.W.: Interpersonal Effects in Computer-Mediated Interaction: A Meta-Analysis of Social and Antisocial Communication. Communication Research 21, 460–487 (1994)

5. Walther, J.B.: Computer-Mediated Communication: Impersonal, Interpersonal, and Hyperpersonal Interaction. Communication Research 23, 3–43 (1996)

6. Chidambaram, L.: Relational Development in Computer Supported Groups. MIS Quarterly 20, 142–165 (1996)

7. Wilson, J.M., Straus, S.G., McEvily, B.: All in Due Time: The Development of Trust in Computer-Mediated and Face-to-Face Teams. Organizational Behavior and Human Decision Processes 99, 16–33 (2006)

8. Postmes, T., Spears, R., Lea, M.: Breaching or Building Social Boundaries? SIDE-Effects of Computer-Mediated Communication. Communication Research 25, 689–715 (1998)

9. Spears, R., Lea, M.: Panacea or Panopticon? The Hidden Power in Computer-Mediated Communication. Communication Research 21, 427–459 (1994)

10. Watt, S.E., Lea, M., Spears, R.: How Social is Internet Communication? A Reappraisal of Bandwidth and Anonymity Effects. In: Woolgar, S. (ed.) Virtual Society?, pp. 61–77. Oxford University Press, New York (2002)

11. Amichai-Hamburger, Y.: Personality and the Internet. In: Amichai-Hamburger, Y. (ed.) The Social Net: Human Behavior in Cyberspace, pp. 27–55. Oxford University Press, New York (2005)

12. Amichai-Hamburger, Y., Kaplan, H., Dorpatcheon, N.: Click to the Past: The Impact of Extroversion by Users of Nostalgic Website on the Use of Internet Social Services. Computers in Human Behavior 24, 1907–1912 (2008)

13. Bargh, J.A., McKenna, K.Y.A., Fitzsimons, G.M.: Can you See the Real me? Activation and Expression of the 'True Self' on the Internet. Journal of Social Issues 58, 33–48 (2002)

14. McKenna, K.Y.A., Bargh, J.A.: Coming Out in the Age of the Internet: Identity Demarginalization through Virtual Group Participation. Journal of Personality and Social Psychology 75(3), 681–694 (1998)

15. Leung, Z., Lam, C.W., Yau, T.Y., Chu, W.: Re-empowering Social Workers through the Online Community: The Experience of SWForum in Hong Kong. Critical Social Policy 30(1), 48–73 (2010)

16. Eaglestein, A., Teitelbaum, R., Shor, D.: Informational Needs of Social Workers in Jerusalem. Ministry of Social Services and Sold Institute, Jerusalem (2007)

17. Wright, S., Street, J.: Democracy, Deliberation and Design: The Case of Online Discussion Forums. New Media and Society 9(5), 849–869 (2007)

18. Christopherson, K.M.: The Positive and Negative Implications of Anonymity in Internet Social Interactions: "On the Internet, Nobody Knows You're a Dog". Computers in Human Behavior 23(6), 3038–3056 (2007)

19. Cook-Craig, P.G., Sabah, Y.: The Role of Virtual Communities of Practice in Supporting Collaborative Learning among Social Workers. British Journal of Social Work 39(4), 725–739 (2009)

20. Haber, K.: Organizational Culture Obstacles for Implementing Open Governance Policy. Israel Democracy Institute, Jerusalem (2013)

21. Sabah, Y., Sharif, I., Fein, T.: Dilemmas of Establishing and Maintaining Online Communities of Practice in the Social Services: The Case of the Israeli Ministry of Social Services. In: Lev-On, A. (ed.) Online Communities. Pardess, Haifa (forthcoming)

22. Strauss, A.L., Corbin, J.M.: Basics of Qualitative Research: Techniques and Procedures for Developing Grounded Theory. Sage Publications, Thousand Oaks (1998)
23. Osimo, D.: Web 2.0 in Government: Why and How? JRC Scientific and Technical Reports. European Commission, Joint Research Centre, Institute for Prospective Technological Studies (2008), http://ftp.jrc.es/EURdoc/JRC45269.pdf (retrieved July 23, 2012)
24. Nonnecke, B., Preece, J.: Lurker Demographics: Counting the Silent. In: Proceedings of the SIGCHI Conference on Human Factors in Computing Systems, The Hague, The Netherlands, pp. 73–80. ACM Press, New York (2000)
25. Amin, A., Roberts, J.: Knowing in Action: Beyond Communities of Practice. Research Policy 37(2), 353–369 (2008)
26. Fein, T.: Online Communities of Practice in the Social Services: A Tool for Sharing and Knowledge Circulation between Employees. MA Thesis, Hebrew University of Jerusalem (2011)
27. Ardichvili, A., Page, V., Wentling, T.: Motivation and Barriers to Participation on Virtual Knowledge-Sharing Communities of Practice. Journal of Knowledge Management 7(1), 64–77 (2003)
28. Ridings, C., Gefen, D., Arinze, B.: Psychological Barriers: Lurker and Poster Motivation and Behavior in Online Communities. Communications of AIS 18(16) (2006)
29. Sharratt, M., Usoro, A.: Understanding Knowledge Sharing in Online Communities of Practice. Electronic Journal of Knowledge Management 1(2), 187–196 (2003)
30. Haythornthwaite, C.: Social Networks and Internet Connectivity Effects. Information, Communication & Society 8(2), 125–147 (2005)
31. Rheingold, H.: A Slice of Life in My Virtual Community. In: Harasim, L.M. (ed.) Global Networks: Computers and International Communication, pp. 37–80. MIT Press, Cambridge (1993)

# Analyzing the Centralised Use of Multiple Social Media by Government from Innovations Diffusion Theory Perspective

Enrico Ferro[1], Euripidis Loukis[2], Yannis Charalabidis[2], and Michele Osella[1]

[1] Istituto Superiore Mario Boella, Via Boggio 61, 10138 Turin, Italy
{ferro,osella}@ismb.it
[2] University of Aegean, Department of Information and Communication Technologies Engineering, Gorgyras and Palama Str., 83200 Karlovassi, Samos, Greece
{eloukis,yannisx}@aegean.gr

**Abstract.** Governments have started increasingly using web 2.0 social media as a new channel of interaction with citizens in various phases of public policies lifecycle. In this direction they have started moving from simpler forms of exploitation of these strong bi-directional communication channels to more complex and sophisticated ones. These attempts constitute important innovations for government agencies, so it is necessary to analyse them from this perspective as well. This paper analyzes an advanced form of centralised use of multiple social media by government agencies from this perspective, using the well established Diffusion of Innovations Theory of Rogers. It is based on a pilot application of the above approach for conducting a consultation campaign in multiple social media concerning the large scale application of a telemedicine program of the Piedmont Regional Government, Italy. It has been concluded that this approach has the fundamental preconditions for a wide diffusion (relative advantage, compatibility with existing values and processes, reasonable complexity, trialability and observability), at least in government organizations having a tradition of bi-directional communication with citizens in all phases of policy making, and also some experience in using social media for this purpose.

## 1 Introduction

Governments have started increasingly using web 2.0 social media as a new channel of interaction with citizens in various phases of public policies life-cycle (agenda setting, policy design, adoption, implementation and monitoring - evaluation) [1-5]. Initially they adopted simpler forms of expoitation of these strong bi-directional communication channels, which involved setting up and operating manually accounts in some social media, posting manually content to them and then reading citizens' comments in order to draw conclusions. Recently they tend to shift towards more complex and sophisticated forms of social media use; they are based on the automated posting of content to multiple social media, and also the retrieval of various types of citizens' interactions with it (e.g. numbers of views, likes, retransmissions, etc.) and relevant content, using the Application Progamming Interfaces (APIs) of these social media, and finally highly sophisticated processing of them [6-9].

M.A. Wimmer, E. Tambouris, and A. Macintosh (Eds.): ePart 2013, LNCS 8075, pp. 95–108, 2013.
© IFIP International Federation for Information Processing 2013

These attempts constitute important innovations for government agencies, so it is necessary to analyse them from this perspective as well. It is important to investigate to what extent they have the fundamental preconditions for a wider diffusion in government. For this purpose we can use methods and frameworks developed by the extensive previous research on innovation diffusion [10]. Such research can reveal both 'strengths and weaknesses' from this perspective, i.e. characteristics and contextual factors that favour diffusion in government, and also characteristics and contextual factors that hinder it, so it can provide guidelines concerning required improvements in relevant systems and methods, and also the contexts they are more suitable for.

This paper makes a contribution in this direction. It analyzes an advanced form of multiple social media use by government agencies, based on a central system that uses social media APIs (a more detailed description of it is provided in section 3), from an innovation perspective, using the well established Diffusion of Innovations Theory of Rogers [11]. Our analysis is based on a pilot application of the above approach for conducting a consultation campaign in multiple social media concerning the large scale application of a telemedicine program of the Piedmont Regional Government, Italy. This research has been conducted as part of project PADGETS ('Policy Gadgets Mashing Underlying Group Knowledge in Web 2.0 Media' – www.padgets.eu), supported by the 'ICT for Governance and Policy Modeling' research initiative of the European Commission.

The paper is organized in seven sections. In the following section 2 the background of this study is outlined. It is followed by a brief description of the abovementioned advanced form of social media use in government in section 3, and its pilot application in section 4. Then in section 5 the research methodology is described, while in the following section 6 the results are presented. The final section 7 contains conclusions and future research directions.

## 2    Background

### 2.1    Social Media in Government

As mentioned in the introduction, social media, though they were initially used mainly by private sector firms in their marketing and customer service activities, are increasingly adopted and utilised by government agencies. It is gradually recognised that social media offer to government agencies significant opportunities for: i) increasing citizens' participation and engagement in public policy making, by providing to more groups a voice in discussions of policy development, implementation and evaluation; ii) promoting transparence and accountability, and reducing corruption, by enabling governments to open up large quantities of activity and spending related data, and at the same time citizens to collectively take part in monitoring the activities of their governments; iii) public services co-production, by enabling government agencies and the public to develop and design jointly government services; iv) crowdsourcing solutions and innovations, by exploiting public knowledge and talent in order to develop innovative solutions to the increasingly complex societal problems [3,12-14].

Highly useful for public policy making can be the capabilities offered by social media to apply the 'crowdsourcing' ideas [15,16], which have been initially developed in the private sector, but have subsequently taken root in the public sector as well (with appropriate adaptations to the specificities of government); these Web 2.0 platforms enable government agencies to mine useful fresh ideas from large numbers of citizens concerning possible solutions to social needs and problems, new public services or improvements of existing ones, or other types of innovations [14,17-23]. This can lead to the application of open innovation ideas in the public sector [21], and gradually result in 'co-production' of public services by government and citizens in cooperation [14,17]. According to [19] such 'citizen-sourcing' may change the government's perspective from viewing citizens as "users and choosers" of government services to "makers and shapers" of them.

However, at the same time relevant literature notes that social media not only offer important opportunities to government agencies, but also might pose some risks under specific circumstances [24]. It is widely recognized that further research is required both for developing new advanced and more efficient and effective forms of exploiting the capabilities offered by social media in government, and also for evaluating them from various perspectives in order to understand better their capabilities and strengths on one hand, and their weaknesses and risks on the other [3,25]. The research presented in this paper contributes in this direction, focusing on the the evaluation of an advanced form of social media use by government from an innovation diffusion perspective.

## 2.2    Diffusion of Innovations Theory

Extensive research has been conducted on innovation diffusion, in order to understand it better and identify factors that favor it [10]. One of the most widely accepted and use theories of innovations diffusion is the one proposed by [11], which has been extensively employed for analyzing ICT-related innovations in both the public and the private sector [26-29]. According to this theory, there are five critical characteristics of an innovation that determine the degree of its adoption, which are shown with their definitions in Table 1.

**Table 1.** Innovation characteristics that determine the degree of its adoption

| Characteristic | Definition |
| --- | --- |
| Relative Advantage | The degree to which an innovation is perceived as better than the idea, work practice or object it supersedes |
| Compatibility | The degree to which an innovation is perceived as being consistent with the existing values, past experiences, and needs of potential adopters |
| Complexity | The degree to which an innovation is perceived as difficult to understand, implement and use |
| Trialability | The degree to which an innovation may be experimented with on a limited scale basis |
| Observability | The degree to which the results of an innovation are visible to others |

Therefore it is paramount to assess to what extent various both simpler and advanced proposed approaches to social media usage by government agencies for supporting public policy making have the above characteristics, which result in higher levels of adoption and diffusion.

## 3     An Advanced Form of Multiple Social Media Use in Government

An advanced form of social media exploitation by government is under development in the abovementioned European project PADGETS (for more details on it see [6] and [7]), which is shown schematically in Figure 1. It hinges on the use of a central system for conducting consultation campaigns on a policy-related topic in multiple social media, carefully selected so that each of them attracts a different targeted group of citizens. In particular, the frontend of this systems allows a policy maker to create a consultation campaign, which includes definition of its topic, the targeted social media and relevant multimedia content (e.g. a short and a longer textual description, images, videos, etc.), termed as 'Policy Gadgets' (or 'Padgets'). The backend of the system using the APIs of these social media is posting to each of them the appropriate subset of this content (e.g. the short text to Twitter, the longer text to Blogger, the video to YouTube), and then retrieves data on citizens' interactions with it (e.g. numbers of views, likes, ratings, comments) from the afore-mentioned social media. Finally these data undergo in the backend three levels of processing in order to extract from them to useful information for policy makers:

1. calculation of various analytics (e.g. numbers of views, likes, ratings, comments, etc., per region, gender, age and education group, for each of the social media and in total),

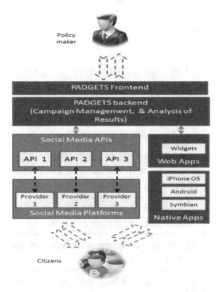

**Fig. 1.** An advanced form of centrally managed multiple social media use in government

2. text mining of the textual comments based on opinion mining techniques (for a review of them see [30]), in order to determine the 'sentiment' of citizens' comments (positive or negative), and the main issues and suggestions expressed by them,
3. future projections through simulation (e.g. using system dynamics or agent-based simulation - for more details see [31]).

# 4    A Pilot Application

In order to evaluate the abovementioned advanced form of centralised multiple social media use by government agencies from an innovation perspective, a pilot application of it was made in cooperation with Piedmont's Regional Government, Italy. One of its major problems has been for long time its high levels of spending for providing health services to its citizens (on average about 80% of its total budget). The increasing budget reductions currently experienced at local and at national level require regional governments to face a major challenge: to significantly reduce health related expenditures without deteriorating quality of service. For achieving these conflicting objectives Piedmont's Regional Government examined various measures, one of them being the introduction of telemedicine methods. In this direction it launched a pioneering telemedicine small scale project in one of the least populated and most mountainous of its provinces, Verbano-Cusio-Ossola (VCO). This telemedicine project was supported by the Local Health Authority of VCO that serves a population of about 172,000 citizens, with 23% of them being over 65 years old. The evaluation of this small scale project was positive, so Piedmont's Regional Government had to decide whether it should proceed to the large scale application of telemedicine practices in the whole Piedmont. Since this was a difficult and complex decision, for which a plethora of factors had to be taken into account, and also due to their long tradition of bi-directional communication with citizens in policy making (mainly using off-line methods, while recently they had some experience in using social media for this purpose), they decided to conduct a consultation with citizens on this in multiple social media, using the approach and the supporting central system described in the previous section. In this way they expected to take advantage of the high penetration of social media (at the level of 30% of ist population) in this region.

In particular, the objective of this social media campaign was to convey information on the planned extension of the telemedicine initiative in the whole Piedmont region to interested and affected citizens (e.g., patients and their families, doctors, health management emloyees), and then to collect feedback from them. The regional government expected through this campaign to gain a better understanding about the levels of final users' interest in and acceptance of these telemedicine services and the technology mediated model proposed for their provision; also, to identify possible barriers due to practical problems or internal organizational resistance, so that approppriate actions could be taken for addressing them. This project was associated with competences of four different departments of the Piedmont Regional Government, the Public Health, Budget and Finance, Institutional Communication and Regional Innovation ones, so it was decided all of them to be involved in it. For this consultation campaign Facebook was used as the central channel, due to both its peculiar interaction patterns as well as its noteworthy penetration rate in Piedmont's population. Beside Facebook, the campaign has made use of Twitter and YouTube. Also, Flickr and LinkedIn assumed an ancillary role. For all these five social media the existing accounts of the Piedmont Regional Goverment were used. The duration of this campaign was one month, during which six videos on telemedicine were created and published in YouTube, and ten policy messages were published via Twitter and Facebook. This campaign was promoted through the websites and the social media accounts of Piedmont Regional Goverment and other local organizations.

## 5    Research Methodology

After the end of this consultation campaign an analysis of it was conducted, which included three stages:

1. Initially we examined the analytics of this campaign provided by each of the above social media, with main emphasis on the following:

   – for Facebook: impressions per post, unique users per post, engaged users per post, users who generated 'stories' per post (sharings, likes, comments), organic reach per post, viral reach per post, virality percentage per post (number of storytellers divided by reach),
   – for YouTube: impressions per video, unique users per video, active interactions per video (likes, dislikes, comments, sharings),
   – or Twitter: retweets, replies and mentions, click-throughs on links included in twits.

2. Next we examined the results of the text mining performed for the textual comments of the citizens, with main emphasis on the issues and suggestions it extracted; for each of them we identified and examined the most representative of the comments mentioning it.
3. Finally, two semi-structured interviews were conducted with the most involved senior staff in this pilot: the Head of Public Health Department and a senior member of the Regional Innovation Department. The main objective of these interviews was to assess to what extent the proposed approach (centralised automated use of multiple social media), viewed as an innovation in government agencies policy making processes, has the five preconditions - characteristics for wide diffusion and adoption proposed by the innovations diffusions theory of [11] (in particular, the part of it that deals with the intrinsic characteristics of an innovation that influence an individual's decision to adopt or reject it): relative advantage, compatibility, complexity, trialability and observability. The main questions discussed are shown in Table 2. Each interview lasted about one hour, was tape-recorded and then transcribed. Open coding [32] of interviews transcripts followed, in order to extract the main points.

**Table 2.** Main questions of the interviews

| To what extent the proposed approach: |
|---|
| - is a better way for consultations with citizens on various public policies than the other existing 'physical' (i.e. through 'physical' meetings) or 'electronic' ways for this (relative advantage)? What are its advantages and also disadvantages?<br><br>- is compatible with the values and the policy formulation processes of government agencies (compatibility)?<br><br>- can be applied practically by government agencies policy makers without requiring much effort (complexity)?<br><br>- can be initially applied in small scale pilot applications by government agencies, in order to assess its capabilities, advantages and disadvantages, before proceeding to a larger scale application (trialability)?<br><br>- is an innovation highly visible to other public agencies, policy makers and the society in general, which can create positive impressions and comments (observability)? |

# 6    Results

## 6.1    Citizens' Reach and Engagement

In terms of reach, the policy messages of this campaign that were posted in the above social media have generated 28,165 impressions. This figure, that has to do with the mere reception of the policy message in the social media realm, is characterized by a cross-platform nature. In Facebook, the figure encompasses the views of posts associated to the campaign which are located on the fan page chosen by the policy makers (we had 27,320 views). Regarding YouTube, here the principle does not change, therefore the indicator includes views of the telemedicine related videos uploaded as part of this campaignv (we had 783). With respect to Twitter it is important to point out that the number of impressions of a given message ("tweet") cannot be computed resorting to either native or third parties' tools. In this platform, the only viable solution has been to estimate impressions using click-throughs on links as well as YouTube referrals (we had 62): as a consequence, this value represents a significant underestimation (at least one order of magnitude) of the actual performance expressed on the specific platform. Translating impressions into unique user accounts, the data from platforms' analytics show that over 11,000 accounts have been reached.

Moving from passive interactions to active engagement, platforms' analytics reveal the participation of more than 300 (unique) individuals during the campaign lifecycle. The inherent cross-platform nature of this consultation campaign implies the use of different measures from each platform for the calculation of this indicator: unique users who generated a story through comments, likes, and public sharing in Facebook, unique users who performed actions such as like, dislike, comments and sharing in YouTube and, in Twitter, unique users who re-tweeted or replied to tweets representing policy messages published by the campaign initiator.

As a supplement to afore-mentioned figures, it is relevant to stress that performances exhibited by campaign messages published during the pilot on Piedmont Regional Government's accounts have been remarkably superior to other messages posted in the same period apart from the institutional campaign, which may be seen in the guise of a control group. A quintessential example in this vein has to do with Facebook regional channel: taking into account this platform, the messages of this campaign had a reach three times larger than others (on average), while in terms of active engagement, they generated reactions about twenty times more than usual.

Going beyond reach and engagement numbers, precious stimuli for policy makers derive from the main perceptions, issues and suggestions extracted through text mining of citizens' textual commens. First of all, telemedicine is percived as a useful means for the rationalization of public spending, especially in a period when budget constraints are tighter than ever. Some messages in this vein are as follows:

*'The project has very good prospects and it can certainly represent an efficient way to reduce the cost of public health and prevention services'.*

*'An example to follow for regions like mine, Lazio, where – more and more frequently – past and present spending reviews are leading to closure of hospitals'.*

Also, substantial benefits are expected to arise also for the patients: whilst the continuous remote supervision of the patient's conditions is expected to result in an improvement of the quality of healthcare provision and patien's life, a reduction in the number of trips between dwelling places and local hospitals, and will have a remarkable impact in terms of savings (i.e., time devoted to mobility and cost of fuel) and environmental footprint (i.e., containment of $CO_2$ emissions). For instance, one message remarks that:

*'Telemedicine can remarkably reduce the queue for particular clinical examinations whose waiting time has now become eternal'.*

However, despite rosy expectations and fervent impulses coming from technophiles, there are still some major roadblocks clearly perceived by the population. In fact, a number of concerns have been expressed about the uneven technological literacy among patients, in light of the relentless aging phenomenon. A message on this states that:

*'Technology scares, especially those who are not born with the PC in the cradle'.*

Finally, citizens involved in the campaign outlined the risk of applying a technocratic approach that does not take into account the human aspects of the physician-patient relationship, or having problems due to insufficient training of healthcare personnel:

*'In any case, data interpretation – especially in more complex situations – requires always a thorough (and human) assessment'.*

## 6.2    Innovation Diffusion Determinants Assessment

The interviewees agreed that this approach (centralised automated use of multiple social media) offers strong relative advantages, in comparison with existing both 'physical' alternatives (e.g. physical meetings for communicating with citizens concerning various public policies under design or implementation) and 'electronic' ones (e.g. government e-participation/e-consultation portals). The inherent nature of this approach is perceived as going beyond the traditional schemes of 'official' e-participation/e-consultation portals developed and operated by government organizations. It was stressed that such a 'formal' e-consultation gives citizens some opportunities to offer comments in response to a limited set of questions posed by government. However, these designated 'official' e-consultation spaces are largely unknown to the general public due to the high costs of promotion and the slow pace of dissemination. Furthermore the tools they provide are not sufficiently user-friendly, and are often usable only by an affluent and acculturate minority. Another problem is that when the consultation period ends, policy makers are hit by a wave of textual comments, without obtaining a clear picture of *vox populi*. However, the examined novell approach is perceived as overcoming the above weaknesses and problems. It leverages already established installed large bases of social media users, and paves the way to a friction-less (i.e., faster and more frequent) interaction between policy makers and society. A substantial relative advantage arises with respect to previous generation of e-participation models due to the fact that the government makes a first step towards citizens (moving to the electronic spaces they chose for discussion and content production), rather than expecting the citizenry to move their content production activity onto the 'official' spaces created for e-Participation. It was also mentioned that the high levels of citizens' reach and engagement achieved in this pilot application of the examined approach, and the useful insights offered by citizens' textual comments and opinions, as discussed in previous section 6.1, are indicative the significant relative advantages that the examined approach provides. In general, the interviewees agree that this pilot confirms the expectations of relevant literature, as mentioned in 2.1, concerning the potential of social media in government along four dimensions: increasing citizens' participation and engagement in public policy making, promoting transparence and accountability (as the main advantages and disadvantages of various policy options can be widely communicated and discussed), public services co-production, and crowdsourcing solutions and innovations.

With respect to compatibility, the interviewees found that the pronounced cross-sectoral nature of this approach renders it a precious decision support tool capable to maximize the 'horizontality' in terms of application scope, and, as a consequence, it may be easily and effectively employed for any kind or thematic area of public policy. Furthermore, it can be used in every stage of the policy life-cycle (agenda setting, policy design, adoption, implementation and monitoring and evaluation). As a result, with regard to compatibility, the recourse to multiple social media seems to fit in with the policy formulation processes of government agencies. Interviewees concluded that the whole approach was compatible with the values and policy formulation processes of Piedmont Regional Government.

However, it was mentioned that the above relative advantages and compatibility are to a significant extent associated with two positive characteristics of the particular government agency, which might not exist in other other contexts: i) their long tradition and culture of bi-directional communication with citizens in all phases of policy making, and ii) their previous familiarity with and experience in using social media for the above purpose. If these do not exist, then it is likely that the above relative advantage and compatibility might be lower, or even there might be important relative disadvantages in comparison with existing alternative channels. Most government agencies have already developed some 'organizational capabilities' in using the abovementioned alternative physical and electronic channels of communication with citizens, but this has not happened yet with social media. The interviewees stressed that a 'typical public servant' might initially not feel 'culturally fit' for and familiar with the language and style of dialogue of most social media, and find it difficult to participate effectively in such dialogues; so if adequate training is not provided to them, there might be a risk of ineffective or even problematic communication between government agencies and citizens in the social media, which would have negative impact on the public image of the former. Furthermore, if there is a lack of tradition and culture of bi-directional communication with citizens in some government agencies, this might become more visible to the citizens due to the extensive, direct and informal interaction that characterises the social media, with negative consequences.

With respect to complexity, it was mentioned that the proposed approach, in combination with the ICT tools supporting it, have the distinctive trait of keeping moderate the cognitive effort required to policy makers. Despite processing data in behind the scene and provide decision makers with a set of synthetic, fresh and relevant data through intuitive visual outputs. The easily understandable way of reporting campaign results determines a substantial simplicity in usage that clears the hurdle of complexity, creating a fertile soil for a smooth adoption by every policymaker inclined to embrace 'open' policy making.

Furthermore, the successful completion of the pilot held in Piedmont Region corroborates the *a priori* conviction that this approach might take advantage of a noticeable scalability that allows to move all along the continuum ranging from small scale to full scale. All interviewees agreed that this innovation may be experimented without particular obstacles, since there does not exist a 'minimum efficient scale' for running a campaign, so it is characterised by trialability. It was recognised that this approach can be initially applied by government agencies in small scale pilot applications, in order to assess its capabilities and to fine-tune the underpinning mechanisms, before proceeding to larger scale applications.

Finally, the interviewees mentioned that the unprecedented exposure (at least in the digital world) given by social media to public policy campaigns makes this innovation highly visible to other public agencies, policy makers and the society in general. In fact, policy messages make their appearance on public pages accessible by everyone (i.e., Facebook Fan Pages, Twitter Pages, YouTube Channels) and viral 'contagious' phenomena occurring in the social media realm in light of intertwined social connections play their part in garnering a rapid and vast spreading of the policy proposal at stake. The resulting observability of the innovation has according to the interviewees a twofold advantage: on one hand, it stimulates the citizenry to step in the debate boosting the adoption rate, and, on the other hand, the opportunity to observe how the tool works on the field can create awareness in the public realm about the opportunity to tap social media in order to let 'collective intelligence' percolate across governmental boundaries.

# 7 Conclusions

The increasing adoption of social media by government agencies, initially simpler but gradually becoming more and more complex and sophisticated, constitutes an important innovation in their public policy making processes. Therefore it is important to analyse it from an innovation diffusion perspective as well, taking advantage of the extensive previous research in this area. This will allow us to understand to what extent various existing or emerging forms of social media exploitation in government, simpler or sophisticated ones, have the fundamental preconditions for a wider diffusion. Also, it will allow identifying characteristics of these approaches and the supporting systems, or of their context (e.g. characteristics of the adopting government organizations or the targeted citizens' groups), which do not favour their diffusion, and take appropriate actions for addressing them.

This paper aims to make a contribution in this direction. It analyses an advanced approach of using social media by government agencies, which includes centralized combined exploitation of multiple complementary social media platforms, in an automated manner taking advantage of their APIs, initially for posting to them various types of policy-related content, and then for retrieving users' interactions with them in these social media platforms, which finally undergo sophisticated processing. As theoretical foundation for our research we use the Diffusion of Innovations Theory proposed by [11]. Our analysis is based on a pilot application of this approach for conducting a consultation campaign concerning the large scale application of a telemedicine program of the Piedmont Regional Government, Italy.

It has been concluded that this approach has the fundamental preconditions for a wide diffusion according to the above theory: relative advantage, compatibility with existing values and processes, reasonable complexity, trialability and observability. However, its relative advantage and compatibility relies to a significant extent on the context on: i) the history and tradition of the adopting government agency with respect to bi-directional communication with citizens, and ii) on its familarity with and experience in using social media for this purpose. If these do not exist, the relative advantage and compatibility might be lower, or even there might be relative disadvantages in comparison with the alternative physical and electronic channels of communication with citizens. The use of social media by government agencies without sufficient preparation, training of the responsible staff, and in general development of 'organizational capabilities' in this area, and culture of bi-directional communication with citizens, might have negative impact on the image of government agencies.

The findings of this paper have interesting implications for research and management. With respect to research, it provides a framework for future analysis of existing or emerging forms, systems and methods of social media use by government agencies from an innovation diffusion perspective, which is definitely a quite important one. In general it opens up a new research direction, which combines theories, frameworks and methods from innovation, political sciences and e-participation research, in order to provide a deeper understanding of social media based innovations in political communication. With respect to management of government agencies, findings indicate that such a complex and sophisticated form of multiple social media use for bi-directional communication with citizens has the fundamental preconditions for a wide diffusion and adoption. However this might depend from previous history and tradition in communication with citizens, and at the same time might necessitate training and familiarization with a new language and style of dialogue with citizens, quite different from the ones dominant previously.

Further research is required on the existing and the emerging more complex and sophisticated forms of social media use in government from various innovation related perspectives, in different contexts (e.g. different government agencies with different cultural - organizational characteristics and relevant experiences, for different types of topics), examining the viewpoints of all stakeholders (politicians, public servants and citizens) and using both qualitative and quantitative methodologies.

# References

1. Osimo, D.: Web 2.0 in Government: Why and How? European Commission Joint Research Center - Institute for Prospective Technological Studies. Office for Official Publications of the European Communities, Luxembourg (2008)
2. Punie, Y., Misuraca, G., Osimo, D.: Public Services 2.0: The Impact of Social Computing on Public Services. JRC Scientific and Technical Reports. European Commission, Joint Research Centre, Institute for Prospective Technological Studies (2009)
3. Bertot, J.C., Jaeger, P.T., Hansen, D.: The impact of policies on government social media usage: Issues, challenges and recommendations. Government Information Quarterly 29, 30–40 (2012)
4. Bonsón, E., Torres, L., Royo, S., Flores, F.: Local e-government 2. 0: Social media and corporate transparency in municipalities. Government Information Quarterly 29, 123–132 (2012)
5. Snead, J.T.: Social media use in the U.S. Executive branch. Government Information Quarterly 30, 56–63 (2013)
6. Ferro, E., Osella, M., Charalabidis, Y., Loukis, E., Boero, R.: Policy Gadgets: Paving the Way for Next-Generation Policy Making. In: IFIP Third International Conference on e-Participation - ePart 2011, Delft, The Netherlands (2011)
7. Charalabidis, Y., Loukis, E.: Participative Public Policy Making Through Multiple Social Media Platforms Utilization. International Journal of Electronic Government Research 8(3), 78–97 (2012)

8. Wandhöfer, T., Taylor, S., Alani, H., Joshi, S., Sizov, S., Walland, P., Thamm, M., Bleier, A., Mutschke, P.: Engaging Politicians with Citizens on Social Networking Sites: The WeGov Toolbox. International Journal of Electronic Government Research 8(3), 22–43 (2012)

9. Charalabidis, Y., Triantafillou, A., Karkaletsis, V., Loukis, E.: Public Policy Formulation Through Non-Moderated Crowdsourcing in Social Media. In: Proceedings of IFIP Fourth International Conference on e-Participation - ePart 2012, Kristiansand, Norway, September 3-6 (2012)

10. MacVaugh, J., Schiavone, F.: Limits to the diffusion of innovation - A literature review and integrative model. European Journal of Innovation Management 13(2), 197–221 (2010)

11. Rogers, E.: Diffusion of Innovations, 5th edn. The Free Press, New York (2003)

12. Bertot, J.C., Jaeger, P.T., Munson, S., Glaisyer, T.: Engaging the public in open government: The policy and government application of social media technology for government transparency. IEEE Computer 43(11), 53–59 (2010)

13. Bertot, J.C., Jaeger, P.T., Grimes, J.M.: Promoting transparency and accountability through ICTs, social media, and collaborative e-government. Transforming Government: People, Process and Policy 6(1), 78–91 (2012)

14. Linders, D.: From e-government to we-government: Defining a typology for citizen coproduction in the age of social media. Government Information Quarterly 29, 446–454 (2012)

15. Surowiecki, J.: The wisdom of crowds. Doubleday, New York (2004)

16. Brabham, D.C.: Crowdsourcing as a Model for Problem Solving: An Introduction and Cases. Convergence: The International Journal of Research into New Media Technologies 14(1), 75–90 (2008)

17. Bovaird, T.: Beyond engagement and participation: User and community coproduction of public services. Public Administration Review 67(5), 846–860 (2007)

18. Torres, L.H.: Citizen sourcing in the public interest. Knowledge Management for Development Journal 3(1), 134–145 (2007)

19. Lukensmeyer, C.J., Torres, L.H.: Citizensourcing: Citizen participation in a networked nation. In: Yang, K., Bergrud, E. (eds.) Civic Engagement in a Network Society, pp. 207–233. Information Age Publishing, Charlotte (2008)

20. Chun, S.A., Shulman, S., Sandoval, R., Hovy, E.: Government 2.0: Making connections between citizens, data and government. Information Polity 15(1/2), 1–9 (2010)

21. Hilgers, D., Ihl, C.: Citizensourcing: Applying the concept of open innovation to the public sector. The International Journal of Public Participation 4(1), 67–88 (2010)

22. Nam, T.: Suggesting frameworks of citizen-sourcing via Government 2.0. Government Information Quarterly 29, 12–20 (2012)

23. Margo, M.J.: A Review of Social Media Use in E-Government. Administrative Sciences. Administrative Sciences 2(2), 148–161 (2012)

24. Picazo-Vela, S., Gutiérrez-Martínez, I., Luna-Reyes, L.F.: Understanding risks, benefits, and strategic alternatives of social media applications in the public sector. Government Information Quarterly 29, 504–511 (2012)

25. Chun, S.A., Luna Reyes, L.F.: Editorial - Social media in government. Government Information Quarterly 29, 441–445 (2012)

26. Wonglimpiyarata, J., Yuberk, N.: In support of innovation management and Roger's Innovation Diffusion theory. Government Information Quarterly 22, 411–422 (2005)

27. Raus, M., Flügge, B., Boutellier, R.: Electronic customs innovation: An improvement of governmental infrastructures. Government Information Quarterly 26, 246–256 (2009)

28. Loukis, E., Spinellis, D., Katsigiannis, A.: Barriers to the adoption of B2B e-marketplaces by large enterprises: lessons learnt from the Hellenic Aerospace Industry. Information Systems Management 28(2), 130–146 (2011)
29. Al-Jabri, I.M., Sohail, M.S.: Mobile Banking Adoption: Application of Diffudion of Innovation Theory. Journal of Electronic Commerce Research 13(4), 373–385 (2012)
30. Maragoudakis, M., Loukis, E., Charalabidis, Y.: A Review of Opinion Mining Methods for Analyzing Citizens' Contributions in Public Policy Debate. In: IFIP Third International Conference on e-Participation - ePart 2011, Delft, The Netherlands (2011)
31. Charalabidis, Y., Loukis, E., Androutsopoulou, A.: Enhancing Participative Policy Making Through Simulation Modelling – A State of the Art Review. In: Proceedings of European Mediterranean Conference on Information Systems (EMCIS) 2011, Athens, Greece, May 30-31 (2011)
32. Maylor, H., Blackmon, K.: Researching Business and Management. Palgrave-Macmillan, New York (2005)

# Approaches to Assessing Public Concerns: Building Linked Data for Public Goals and Criteria Extracted from Textual Content

Shun Shiramatsu, Tadachika Ozono, and Toramatsu Shintani

Graduate School of Engineering, Nagoya Institute of Technology, Japan
{siramatu,ozono,tora}@nitech.ac.jp

**Abstract.** The importance of public involvement in Japanese regional societies is increasing because they currently face complicated and ongoing social issues due to the post-maturity stage of these societies. Since citizens who have beneficial awareness or knowledge are not always experts on relevant social issues, assessing and sharing public concerns are needed to reduce barriers to public participation. We propose two approaches to assess public concerns. The first is building a linked open data set by extracting public goals for a specific social issue aimed at by citizens or agents from articles or public opinions. This paper deals with hierarchical goals and subgoals for recovery and revitalization from the Great East Japan Earthquake manually extracted from related articles. The data set can be used for developing services to match citizens and agents who aim at similar goals to facilitate collaboration. The second approach is building a linked data set by extracting assessment criteria for a specific social issue from public opinions. This paper deals with candidate terms that potentially represent such criteria for a specific public project automatically extracted from clusters of citizens' opinions. The data set can be used as evidence for policy-making about the target project.

**Keywords:** Linked Data, Public Involvement, Concern Assessment, Goal Matching Service, Text Mining.

## 1 Introduction

Japanese regional societies currently face complicated and ongoing social issues, e.g., disaster risks, dilapidated infrastructures, radiation pollution, and an aging population. Some Japanese researchers regard such troubling situations, that are partially due to the post-maturity stage of societies, as "a front-runner of emerging issues" [1]. Public involvement is an interactive communication process between stakeholders in deciding public policy [2] and has thus become more important to explore optimal solutions to complicated issues. For example, interactive and bottom-up communication is essential to design an optimal policy toward recovery and revitalization from the Great East Japan Earthquake [3].

Since citizens who have beneficial awareness or knowledge are not always experts on relevant social issues, public concerns need to be assessed and shared

M.A. Wimmer, E. Tambouris, and A. Macintosh (Eds.): ePart 2013, LNCS 8075, pp. 109–121, 2013.

to reduce barriers to public participation. It is difficult to participate in issues without contextual or background information. Linked open data (LOD), which are semantically connected data on the basis of universal resource identifiers (URIs) and the resource description framework (RDF), plays an important role in fostering open government [4]. We aim to accrue LOD to share public concerns among citizens, governments, and experts to increase transparency that facilitates eParticipation. The structure of public concerns is an important context when building consensus. In this paper, we call the process of structuring public concerns "*concern assessment*".

Social networking systems (SNSs) such as Facebook are used for developing collaborative relationships not only in private but also in public spheres. To reduce barriers to participation and collaboration in public spheres, we consider that SNSs need to incorporate functions to share public concerns. In this paper, we focus on two types of public concerns, i.e., public goals and assessment criteria. Public goals that are aimed at by citizens are important for facilitating public collaboration. Assessment criteria for a specific social issue are also important for comparing and deliberating on multiple options to solve the issue.

We have developed an LOD set called SOCIA (Social Opinions and Concerns for Ideal Argumentation) that consists of Web content related to Japanese geographic regions, e.g., regional news articles, microblog posts, and minutes of city council meetings. The vocabularies for structuring relationships among such content and opinions are partially defined in the SOCIA ontology that we designed.

The main reason SOCIA deals with such web content is to share background context behind regional social issues. The background context that should be supported, however, includes not only relationships among content but also personal context, e.g., public goals and assessment criteria. The conventional SOCIA dataset and ontology could not yet support these kinds of personal context. In this paper, we expand the SOCIA ontology for structuring public goals and criteria and presents and present a prototyped dataset consistings of goals for revitalization from the Great East Japan Earthquake.

## 2   Literature Review

The International Association for Public Participation (IAP2) [5] and the Obama administration's Open Government Initiative (OGI) [6] have presented similar stages for public participation, i.e., the Spectrum of Public Participation and the Principles of Open Government shown in Fig. 1. The gradation in the figure represents the public impact of each stage. The figure also indicates the expected coverage of the use of LOD. Open data generally contributes to transparency and informativity, i.e., to the first stage. However, non-linked open data (e.g., CSV table data) generally lack interoperability. LOD is expected to be able to also contribute to the higher/collaborative stages because semantic links compliant with RDF increase the interoperability of data and help us to reuse data for interorganizational collaboration. Contextual information provided by the semantic

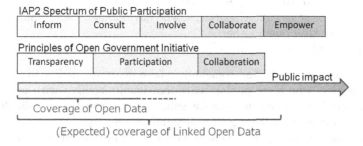

**Fig. 1.** Expected coverage of Linked Open Data

links provides the potential for developing social web services to facilitate public collaboratoin. For example, an architecture based on linked data paradigm for participatory decision-making proposed by Kalampokis et al [7] can potentially be expanded to an architecture for supporting inter-organizational collaboration.

Over 40 countries currently have open data portals.[1] The number of open data portals has been increasing since 2009. In Japan, the Ministry of Economy, Trade and Industry operates a web site called the "Open Government Laboratory"[2] as an experimental Web site towards achieving eParticipation and eGovernment. The LOD Challenge Japan has been held since 2011, which is modeled on the Open Data Challenge in Europe. SOCIA and our system [8] received the ChallengeDay Award at the LOD Challenge Japan 2011.[3] Utilizing open data is rapidly promoted by "e-Government Open Data Strategy" of the IT Strategy Headquarters of the Japanese Government since 2012.

There are several vocabularies that can be used for public participation or collaboration, e.g., the participation schema [9] and the weighted interests vocabulary [10]. However, these vocabularies have not focused on assessing public concerns to facilitate public collaboration. This study presents how to deal with public goals and assessment criteria on the basis of LOD.

## 3    Manual Extraction of Public Goals

Public collaboration and consensus building between stakeholders are essential to enable revitalization from disasters, e.g., the Great East Japan Earthquake. Collaboration between multiple agents generally requires the following conditions:

- Similarity of the agents' goals or objectives
- Complementarity of the agents' skills, abilities, or resources

---

[1] http://www.data.gov/opendatasites

[2] http://openlabs.go.jp/ (in Japanese)

[3] http://lod.sfc.keio.ac.jp/challenge2011/result2011.html (in Japanese)

As the first step, this study focuses on the similarity of the goals. Sharing a data set of public goals can help citizens, who have similar goals, build consensus and collaborate with one another.

We focus on the following three problems related to public collaboration.

1. Citizens cannot easily find somebody whose goals are similar to their ones.
2. Stakeholders who have similar goals occasionally conflict with one another when building consensus because subgoals are sometimes difficult to be agreed on even if the final goal is generally agreed on.
3. A too abstract and general goal is hard to be contributed collaboratively.

We presume that the hierarchies of goals and subgoals play important roles to address these problems. First, the hierarchical structure can make methods of calculating the similarity between public goals more sophisticated. The hierarchy provides rich context to improve retrieval of similar goals. If the data set of public goals had only short textual descriptions without hierarchical structures, calculating the similarity between goals would be difficult and the recall ratio in retrieving similar goals would be lower. Second, visualizing the hierarchies is expected to support people in conflict to attain compromises. Third, dividing goals into fine-grained subgoals reduces barriers to participation and collaboration because small contributions to fine-grained subgoals are more easily provided.

We are planning to develop a Web service to match citizens and agents who are aiming at similar goals to facilitate collaboration. Toward this end, we expanded the SOCIA ontology to describe the public goals in Fig. 2. The property socia:subgoal enables us to describe the hierarchical structure of goals and

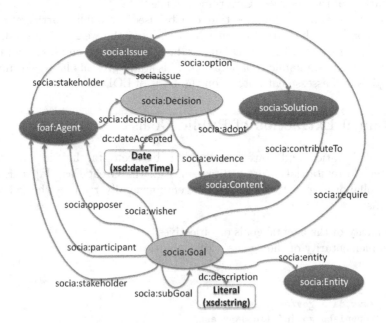

**Fig. 2.** Expanded classes in SOCIA ontology to represent public goals

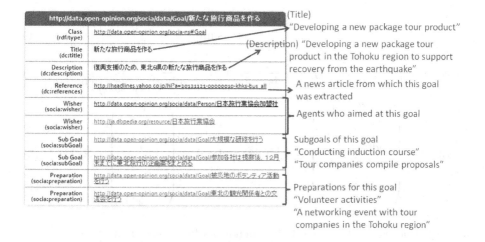

**Fig. 3.** Instance of public goal: "Developing new package tour product"

subgoals. The public goal matching service that we aim to develop requires high-recall retrieval of similar goals to facilitate inter-domain, inter-area, and inter-organizational collaboration.

To develop a service for matching public goals, data on public goals need to be input by stakeholders who are aiming at the goals in person. Before developing such an SNS like mechanism to input stakeholders' goals and match them, we built an LOD set[4] by manually extracting public goals from news articles and related documents. The 657 public goals and 4349 RDF triples were manually extracted from 96 news articles and two related documents by one human annotator. The most abstract goal that is the root node of the goal-subgoal hierarchy is "revitalization from the earthquake".[5] The subgoals are linked from this goal with the `socia:subgoal` property.

The manually built LOD set can be used for developing a method of calculating the similarities between public goals. It can also be used as example seed data when citizen users input their own goals for revitalization. Fig. 3 shows an instance of a public goal to revitalize the Tohoku region from the Great East Japan Earthquake. This goal of "developing a new package tour product", has a title in Japanese, a description in Japanese, and two subgoal data resources.

The cosine similarity between public goals can be calculated on the basis of a recursive definition of a bag-of-features vector as:

---

[4] `http://data.open-opinion.org/socia/data/`
`Goal?rdf:type=socia:Goal&limit=100` (in Japanese)

[5] `http://data.open-opinion.org/socia/data/Goal/%E9%9C%87%E7%81%BD`
`%E5%BE%A9%E8%88%88` (in Japanese)

$$\text{sim}(g_i, g_j) = \frac{\text{bof}(g_i) \cdot \text{bof}(g_j)}{\|\text{bof}(g_i)\|\|\text{bof}(g_j)\|} \quad (1)$$

$$\text{bof}(g) = \frac{\alpha}{\|\text{tfidf}(g)\|}\text{tfidf}(g) + \frac{\beta}{\|\text{lda}(g)\|}\text{lda}(g) + \frac{\gamma}{|\text{sub}(g)|} \sum_{sg \in \text{sub}(g)} \frac{\text{bof}(sg)}{\|\text{bof}(sg)\|} \quad (2)$$

$$\text{tfidf}(g) = \begin{pmatrix} \text{tfidf}(w_1, g) \\ \vdots \\ \text{tfidf}(w_{|W|}, g) \\ 0 \\ \vdots \\ 0 \end{pmatrix} \in \mathbb{R}^{|W|+|Z|}, \quad \text{lda}(g) = \begin{pmatrix} 0 \\ \vdots \\ 0 \\ \text{p}(z_1|g) \\ \vdots \\ \text{p}(z_{|Z|}|g) \end{pmatrix} \in \mathbb{R}^{|W|+|Z|}, (3)$$

where $g$ denotes a public goal, $\text{bof}(g)$ denotes a bag-of-features vector of $g$, and $\text{sub}(g)$ denotes a set of subgoals of $g$. Here, $w \in W$ denotes a term, $z \in Z$ denotes a latent topic derived by a latent topic model [11], and $\text{tfidf}(w, g)$ denotes the TF-IDF, i.e., the product of term frequency and inverse document frequency, of $w$ in a title and a description of $g$. The $\text{p}(z|g)$ denotes the probability of $z$ given $g$, $0 \leq \alpha, \beta, \gamma \leq 1$, and $\alpha + \beta + \gamma = 1$. The reason this definition incorporates a latent topic model is to enable short descriptions of goals to be dealt with because TF-IDF is insufficient for calculating similarities in short texts. The parameters $\alpha$, $\beta$, and $\gamma$ are empirically determined on the basis of actual data.

This prototyped method of calculating similarities should be tested, verified, and refined though experiments in future work using the LOD set of public goals that we present.

## 4    Automatic Extraction of Assessment Criteria

Citispe@k, which is our system for online public debate, supports manual tagging of assessment criteria for public opinions and Web content [12]. Transparent and participatory management of public issues requires assessing public concerns about the issue and criteria for the assessment. We call the criteria for the concern assessment "assessment criteria" in this paper. Although assessment criteria are diversified for each public issue, citispe@k does not yet support suggestion functions for setting new criteria. Here, we investigate the ability to apply text mining to extract assessment criteria from public opinions gathered from public workshops about a specific public project to maintain mountainous areas.

These workshops were held four times in four different areas. Participants at each workshop were divided into three to four debate teams. There were a total of 15 debate teams in these workshops. There were about five to six participants for each debate team, and one of them was a facilitator who did not state opinions. The opinions stated in each debate were manually structured according to the KJ-method [13], which consisted of brainstorming and grouping phases. The opinions were written on colored cards in the brainstorming phase. Red cards

**Table 1.** Citizens' opinions written on sticky notes with KJ method

|  | Area A | Area B | Area C | Area D | Total |
|---|---|---|---|---|---|
| No. of debate teams | 4 | 4 | 3 | 4 | 15 |
| Positive (red) | 50 | 63 | 45 | 54 | 212 |
| Negative (blue) | 40 | 57 | 48 | 59 | 194 |
| Demand (yellow) | 37 | 48 | 57 | 53 | 205 |
| Total | 127 | 168 | 150 | 166 | 611 |

**Table 2.** Utterances in debate transcripts

|  | Area A | Area B | Area C | Area D | Total |
|---|---|---|---|---|---|
| No. of debate teams | 4 | 4 | 3 | 4 | 15 |
| In-range, citizens | 678 | 685 | 450 | 681 | 2494 |
| In-range, facilitators | 509 | 401 | 279 | 279 | 1468 |
| Out-of-range | 293 | 534 | 288 | 252 | 1367 |
| Total | 1480 | 1620 | 1017 | 1212 | 5329 |

were for positive opinions, blue cards were for negative ones, and yellow cards were for demands or hopes. The opinions on the cards were manually classified into several groups in the grouping phase. The opinion groups had manually assigned labels. Although the group labels potentially represented assessment criteria if their expressions were uniform, their expressions were actually non-uniform and different for each debate team. Hence, we should apply text mining techniques to automatically extract candidate terms for assessment criteria. We employed a method of cluster analysis using text mining techniques, i.e., we clustered the opinions and extracted feature terms for each cluster.

The frequency of terms for short texts was insufficient for calculating similarities. The shorter the text content became, the lower the probability of the same term concurrently occurring in two kinds of content became, even if they were semantically close. Actually, participants at the workshops could not write lengthy opinions on the cards. The average number of morphemes in each opinion on a card was only 13.4. To address this problem, we used the latent Dirichlet allocation (LDA) [11], which is a frequently used model of latent topics in a document set. We used an implementation of the hierarchical Dirichlet process-LDA (HDP-LDA)[6] in the training phase of a topic model [14]. Although conventional LDA needs to be manually given the number of latent topics, HDP-LDA can determine this automatically.

Table 1 summarizes the number of opinions written on cards for each area. A total of 611 opinions were written by 15 debate teams. Since there were insufficient opinions to train the latent topic model, we also used utterances that were related to opinions on the cards in 15 debate transcripts. Table 2 lists the number of utterances in debate transcripts for each area. We regarded adjacent

---

[6] http://www.cs.princeton.edu/~blei/topicmodeling.html

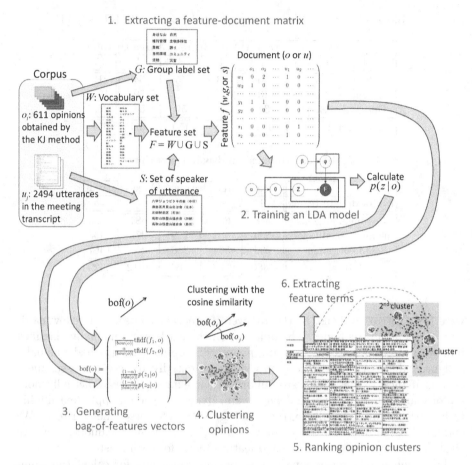

**Fig. 4.** Clustering opinions and extracting feature terms that potentially represent assessment criteria

sentences sandwiched by interlocutors' names as one utterance. Although there were a total of 5329 utterances, the transcripts also included irrelevant utterances, e.g., introductory and concluding remarks and facilitators' utterances. To divide transcripts into relevant (in-range) and irrelevant segments (out-of-range), we appended boundary markers to them. There were 2494 utterances other than those by facilitators in the in-range segment. These 611 opinions and 2494 utterances were used as a corpus to train HDP-LDA.

The procedure for clustering opinions and extracting feature terms that potentially represent assessment criteria is detailed in Fig. 4 Hereafter, let $o \in O$ be an opinion written on a card, $u \in U$ be an utterance in transcripts of the debate, and $d \in D = O \cup U$ be a document (i.e., $d$ is any one of $o$ or $u$). Let $w \in W$ be a morpheme $N$-gram ($N = 1, 2, 3$), $g \in G$ be a label for an opinion group manually assigned, $s \in S$ be a speaker (interlocutor) of an utterance in the debate transcripts, and $z \in Z$ be a latent topic derived by HDP-LDA.

To prepare for step 1 in the figure, determine feature set $F = W \cup G \cup S$ and document set $D = O \cup U$ appearing in the corpus. $w \in W$ can be extracted from the corpus through morphological analysis by using MeCab[7], which is a morphological analyzer. Morpheme $N$-grams that appear less than three times in the corpus are excluded because such rare expressions are not suitable for statistical processing. In the step 1, the feature-document matrix consists of frequencies of features in each document (i.e., opinion on cards or utterances in transcripts). In the step 2, an LDA model is trained from the feature-document matrix with the HDP-LDA tool. Probability $p(z|o)$ is calculated using the parameters obtained with the trained model. In the step 3, the bof($o$), which is a bag-of-features vector for $o$, is generated as:

**Table 3.** Feature terms of top four clusters that potentially represent assessment criteria

|  | 1st cluster | 2nd cluster |
|---|---|---|
| Feature N-grams (translated from Japanese) | Desirable, climbable, near, stroll, mountain, everyday climbing, hiking trail, Suma Alps | Far, break, Osaka, mountains, foliage tree, observation deck, broad-leafed tree, landscape, seasons |
| Interpretation by a user | Maintaining hiking trails | Landscapes of mountains |
| No. of opinions | 82 | 54 |
| (Negative+demand) ratio | 0.488 | 0.315 |
| Opinions near to cluster centroid (translated from Japanese) | The climbing trails are maintained → ease of use | Are there any collaborative tasks to make Mt. Takatori better |
|  | The hiking trails are maintained. | Great because the sea, mountain, and town can all be seen. Good perspective from the sea. |
|  | There are no handrails on the climbing trails. | I have a view of Mt. Takatori every morning. The mountain's green surroundings are pleasant. |

|  | 3rd cluster | 4th cluster |
|---|---|---|
| Feature N-grams (translated from Japanese) | Crow, young people, dragonfly, decrease, increase, environment - creation, a lot of greenery | Grow forest, artificial, harvested, project, citizen, important, green belt, safety, animal |
| Interpretation by a user | Ecosystem | Growing forest and nature |
| No. of opinions | 31 | 25 |
| (Negative+demand) ratio | 0.614 | 0.882 |
| Opinions near to cluster centroid (translated from Japanese) | Number of boars increased. | Maintain artificially constructed things. |
|  | Number of crows increased. | Artificial forests increased. |
|  | Now there is a lot of greenery, more than when the Hanshin earthquake occurred. | Citizens groups for vitalizing mountainous areas need government financial help. |

---

[7] https://code.google.com/p/mecab/ (in Japanese)

$$\text{bof}(o) = \frac{\alpha}{\|\text{tfidf}(o)\|}\text{tfidf}(o) + \frac{1-\alpha}{\|\text{lda}(o)\|}\text{lda}(o), \tag{4}$$

where vectors $\text{tfidf}(o)$ and $\text{lda}(o)$ are defined in the same way as that in Eq. (3) in the previous section. Parameter $\alpha$ satisfies $0 \le \alpha \le 1$. In the step 4, opinions $o_i$ and $o_j$ whose cosine similarity is greater than a particular threshold, $\theta$, are grouped as cluster $c$. Clusters whose cosine similarity between their centroids is greater than $\theta$ are also grouped as one cluster. One opinion can belong to multiple clusters, i.e., this method is a kind of soft clustering. In the step 5, opinion clusters $c \in C$ are ranked in descending order of the number of opinions. In the step 6, $w$ as candidate feature terms for each opinion cluster $c$ are ranked with the following score based on pointwise mutual information (PMI):

$$\text{score}(w, c) = \frac{\text{PMI}(w, c) - E_w}{\sigma_w} \quad \text{and} \tag{5}$$

$$\text{PMI}(w, c) = \log \frac{\text{p}(w, c)}{\text{p}(w)\text{p}(c)}, \tag{6}$$

where $E_w = \frac{1}{|C|}\sum_{c \in C}\text{PMI}(w, c)$ and $\sigma_w = \frac{1}{|C|}\sqrt{\sum_{c \in C}(\text{PMI}(w, c) - E_w)^2}$. Canonicalization by using standard variation $\sigma_w$ in Eq. (5) is necessary because rare terms tend to be over-emphasized by only the PMI value.

We empirically set $\alpha = 0.5$ and $\theta = 0.65$ in this experiment , and the four top-ranked clusters and extracted feature terms with high scores are listed in Table 3. The feature terms for each cluster represent kinds of facets of opinions in the cluster. They potentially represent assessment criteria that are focused on by the opinion cluster. For example, the feature terms in the first cluster can be interpreted as "maintaining hiking trails" and those in the second cluster can be interpreted as "landscapes of mountains". The obtained clusters can be

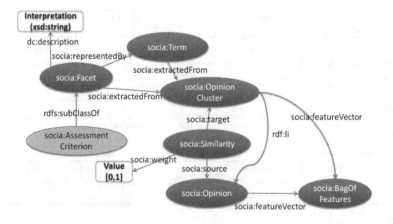

**Fig. 5.** Expanded classes in SOCIA ontology to represent assessment criteria

interpreted as facets or assessment criteria of opinions. The ratio for negative opinions and demand (blue and yellow cards), which is weighted according to the distance from cluster centroids, represents the degree of needs to be addressed by the target public project. For example, the ratio for the second cluster is low because the participants are satisfying the landscapes of mountains.

Fig. 5 outlines classes that are newly needed in SOCIA to describe the assessment criteria extracted from opinions. All opinion clusters correspond to `socia:Facet`. Clusters interpreted as assessment criteria can be instances of `socia:AssessmentCriterion`, which is the subclass of `socia:Facet`. An LOD set for assessment criteria can be built according to the classes in the figure. The links between assessment criteria and opinion clusters enable government and citizens to check context behind the concern assessment. Such structure can be utilized to develop tools for assessing and sharing public concerns.

Furthermore, we visualized the distribution of opinions to enable users to understand the overview using non-metric multidimensional scaling (NMDS) based on the inverse cosine similarity of $bof(o)$ shown in Fig. 6. The colors of the points in the figure correspond to the colors of cards. Semantically close opinions are closely located by the NMDS algorithm. We use function `isoMDS` for NMDS, which is included in the library MASS in the statistical software R.[8] On the basis of this visualization, we developed an exploratory browsing interface on the Web browser shown in Fig. 7. Users can interactively browse neighboring opinion clusters of their clicked points in this browsing interface.

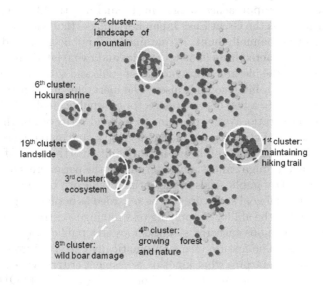

**Fig. 6.** Visualizing opinion distribution based on NMDS

---

[8] http://www.r-project.org/

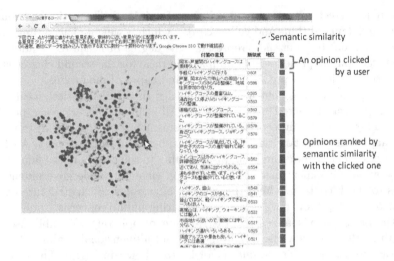

**Fig. 7.** Web application for exploratory browsing of opinions based on NMDS visualization

## 5    Conclusion

We focused on two types of public concerns, i.e., public goals and assessment criteria, and presented our approaches to assessing them. First, the LOD of public goals for revitalization from the Great East Japan Earthquake that was aimed at by citizens or agents was manually built. It contained 657 public goals and 4349 RDF triples manually extracted from 96 news articles and two related documents. The data set dealt with the hierarchical structure of goals and subgoals, which played important roles in attaining compromises. The hierarchy of subgoals was recursively used to generate a bag-of-features vector of a public goal in order to avoid decreasing the recall ratio. We are planning to test and verify our method of calculating the similarities between goals and to develop a goal matching service using this data set. The effectiveness of the recursive definition of the bag-of-features vector can be verified through empirically determining the parameters $\alpha$, $\beta$, and $\gamma$ on the basis of the LOD of public goals. If the optimal value of $\gamma$ becomes significantly greater than 0, the subgoal structure can be regarded as actually significant. Second, we investigated the ability of applying text mining to extract assessment criteria from public opinions gathered at workshops on a public project to maintain mountainous areas. The feature terms automatically extracted from an opinion cluster helped us to interpret what kinds of assessment criteria were indicated by clusters. We also presented an extension of our ontology to build LOD for assessment criteria. Moreover, we developed an exploratory browsing interface to enable overviews of opinion clusters to be understood.

**Acknowledgments.** This work was supported by the Revitalization Promotion Program (A-STEP) (No. 241FT0304) of JST, the Grant-in-Aid for Young Scientists (B)

(No. 25870321) from JSPS, the SCOPE from the Ministry of Internal Affairs and Communications, the Rokko Sabo office of the Ministry of Land, Infrastructure, Transport and Tourism, and Yachiyo Engineering Co., Ltd. We would also like to sincerely thank Dr. Hayeong JEONG for her valuable advices.

# References

1. Komiyama, H.: Vision 2050 and the role of japan toward the sustainable society. In: Proceedings of the 4th International Symposium on Environmentally Conscious Design and Inverse Manufacturing, pp. 2–4 (2005)
2. Jeong, H., Hatori, T., Kobayashi, K.: Discourse analysis of public debates: A corpus-based approach. In: Proceedings of 2007 IEEE International Conference on Systems, Man and Cybernetics, pp. 1782–1793 (2007)
3. Nishimori, M., Kanke, M., Tsutsuki, A., Kotake, N., Shirasaka, S., Yasui, T.: Optimal policy design for disaster-hit area of japan: bottom-up systems analysis of special zone for reconstruction by the isdm. In: Proceedings of the CESUN 3rd International Engineering Systems Symposium (2012)
4. Höchtl, J., Reichstädter, P.: Linked open data - A means for public sector information management. In: Andersen, K.N., Francesconi, E., Grönlund, Å., van Engers, T.M. (eds.) EGOVIS 2011. LNCS, vol. 6866, pp. 330–343. Springer, Heidelberg (2011)
5. IAP2: Iap2 spectrum of public participation (2007), http://www.iap2.org/associations/4748/files/IAP2%20Spectrum_vertical.pdf
6. WhiteHouse: Open government initiative (2009), http://www.whitehouse.gov/open
7. Kalampokis, E., Hausenblas, M., Tarabanis, K.: Combining social and government open data for participatory decision-making. In: Tambouris, E., Macintosh, A., de Bruijn, H. (eds.) ePart 2011. LNCS, vol. 6847, pp. 36–47. Springer, Heidelberg (2011)
8. Shiramatsu, S., Swezey, R.M.E., Sano, H., Hirata, N., Ozono, T., Shintani, T.: Structuring japanese regional information gathered from the web as linked open data for use in concern assessment. In: Tambouris, E., Macintosh, A., Sæbø, Ø. (eds.) ePart 2012. LNCS, vol. 7444, pp. 73–84. Springer, Heidelberg (2012)
9. Styles, R., Wallace, C., Moeller, K.: Participation schema (2008), http://purl.org//vocab//participation/schema
10. Brickley, D., Miller, L., Inkster, T., Zeng, Y., Wang, Y., Damljanovic, D., Huang, Z., Kinsella, S., Breslin, J., Ferris, B.: The weighted interests vocabulary 0.5 (2010), http://purl.org/ontology/w/core
11. Blei, D.M., Ng, A.Y., Jordan, M.I.: Latent Dirichlet Allocation. Journal of Machine Learning Research 3, 993–1022 (2003)
12. Swezey, R., Sano, H., Hirata, N., Shiramatsu, S., Ozono, T., Shintani, T.: An e-participation support system for regional communities based on linked open data, classification and clustering. In: Proceedings of the 11th IEEE International Conference on Cognitive Informatics & Cognitive Computing, pp. 211–218 (2012)
13. Kunifuji, S., Kato, N.: Consensus-making support systems dedicated to creative problem solving. International Journal of Information Technology and Decision Making 6(3), 459–474 (2007)
14. Teh, Y., Jordan, M., Beal, M., Blei, D.: Hierarchical dirichlet processes. Journal of the American Statistical Association 101(476), 1566–1581 (2006)

# Online Political Debate: Motivating Factors and Impact on Political Engagement

Asbjørn Følstad and Marika Lüders

SINTEF
PB 124, Blindern
0314 Oslo, Norway
{asbjorn.folstad,marika.lueders}@sintef.no

**Abstract.** Online political debate is increasing in importance, both as a real world phenomenon and as an object of scientific study. We present a survey study exploring people's motivations for engaging in online political debate and how such debate may impact their general political engagement. The survey was conducted among 90 participants of an online environment for political debate hosted by one of the main Norwegian political parties. We found four motivational factors with relevance for participation in online political debate: engaging topic, want to contribute, frustration, and reciprocal learning. Sixty-four per cent of the participants answered that the online environment for political debate could make them more politically engaged. These participants reported that such an increase in political engagement could be due to the online environment providing a sense of influence, access to political debate, a means for getting updated, a lowered threshold for participation, motivating local political engagement, and awareness concerning political events.

## 1 Introduction

Political debate is increasingly conducted online. This trend has been welcomed with enthusiasm as it has been assumed that such political debate may lower the threshold for participation, increase citizen involvement, and, in consequence, strengthen democracy [8]. The enthusiasm has seemed warranted as citizens do make use of online arenas for political debate to share their opinions and engage themselves politically [5; 7]. It is suggested that online political debate may be beneficial to public involvement in policymaking [11]. Also, it has been suggested that online arenas for political debate may serve as a public sphere supporting rational-critical discourse among its participants [3], though this has been severely criticized [11].

A range of studies have been conducted to characterize those that engage in online political debate, for example in terms of gender, age, and education. Also, efforts have been made to assess the quality of such online debate [11]. The contribution of this study is to provide insight into the motivation of those engaging in online political debate and the perceived impact of such debate on the debaters' political engagement. Thus, this study extends the current knowledge of online political debate as it provides knowledge on how such political debate is perceived from the

M.A. Wimmer, E. Tambouris, and A. Macintosh (Eds.): ePart 2013, LNCS 8075, pp. 122–133, 2013.

perspective of those who engage in it. Furthermore, it suggests how online political debate may strengthen the participants' general political engagement; the latter being a needed addition to the current literature on the correlation between online and offline political engagement [1; 13].

The remainder of the paper is structured as follows: first we provide an overview of previous work. Then we formalize the research questions and present our research method, followed by a presentation of the results of our study. Finally, we discuss the results, their implications, and the study limitations, as well as suggest future work.

## 2    Previous Work

### 2.1    Online Political Participation

Political participation is hardly an unambiguous term in the scientific literature. Teorell [12] distinguished between responsive, participatory and deliberative models of democracy. Voting and participation in election campaigns are key aspects of a responsive democratic model [14]. Taking part in decision-making processes is at the core of a participatory model [16]. Participating in the political opinion formation is central to a deliberative model [12].

Participatory and deliberative democracy depends on debate and dialogue between citizens. Significant participatory divides have been found concerning gender and education, with males being more active in online political debates, and with educational levels correlating with online political participation [11; 15]. Yet, in multiple regression analyses, demographic variables (such as gender and age) have been found to explain far less of the variance in online political participation than factors associated with political engagement in general [13].

Individuals' general political interest, offline political engagement, and civic engagement may be better predictors of online political participation than mere demographic variables. Vesnic-Alujevic [15], in a survey study among citizens using the European parliament Facebook pages, found that online political participation correlated strongly with political interest. Likewise, Conroy, Feezell, and Guerrero [1] found a strong correlation between online and offline political engagement in their study of political Facebook groups. De Zúñiga, Jung, and Valenzuela [18] found strong correlations between online political engagement, offline political participation, civic engagement, and the use of social networking sites for news. An experimental study by Min [9] showed that online deliberation may increase the participants' sense of political efficacy and willingness to participate in politics.

Motivated by the promise that online political debate, adhering to the principles of deliberative democracy [12], may strengthen the public sphere, several studies have analysed the quality of such debate. Stromer-Galley and Wichowski [11] summarized this literature, and concluded that "online political debate, created by and for citizens left to their own devices tends not to produce high-quality discussions" [ibid., p. 180]. However, the quality of the discussion, that is, the discussion's adherence to the principles of deliberative democracy, may be higher for debates involving both ordinary citizens and politicians [ibid., p. 179]. Also, the design of the online environment for political debate may affect the quality of the discussions; higher quality discussions are found in online environments such as blogs that motivate more contemplative comments rather than a speedy exchange of messages [ibid., p. 178].

## 2.2    Online Debate Connecting Citizens and Politicians

It is noteworthy that the involvement of politicians in online political debate among citizens may improve the quality of the debate. As politicians are elected to represent citizens, they also need to listen to the opinions of the same citizens [4; 17]. Furthermore, politicians listening to, and debating with, ordinary citizens may strengthen the involvement of citizens in policymaking. Stromer-Galley and Wichowski suggest that online discussions "hosted by government agencies or policymakers, enact democracy by situating citizens as agents within the policymaking process" [11, p. 182].

The possible use of online political debate as a means to involve citizens in policymaking may be a way to implement Dahl's [3] characteristic of democratic participation, where all citizens should have the same opportunity to set political agendas and influence political decision-making. Furthermore, online political debate involving ordinary citizens and politicians could have an added democratic value as it may strengthen the openness of political processes [10].

## 3    Research Questions

Our research questions are designed to fill what we perceive as two gaps in the current knowledge on online political debate: the motivation for participating in such debates and the impact of such participation on the debaters' political engagement. Two research questions were formulated.

*RQ1: Which factors motivate participation in online political debate?*

The current literature provides ample insight into the characteristics of online political debaters. However, the current knowledge on motivational factors is limited. Extending this knowledge is important as it may help us improve the online environments for such debates, as well as understand the role such debates may have in society.

*RQ2: How may participation in online political debate impact the general political engagement of the debaters?*

From the current literature we know that the tendency to participate in online political debate is closely associated with political engagement in general. However, we find that there is a lack of knowledge concerning how online political debate may come to affect such general political engagement. Extending our knowledge on this issue is relevant both for understanding the role of online political engagement for the individual debater as well as to set up political debate so as to increase general political engagement in the population.

As the literature suggests that the quality of online political debate may be positively affected by involving both politicians and ordinary citizens, we wanted to investigate our research questions in a context where both these groups participated; this to prevent our findings from being unduly biased by the participants' perception of the online political debate as of low quality.

Furthermore, we wanted to investigate our research questions in an online environment promoting contemplative comments rather than a fast exchange of messages, also for the purpose of controlling against low-quality political debate.

# 4     Method

To gain in-depth understanding of online debaters' motivation, and the impact of such debate on general political engagement, this study was conducted in the context of a single case: an online environment for political debate run by one of the main political parties in Norway.

We wanted to gather data from a relatively large number of participants. Consequently, we decided to conduct an online questionnaire survey. As we wanted the study to be exploratory, we included questionnaire items with free-text answers to gather qualitative data.

## 4.1     The Case

The case was an online environment for political debate hosted by one of the main political parties in Norway. The environment was divided into sections concerning specific topics (such as education, health, employment), specific parts of the party organization (local and higher level party bodies), and blogs for individual politicians.

The online environment was set up to foster deliberative dialogue involving central party members / politicians, peripheral party members, and politically interested citizens who are not members of the party organization. The overall design of the online environment was a portal structure including a number of blogs for specific topics or parts of the party organization. In the separate blogs, discussions were organized as threads following an introductory text. The comment field was located below the discussion thread, to motivate the participants to read others' comments before posting their own. Upon posting a comment, the online debater by default was set to follow the discussion, and notified by e-mail when new comments were posted. The online debaters had to log in to comment, either as a user of the online environment or through their Facebook or Twitter accounts. The vast majority of debaters participated in their own full name.

## 4.2     The Participants and Recruitment Process

The participants were selected on the basis of their participation in four sections of the online environment; three thematic sections (foreign affairs, education, and employment) and a section serving as the blog for the party leader. In total, 464 persons had made one or more comments in the four sections during a given two month period in 2010; 87 in the three thematic sections, the others in the party leader blog only. Those that had commented in the three thematic sections, or that had made two or more comments in the party leader blog, were invited. Furthermore, among those that had made only one comment in the party leader blog, 40 were randomly selected. We did not invite persons that had published blog posts (in addition to comments) in the online environment, as we assumed these to be closer to the central party administration. Furthermore, we did not invite persons that had logged in with Twitter or Facebook accounts, as we wanted our participants to be regular visitors of the online environment. These filters excluded 48 of the 464 commenters.

In total we invited 204 persons to participate in the study by invitations sent through the internal messaging system of the studied online environment. Of these, 90 responded to the invitation (44%). For the purpose of anonymity, no couplings were made in the data set between (a) the debaters and content in the studied online environment and (b) the participants' questionnaire responses.

### 4.3   The Questionnaire

The questionnaire contained 17 questions on demographics, the participants' use of social media, the participants' use of the studied online environment, their motivation for providing comments in the studied online environment, the impact of their online participation on their general political engagement, their experience of the online environment, and suggested changes for the online environment. Due to limited general interest, the findings concerning the latter theme are not presented.

### 4.4   The Analysis Process

The participants' free-text responses concerning their experience of the studied environment, their motivation for commenting, and the impact of their online participation, were subjected to thematic analysis [6]. For each of these questions, an initial set of coding categories was established after the first reading of the comments. The initial categories were then refined following pilot coding. After having established a stable set of coding categories, all comments were coded. Following this, the comments within each coding category were subjected to a second round of analysis for detailed findings.

## 5   Results

### 5.1   The Participants

The average age of the participants was 51 years (SD = 13, min = 22, max = 83). Sixty-three per cent were male. Nearly half of the participants (44%) had used the studied online environment for a year or more. The participants were also active in other social media; 73% reported that they were regular users of Facebook, 21% were regular users of Twitter.

The majority of the participants were members of a political party; 30% reported that they were active members, 27% were passive members. About one-sixth (17%) reported participating in political meetings.

Upon being asked about their experience of the studied online environment, the most prominent themes were statements on satisfaction (16 comments in this category) and critique of the discussions (nine comments). Statements on satisfaction concerned various aspects of the online environment and the way it was run. The critique of the discussions in particular concerned disrespectful treatment of other participants, varying quality in the comments, and difficulties in getting an overview of discussions; the latter having the consequence that themes were seen as repeated multiple times in the same discussion thread.

### 5.2    Which Factors Motivate Participation in Online Political Debate?

The participants were asked to explicate why they had commented in the studied online environment. The participants' answers were found to reflect four overall motivations:

1. **Engaging topic (32%).** These participants reported being engaged by the topic under discussion and/or having strong opinions. Several provided details on the actual topic of interest.
2. **Want to contribute (19%).** These participants reported that they had knowledge or experience that they found to be a needed or useful addition to an on-going debate. They typically also reported a desire for their opinion to have some kind of impact.
3. **Frustration (12%).** These participants typically reported anger or frustration concerning general societal or political issues. Three of these also aired frustration concerning the debate in the studied online environment.
4. **Reciprocal learning (2%).** Two of the participants reported that they found the studied online environment to be an arena for learning.

See **Fehler! Verweisquelle konnte nicht gefunden werden.** for examples of participant reports concerning motivational factors.

Of relevance to the question on motivation, we found that 38% of the participants voiced a general wish for even more engagement on the part of politicians in the studied online environment. This was not the topic of any of the questions in the questionnaire, but something that was reported in response to several of the free-text questions.

In particular, the participants wanted feedback from central party members and politicians in the form of comments in the online discussions, clarity concerning the impact of the participants' comments, and clarifications concerning whom from the party organization one may expect to respond to comments.

**Table 1.** Example participant comments concerning their motivation for commenting in the studied online environment for political debate

| Theme | Example comments (translated from Norwegian) |
|---|---|
| 1. Engaging topic | *It was something that caught my interest. Issues that I have experienced or will experience myself.* |
| | *I am very interested in questions on the politics of drug abuse. I see a connection between drug addiction and sick leave, crime and health in general.* |
| 2. Want to contribute | *I disagreed with the post starting this discussion, and feel that I have both the competency and the engagement.* |
| | *Disagree with many of the comments on the causes for sick leave, and wanted to present my point of view.* |
| 3. Frustration | *I commented out of frustration following this year's election and the subsequent unfulfilled promises concerning students [...]* |
| | *I am annoyed concerning the sick leave discussion.* |
| 4. Reciprocal learning | *I look at the comments as introductions or replies in a knowledge debate where the goal is to reciprocally learn and develops one's own position and opinion in interplay with politically interested people.* |
| | *Interesting and sensible debates are pleasant and instructive to participate in.* |

### 5.3 How May Participation in Online Political Debate Impact the Political Engagement of the Debaters?

The participants were asked whether they thought the studied online environment could affect the strength of their political engagement. Sixty-four per cent answered that the studied online environment could make them more politically engaged, 31% answered that it had no effect, 5% answered that it could make them less politically active.

The participants who answered that the online environment could make them more politically active were asked, in a separate question, to report in free-text on how the environment could have this effect. The other participants were not asked this question. The thematic analysis yielded six answer categories:

1. **Sense of influence** (reported by 17). These participants see the studied online environment as an opportunity for having an influence and communicating their own opinion. This opportunity in turn is reported to motivate an increase in political engagement. However, several of the participants reported that such an increase in their political engagement presupposed an active engagement from central party members and politicians in the studied online environment.

**Table 2.** Example participant comments on how the studied online environment could increase their political engagement

| Theme | Example comments |
| --- | --- |
| 1. Sense of influence | *By this I mean that it is possible for me to reach out with my opinions to a wider audience, I have on several occasions received "likes" on my comments and to me this is motivating.* |
| | *Closeness to the power – provided that the comments are read by someone in charge. Share experiences from the real world.* |
| 2. Access to debate | *It is easier to get an interest in particular issues if you have an arena for speaking out.* |
| | *I have just discovered political blogs, it is a new arena for me. Otherwise, I am engaged in political discussions at work and would like to be more engaged in other (non-political) organizations.* |
| 3. Getting updated | *The website keeps me updated at all times, and keeps my engagement up. [...]* |
| | *I think this gives me the opportunity to follow what is going on [...]* |
| 4. Lowered threshold for participation | *[...] I can participate more actively in discussion where the topic engages me.* |
| | *People spend A LOT of time in front of their computers every day. If we are to have politically active citizens, it must be easier to participate in the political debates. We achieve this through [the studied online environment] and the newspaper comment fields, etc.* |
| 5. Local participation | *That I get sufficiently engaged to associate myself with a local party body, start going to meetings and participate.* |
| | *[...] A lot of members today hold valuable competency and I believe that many virtual discussions, between two-three members, may lead to meetings in local party bodies.* |
| 6. Information on events | *Issues that are discussed and meetings that are announced will contribute to other activities. [...]* |
| | *Information on seminars and campaigns, as well as other events, that I primarily see on [the studied online environment]. [...]* |

2. **Access to debate** (reported by 14). These participants described the access to debate, made possible by the studied online environment in particular or by the general increase in arenas for online political debate, as engaging and inspiring in itself. Three of the participants noted that the discussions in the studied online environment could also serve as a basis for political debate outside this environment. Three explained that the main value of online arenas for political debate is to increase the transparency in political processes and to support grassroots movements.

3. **Getting updated** (reported by 5). These participants reported that the studied online environment helped them to get updated on political issues. Three of these specifically associated such updates with engagement in political activity. The described updates concerned, for example, general political trends, particular topics under debate, and news concerning particular persons.

4. **Lowered threshold for participation** (reported by 4). These participants reported that the studied online environment represents a low-threshold offer for persons who want to engage politically, and that it makes it easier to be politically active.

5. **Local participation** (reported by 4). These participants reported that their activity in the studied online environment could motivate them to participate actively in local politics.

6. **Information on events** (reported by 4). The studied online environment is used for spreading information on events such as meetings, seminars, and campaigns. Some of the participants reported that such information increases their chances for participating in the events.

See **Fehler! Verweisquelle konnte nicht gefunden werden.** for example participant comments concerning how the studied online environment could make them more politically active.

# 6     Discussion

In this section, we will first discuss our findings relative to the two main research questions. Then we will discuss the limitations of the study and suggest future work.

## 6.1     Motivators for Online Political Debate

The participants' responses provided relevant insights into possible motivators for participation in online political debate. We find it consoling that the most frequently reported motivator was an engagement in the discussed topic, and that the second most frequent motivator was a wish to contribute in the debate. Both these motivators are in compliance with the ideals of online deliberation. It is useful for developers and hosts of online environments for political debate to know that engaging topics and a wish to contribute may be key motivators for online debaters. In particular, this may have implications for how topics should be presented and moderated. Given that the findings are general, developers and hosts of such online environments needs to look for topics and content triggering the participants' engagement, and present topics in an engaging manner, rather than, for example, just present content for informational purposes. It may also be important to strengthen participants' opportunities for making contributions that may actually impact political policymaking, thereby "situating citizens as agents within the policymaking process" [11, p. 182].

That said, it is noteworthy that general frustration was the third most frequently reported motivation to make comments in the online environment. While frustration may possibly help people get started in online debate, such motivation is hardly an optimal basis for the rational-critical discourse of deliberative democracy [2]. Possibly, debaters venting their frustration online may be the reason why some of the study participants criticize what they perceive as disrespectful treatment of others in the debates. Although political debate may benefit from having nerve and temperature, it is an important challenge for the hosts of online political debate to reduce the effect of online debaters motivated mainly by their frustration. In particular, this is important in cases such as the one in this study, where frustration only motivates a small proportion of the online debaters.

Finally, it may be noted that there still is a way to go before online deliberation [2] is the backbone reflex of the participants in the studied online environment. Only two participants reported reciprocal learning as their motivation. Being engaged and wanting to contribute are indeed necessary requisites for online political debate. However, in terms of online deliberation, it will also be necessary to listen to others' perspectives and appreciate the possible learning that may come out of the political debate.

## 6.2    Impact on General Political Engagement

From the existing literature we know that participation in online political debate is highly correlated with general political engagement [15; 1; 18]. Furthermore, online deliberation may strengthen political efficacy and willingness to participate in politics [9].

In our study, the majority of the participants reported that their participation in online political debate might strengthen their political engagement. This finding is in line with Min's conclusion that online deliberation may increase political efficacy and willingness to participate in politics [9]. Furthermore, our findings indicate how such increased willingness to engage politically may be explained.

The most frequently reported reason for a strengthened political engagement is the perceived promise of influence associated with an online environment hosted by a political party. This perceived promise may be strengthened by politicians and central party members participating in the same environment. However, although party members indeed were present as debaters, several of the survey participants voiced concern that central party members and politicians were not more active. This concern reflects a scalability-challenge in the interchange between politicians and ordinary citizens in online political debate; as the number of active debaters increases, it will be next to impossible for central party members and politicians to follow up all comments.

Consequently, we need sustainable approaches to support interaction between politicians, central party members, and ordinary citizens in online political debates. One approach may be to clarify the promise of the online political debate: that the online environment is an arena for debate mainly among citizens and local party members; however, central party members and politicians may be active to the extent possible. A second approach may be to conduct regular summaries of the content of political debate, for example as input in political policymaking, and be clear on how the online debaters have contributed to the summaries.

Other reasons for strengthened political engagement included the motivation for involvement in local politics, and an increased awareness of political events. Political parties hosting online environments for political debate may benefit from these effects of the online political debate by making easily available offerings to the online debaters, for example by promoting selected offline political events.

### 6.3    Limitations and Future Research

This study was conducted in an online environment for political debate where ordinary citizens, party members and politicians participated. Furthermore, the online environment was designed to foster contemplative comments rather than a fast-paced exchange of messages. Consequently, the generality of our findings is limited to contexts for online political debate that share these characteristics. Future work comparing the kind of online environment used in this study to other online environments for political debate is needed to make more general claims.

The case of the present study was arguably a suitable object of study for our research questions, in particular as Norway is an egalitarian society with high Internet penetration and online maturity in the population. However, the generality of the findings may depend on the characteristics of the society in which the study was conducted. Consequently, it will be beneficial to replicate the study in other cases, preferably in other countries.

**Acknowledgement.** This work was conducted as part of the research project NETworked Power (http://networkedpower.origo.no) supported by the Norwegian Research Council VERDIKT programme, project number 193090.

# References

1. Conroy, M., Feezell, J.T., Guerrero, M.: Facebook and political engagement: A study of online political group membership and offline political engagement. Computers in Human Behavior 28, 1535–1546 (2012)
2. Dahlgren, P.: The Internet, public spheres, and political communication: Dispersion and deliberation. Political Communication 22, 147–162 (2005)
3. Dahl, R.A.: Democracy and its critics. Yale University Press (1989)
4. Dean, H.: Wikipartia. How the web is restoring democracy to politics. Forbes 179, 94–98 (2007)
5. DeWolfe, C.: The MySpace Generation. Fortune 179, 72–74 (2007)
6. Ezzy, D.: Qualitative analysis. Routledge (2002)

7.  Kahn, R., Kellner, D.: Virtually Democratic: Online Communities and Internet Activism. In: Barney, D., Feenberg, A. (eds.) Community in the Digital Age: Philosophy and Practice, pp. 183–200. Rowman & Littlefield (2004)
8.  Lüders, M.H., Følstad, A., Waldal, E.: Expectations and experiences with MyLabourParty: From right to know to right to participate? Journal of Computer-Mediated Communication (forthcoming)
9.  Min, S.: Online vs. face-to-face deliberation: Effects on civic engagement. Journal of Computer-Mediated Communication 12, article 11 (2007)
10. Sevland, L.J., Berg, D.H., Brosvik, T., Kvaløy, O.A., Moe, B.T., Myrvold, T.M., et al.: Det lokale folkestyret i endring? Om deltaking og engasjement i lokalpolitikken. Departementenes Servicesenter (2006)
11. Stromer-Galley, J., Wichowski, A.: Political Discussion Online. In: Consalvo, M., Ess, C. (eds.) The Handbook of Internet Studies, pp. 168–187. Wiley-Blackwell (2011)
12. Teorell, J.: Political participation and three theories of democracy: A research inventory and agenda. European Journal of Political Research, 787–810 (2006)
13. Valenzuela, S., Kim, Y., de Zúñiga, H.G.: Social networks that matter: Exploring the role of political discussion for online political participation. International Journal of Public Opinion Research 24, 163–184 (2012)
14. Verba, S., Nie, N.H.: Participation in America: Political democracy and social equality. Harper & Row (1972)
15. Vesnic-Alujevic, L.: Political participation and web 2.0 in Europe: A case study of Facebook. Public Relations Review, 466–470 (2012)
16. Vitale, D.: Between deliberative and participatory democracy: A contribution on Habermas. Philosophy & Social Criticism 32, 739–766 (2006)
17. West, D.M.: Digital government: Technology and public sector performance. Princeton University Press (2005)
18. de Zúñiga, H.G., Jung, N., Valenzuela, S.: Social media use for news and individuals' social capital, civic engagement and political participation. Journal of Computer-Mediated Communication 17, 319–336 (2012)

# You Say "Yes", I Say "No": Capturing and Measuring 'Public Opinion' through Citizens' Conversation Online (on the Russian-Language LiveJornal Blogging Platform)

Yuri Misnikov

1B-1-6 Park Str., Minsk, Zhdanovichy, 223033, Belarus
yuri.misnikov@gmail.com

**Abstract.** The paper presents the results of the empirical study devoted to mapping and measuring the aggregated political positions – viewed as a specific form of discursive public opinion – expressed by ordinary citizens on a discussion forum on the Russian internet. The study is considered as part of the broader inquiry into the field of online deliberations. New evidence is discussed in this regard by deepening the empirical side of claim making and validation through studying agreements and disagreements among online discussants using Jurgen Habermas' notion of validity claims to normative rightness. The claim-based approach has helped reveal, firstly, how participants problematize issues of public importance and what these issues are, and, secondly, which intersubjective solidarities (groups) participants form around these issues. The paper concludes by considering both the epistemic and pragmatic aspects of such results for better understanding the participatory value of public discussions online from a perspective of discursive sociology and public trust building.

> *- You say "Yes", I say "No".*
> *You say "Stop" and I say "Go, go, go".*
> *Oh no.*
> *You say "Goodbye" and I say "Hello, hello, hello".*
> *I don't know why you say "Goodbye", I say "Hello, hello, hello".*
> *I say "High", you say "Low".*
> *You say "Why?" And I say "I don't know".*
> *Oh no.*
> *You say "Goodbye" and I say "Hello, hello, hello".*
> THE BEATLES - HELLO GOODBYE song
> By LENNON/ MCCARTNEY

## 1 Theoretical and Analytical Framework

The paper continues testing the practicability of Jurgen Habermas' notion of basic validly claims – as part of his broader theories of communicative action, discourse ethics and, of course, the public sphere –for studying online discourses from a participatory democracy

M.A. Wimmer, E. Tambouris, and A. Macintosh (Eds.): ePart 2013, LNCS 8075, pp. 134–146, 2013.

perspective. While the Habermasian conceptualization of the public sphere has been met with grounded criticism insisting, for example, that there are many public spheres for different social strata rather than just 'bourgeois' one and that the very concept is excessively idealized imposing the 'ideal speech situation' conditions that are impossible to meet in real world [for example, 27, 9, 4], still the democratic value of the public sphere remains as strong as ever, especially in the digital age, which has markedly redrawn the boundaries of the traditional offline publicness. The research that has emerged at the crossroads of new media and the public sphere concept appears to be strong and expanding [2, 10, 25, 28, 29, 30].

## 1.1    Reaffirming Democratic Value of the Pluralistic Public Sphere

Habermas' views on the public sphere have also evolved significantly since his original book *The structural transformation of the public sphere: an inquiry into a category of bourgeois society* was published decades ago. In his later work, he replaced a previous – impossible to implement – requirement for the total participatory equality and inclusiveness with a more realistic condition of non-exclusion [16]. In other words, a condition to engage all those capable of participating in public discourses was no longer necessary. However, the condition of equal participation was still valid; that is, those citizens who are willing to participate should not be excluded from participation, which in turn must be free, non-coerced and safe from intentional self-deception [3, 15].

While Habermas admits that the public sphere is pluralistic by nature, he also insists that disparate public spheres co-constitute each other and thus generate 'emancipatory potential' rather than simply co-exist independently. He demonstrated that using an example of 'plebeian' sphere, which existed in the 19th century alongside with that of the elitist bourgeois one. It was pluralistic in terms that the elitist public sphere could only exist – and distinguish itself – against the background of other public spheres attributed to the social groups excluded from the mainstream one [12, p. 426-7]. Thus Habermas makes a special call to recognise the importance of the public culture and its space created by the ordinary people.

## 1.2    The Virtual Public Sphere as a Space for Democratic Communication

The Internet as a virtual public sphere [6, 256] has attracted the endless numbers of ordinary people to express themselves on the similarly endless number of topics including those of public interest. It is a highly pluralistic public sphere. Many online communities, as well as sub- and counter-cultures that could not have proper place and role in the public communication realm dominated by the corporate mass media in the offline world have emerged and expanded on the Internet ignoring state and social boundaries [1, 7, 8, 10, 19, 20].

This research attempts to study the political culture of the common, ordinary people, of the laymen, who are not professional politicians but nonetheless are active in civic terms online and often offline too. It is essential to know whether the causal online conversations are deliberative in the Habermasian democratic, participatory sense; whether they have an epistemic value and whether they can be studied, for example, sociologically, i.e. as discursively constructed expressed 'opinions' – or even public mood – and to which extent such 'opinion' is 'public'. If so, how can it be mapped and measured?

Habermas makes a clear link between the public sphere and the opinion within it, or rather many opinions. This is how he describes the public sphere sociologically:

'The public sphere can best be described as a network for communicating information and points of view (i.e., opinions expressing affirmative or negative attitudes); the streams of communication are, in the process, filtered and synthesized in such a way that they coalesce into bundles of topically specified *public* opinions. Like the lifeworld as a whole, so, too, the public sphere is reproduced through communicative action; it is tailored to the general comprehensibility of everyday communicative practice' [14, p. 360].

He also notes, that while it is a basic (elementary) 'social phenomenon such as action, actor, association, it does not carry a traditional sociological concept of "social order". It is so because it is not a system, organization or institution and therefore does not have an underlying 'framework of norms' on which memberships, competencies, roles are based upon. The public sphere is a dynamic communicative structure, with the constantly shifting horizons. Otherwise speaking, the public sphere discourses can be described through the streams of circulating opinions.

In this light, the public sphere emerges as a linguistically constituted space of communication actors who generate intersubjective solidarities as a result of their 'cooperatively negotiated interpretations' by 'taking positions on mutual speech act offers and assuming illocutionary obligations' [14, pp. 361-2], i.e. through issuing affirmative or negative statements. Discourse participants mutually grant each other communicative freedom to say "Yes" and "No" and thus to claim certain "truths" as they see it according to their morals and ethics. Habermas believes that by doing so discourse participants grant mutual communicative freedom to each other.    This space, for Habermas, must be open in principle 'for potential partners who are present as bystanders or could come on the scene and join those present' (14, p. 361). This observation well describes Internet discussions that are full of so called 'lurkers' who observe the discussion but contribute rather occasionally.

However, it is not entirely clear how the public sphere opinions can be revealed and understood, let alone reliably measured. One of the options is the use of so called basic validity claimed borrowed from Habermas' ethics discourse theory. Validity claims are the discursive vehicles via which participants connect their personal real-world practices with broader worldview perspectives communicatively.  The study is thus focused on collecting empirical evidence with regards to the 'opinions' generated in the virtual public sphere(s).

## 1.3    Analytical Value of Basic Validity Claims

Basic validity claims are reciprocal and discursive instruments to realise (a rational) communicative (speech) acts. While they are linguistically constructed, their main value semantic in conveying the indirect, intended meaning beyond language aimed at reaching understanding with 'someone with regard to something' in Habermas' terminology. The act of claim making is the articulation of a position, demonstration of certain reasons behind the speech act, transmission of an intentional meaning. Eventually, the speaker seeks the reciprocal validation of the proposed meaning by other discourse participations. From that perspective, claim validation is a rational (logical) exercise rather than linguistic; it is often a moral and ethical act as well to represent a certain worldview. The act of claim validation requires understanding the intentional meaning so as to reveal what is claimed and the reasons behind the claim. It is a subsequent communicative action undertaken by a respondent who is interested in the claim and is ready to respond. Claims are recognised when they validated by a response, but not necessarily agreement [21, 22].

According to Habermas, there are three main types of validity claims reflecting three respective communicative worlds, namely: (1) validity claims that claime propositional truth about the objective world, (2) validity claims that claime normative rightness of certain groups, and (3) validity claims that claime subjective truthfulness about personal intentions (see more on how validity claims can be classified in [22]).

This research focuses on the second type, i.e. the claims to normative rightness. This is the main vehicle of intersubjective communication through speech acts that helps coordinate social actions, seek mutual understanding (not necessarily consensus), and build solidarities among communicators. Such claims manifest public reasoning which emerges as an act of reciprocal recognition among individuals in an ordinary, everyday communicative practice, including on the Internet. As a result, participants construct intersubjective social solidarities, i.e. fluid groups based on shared values as a basis for claiming group-specific interests. This is effectively a reflection of more stable value-based shared social (and political) worlds that exist in a particular society.

The empirical framework of the study is designed to show how the validity claims to normative rightness are used to reveal and measure public opinion discursively.

## 2 Empirical Framework

The main research question has been to test the hypothesis that the validity claims to normative rightness can be used to (a) map out and measure the prevailing opinions expressed by discussants, and (b) disclose issue-based solidarities formed by them and, as a result, reveal political preferences that emerge in the course of online deliberations. In addition, it was assumed (following the previous research in this field) that the articulation of disagreements is the main content of the validation act that drives the debate forward. Otherwise speaking, the assumption was that participants in online discourses prefer to communicate with those holding opposite positions.

### 2.1 Case study Description and Research Approach

The case study was taken from the discussion happened on the Russian-speaking blogging platform LiveJournal (http://nytimesinmoscow.livejournal.com/2245.html)

following a publication on 22 February 2008 by the New York Times of an article criticizing President Putin (his first term in office) for curtailing democracy in Russia. Over 3,000 comments were posted within just a few days by the Russian readers. Some of them were translated into English and posted on the paper's own web site, where, too, a hot discussion unfolded (these were not included into the research analysis). The content of the first 189 out 3,398 all posted messages was coded to (i) reveal validity claims to normative rightness and (ii) assess the discussion deliberative quality including such parameters as civility. The previous research revealed that a relatively small sample of minimum 70-100 posts is generally sufficient for meaningful discourse analysis. Of these 189 posts, the first 100 were analyzed find out the dominant issues raised by the participants and the solidarity groups that are formed around such issues.

The following parameters were used to code the content: (1) unique three-digit identifier of the post; (2) openly uncivil posts; (3) validity claims manifested via (a) agreement and (b) disagreement with others' claims; (4) thematic orientation of validity claims. Each claim – both validated and not validated – was numbered in a chronological order. For example, the coding format "VC-55//3-3-1=*The article is untruthful (Статья неправдивая)* means that "VC-55" is the validity claim number 55; a three-digit sequence "3-3-1" tells it is the 1st post (last digit) of the author number 3 (middle digit) and that it was the 3rd post in a row among all participants. The text "=*The article is* untruthful' is the post's intended meaning that the author does not agree with the article. The post also contains another claim made by the same author "VC-56//3-3-1=*America should better deal with its democracy (Америке лучше заниматься своей демократией)*", which problematizes the issue of broader Russia-American relations. Its intended meaning is to dismiss the paper's opinion of the state of democracy in Russia as unimportant. Others can validate this claim by agreeing or disagreeing with it in a simplified form *For* and *Against*, in the spirit of Habermasian positive and negative attitudes.

All claims were coded in the order of their formulation by the authors, including those that were not validated later. Linguistically, there can be various options to formulate the problematized issue; however, as long as it does not affect significantly the intended meaning of the utterance and falls under the same thematic domain, such differences are acceptable. To choose the right wording usually helps the respondent's perspective; that is, how the claim is perceived at the validation step when the underlying meaning is accepted via agreement or rejected through disagreement.

## 2.2    Analysis

Thematic categorization was applied only to those claims that have been validated by others with the clearly visible affirmative or negative attitude. This also means that the overall number of validation acts is always smaller than the number of claims made. It is up to the participants to decide which claims to validate. Overall, 59 participants made 189 posts; 10% of all the posted messages were uncivil and explicitly rude (and often personal); 70% of the posts contained claims to normative rightness, which amounted to as many as 179 claims (unique and repeated), of which 147 claims were validated (it can be said that the discussion was sufficiently dialogic and reciprocal); 76% (112) were the unique validation acts (the same claim can be validated more than once by a number of participants); 2/3 of claims were validated via disagreement; 10 of 189 posts were discounted on the grounds of either personal character or subjectless, few were deleted by their authors themselves later.

On average, there were 3 posts per participant, which is in line with other discussions analyzed by the author earlier. This means that more posts does not necessarily lead to the increase in deliberative quality. The debate was sufficiently civil, with 1 in 10 posts openly uncivil (usually personal ones), which is also in line with other Internet discussions of much larger size (the percentage of uncivil posts is typically within the range of 6-17 %). The discussion was dialogical, for 4 of 5 claims were validated. It should be noted that both claims and their subsequent validation are sometimes repeated; that is, different participants can pick up on the same claims, which is natural in such discussions. The share of unique validation acts was 76%. Also, 2/3 were validated by disagreement confirming my previous findings that discussants in an anonymous virtual talk prefer interacting with the differently minded people, not with the like minded as is often the case in the offline world.

Thematically categorized were only validated claims via agreement or disagreement. The construction of claim development chain was as follows: if the author "A" in the claim number 1 "VC-1" expressed disagreement, for example, with the paper's stance in relation to the state of democracy in Russia, this author was included into an inter-subjective solidarity *Against* the newspaper. If another author "B" in her claim number "VC-10" supported the paper's view, then she became a virtual member of another solidarity that was *For* the paper. Otherwise speaking, even without direct communication these participants disagree on a certain issue. Anyone else who disagreed with the author "A" was automatically in agreement with the author "B" (unless other claims were made). Figure 1 below illustrates the dialogical process using a real example. The generalized logic of claim development is schematically presented in Figure 2.

Agreements and disagreements are mutually intertwined and even interdependent. They have little sense viewed in isolation from the preceding interactions and claims already made. For example, a participant number 18 claims via VC-38 that there will be no Black Tuesday in Russia any more, and thus supports the government's economic policies – i.e. being *For* authorities, while another participant number 40 disagrees claiming that the Black Tuesday will certainly arrive again (claim VC-39) and that Putin leads the country towards a catastrophe (claim VC-40); he is then Against the government's economic policies. In response, the participant 18 defends the previous position in favour of the authorities by providing an argument that until now Putin did not commit serious errors and therefore deserves support (claim VC-41), noting that the tragedies of Beslan and Kursk submarine are not significant in comparison with the end of the Chechen war (claim VC-42). The latter claim is fiercely disputed by a participant number 42 (claim VC-42) who joins the group of those who are against the government.

As a consequence, agreeing and disagreeing leads to the formation of issue-based intersubjective solidarities; that is, the groups that unite participants around acceptance or rejection of something. If, for example, a participant 1 claims disagreement with the article regarding democracy in Russia – then he founds a group of those who are *Against* (rejection) the paper's policy. If another participant 3 claims disagreement with participant 1 in his criticism, then he belongs to another group which members are united in their solidarity that is *For* (support) the paper's view point. If then participants 5 claims disagreement with participant 3, and participant 6 agrees with participant 1, while participant 8 also agrees with participant 5, they all are part of the same group Against that unites the critics of the newspaper, and in some case America in general. Thus joining this solidarity is possible not only via direct agreement with these critics but also via indirect disagreement with those who reject article; the participants don't need to interact directly to be part of the same issue-based solidarity. In other words, it is possible reveal a bigger picture behind agreements and disagreement.

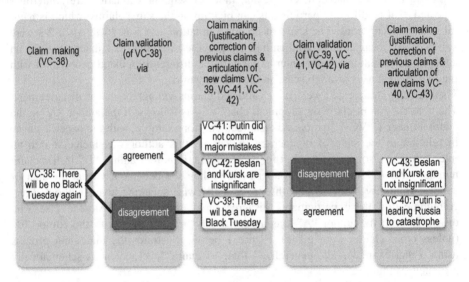

**Fig. 1.** Example of claim making and validation

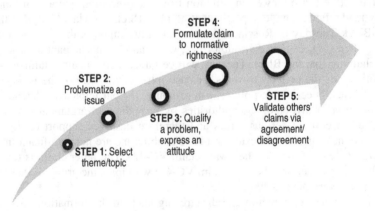

**Fig. 2.** Claim development logic

A range of issues and related inter-subjective solidarities has been revealed as a result of the online discussion. As a result, it's been possible to identify not only the range of issues that they were interested in, but also their attitudes towards these issues. There were six such  issues: (1) Putin's policies, (2) Russian government's policies, (3) role of Russian democrats in general and human rights defenders in particular, (4) the New York Times newspaper that published the article, (5) politics and the state of democracy in America and (6) Russia' military policy.

Using this approach, it has been possible not only reveal the issues that the participants problematize themselves during the debate, but – more importantly – to measure the extent of their support or the lack of it. For example, the least support has been demonstrated in relation to the appositionally (and by default in the participants' eyes) democratically minded human right activists – just 6%. Also, little support was expressed for the *New York Times* paper, which criticized Putin. However, against this background, 24% of support given to America and its democracy was rather paradoxical (see Figure 3).

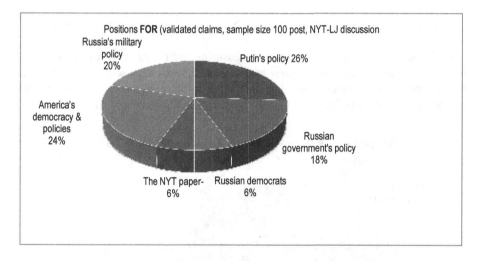

**Fig. 3.** Distribution of discursively articulated Yes (For) positions by discussion themes

Positions "Against" produce naturally similar outcomes, especially regarding Putin's policies – he is the least criticized political actor, while the attitude towards the government was much more negative, as well in relation to Russia's military policies (roughly 20% of all positions). America was criticized most of all – almost 40%. While the participants found positive features of American democracy, the negative assessment prevails (see Figure 4).

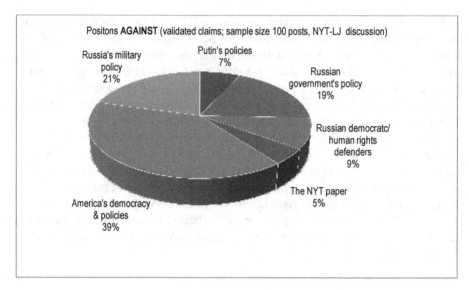

**Fig. 4.** Distribution of discursively articulated No (Against) positions by discussion themes

The claim-based method allows also measuring the discursively expressed 'opinion' about the problematized issues by the size of supportive solidarities. Overall, the distribution of position-based intersubjective solidarities formed by participants mirror the distribution of the positions themselves (see Figures 5 and 6).

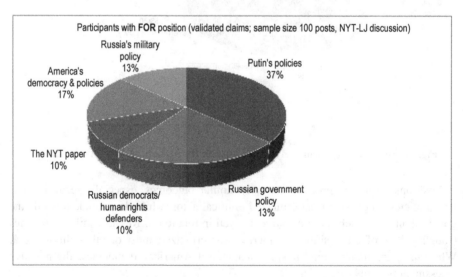

**Fig. 5.** Distribution of holders of discursively articulated Yes (For) positions by discussion themes

The most numerous was the group supporting Putin (37% of all participants), and the least represented was that in support of the Russian human rights defenders (10%). In the same vein, a group with a negative attitude towards America was the largest (37%), while the group that did not like Putin's policies was among the smallest comprising 11% of all participants. Again, paradoxically, the percentage of those who criticized the *New York Times* was even smaller.

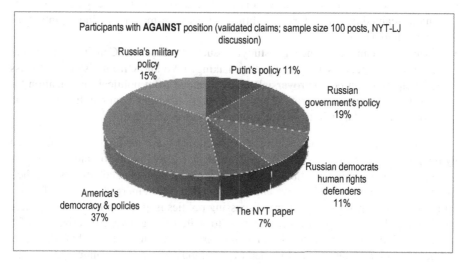

**Fig. 6.** Distribution of holders of discursively articulated No (Against) positions by discussion themes

## 3  Conclusions

It can be concluded that the validity claims to normative rightness are useful to (a) capture an intended meaning of utterances, (b) assess  how deliberative are online debates, (c) measure the scope of public opinion discursively, (d) reveal issue-based intersubjective solidarities. It has been confirmed that disagreements are indeed the discourse drivers.

Overall, the research, regardless of its limitations (e.g. the small sample), has demonstrated not only the analytical efficacy of claims to normative rightness in underpinning the deliberative quality of online debates, but also its practical usefulness in measuring the discursively articulated public opinion. Yet it still needs to be seen how public such opinion is and even more importantly whether it is an opinion in the first place.

The questions for future research could include:

- How different is this discursive form of 'public opinion' from the traditional opinions measured by more traditional sociological polls based on representative samples or random focus groups; can it be part of the emerging sociology of cyberspace (Hi05) or of a discursive sociology? Karen Sanders [4], for example, distinguishes the discursive (consensual) definition of public opinion, which is formed via communicative practices that split society into communities (referring to Susan Herbst) as one of the four models of public opinion (three others are based on (1) majoritarian principles; (2) rejection of the existence of the public opinion as such; and (3) aggregation and measurement of data from sociological polls/public opinion surveys).

- Can the conversational form of online discussions be (a) recognized and (b) mainstreamed both into formal politics and decision-making, including into policy modeling?
- What else can be learned by studying such discussions? Can it be used, not abused, for agenda setting and policy making? (We know from history that mass participation can be controversial). How to move from political mobilization toward democratic socialization and collaboration across communities and civic cultures? Can that help to overcome the "majoritarian tyranny"?

From the Habermasian perspective, the traditional mass media are too influenced by the power forces and thus reflect only a mediated "quasi public opinion". They are not able to engage in earnest the masses of informal, non-organized citizens and their fundamentally "non-public" views and opinions that have emerged in a specific cultural context [12, p. 440]. Therefore, discussing politics is essential not only to ensure and expand democratic pluralism, but also to soften the growing polarization of a modern society via a multi-level and multi-purpose system of the public dialogue. Public communications in the Internet's anonymous virtual environment can be an enabling factor to build trust between the strangers, which is critically important for democratic socialization and public trust – the very basis of democracy [5, 24].

The jury is still out whether such a conversational form of online discussions has legitimate democratic (socialization) value. These they do not necessarily always rational in the strict Habermasian sense, but the very act of participation is a conscious rational choice. It is clear, however, that the extremely large scale of such debates and the seriousness on the part of their participants cannot be ignored if a society continues to remain democratic and maintain public trust by demonstrating the respect to the Other, to the unknown Stranger.

# References

1. Baym, N.: The Emergence of On-line Community. In: Jones, S.G. (ed.) CyberSociety 2.0: Revisiting Computer-Mediated Communication and Community, vol. 2998, pp. 35–68. Sage, Thousand Oaks
2. Berdal, S.: Public Deliberation on the Web: A Habermasian Inquiry into Online Discourse. Hovedfag Thesis. Dept. of Informatics, University of Oslo (2004), http://www.duo.uio.no/publ/informatikk/2004/20535/SimonBerdal.pdf (accessed June 24, 2009)
3. Bohman, J., Rehg, W.: Jürgen Habermas, The Stanford Encyclopaedia of Philosophy, Summer edn. (2009), http://plato.stanford.edu/archives/sum2009/entries/habermas (retrieved July 13, 2009)
4. Calhoun, C.: Habermas and the Public Sphere. MIT Press, Cambridge (1992)

5. Coleman, S., Anthony, S., Morrison, D.E.: Public trust in the news: a constructivist study of the social life of the news. Reuters Institute for the Study of Journalism of the University of Oxford, Oxford (2009)
6. Dahlgren, P.: Internet, Public Spheres and Political communication: Dispersion and Deliberation. Political Communication 22(2), 147–162 (2005)
7. Downey, J., Fenton, N.: New Media, Counter Publicity and the Public Sphere. New Media & Society 5(2), 185–202 (2005)
8. Etling, B., Alexanyan, K., Kelly, J., Faris, R., Palfrey, J., Gasser, U.: Public Discourse in the Russian Blogosphere: Mapping RuNet Politics and Mobilization. Berkman Center Research Publication, No. 2010-11 (October 19, 2010), http://cyber.law.harvard.edu/sites/cyber.law.harvard.edu/files/Public_Discourse_in_the_Russian_Blogosphere_2010.pdf (accessed March 19, 2012)
9. Fraser, N.: Rethinking the Public Sphere: A Contribution to the Critique of Actually Existing Democracy. In: Calhoun, C. (ed.) Habermas and the Public Sphere, pp. 109–142. MIT press, Cambridge (1992)
10. Graham, T.: Needles in a Haystack: A New Approach in Identifying and Assessing Political Talk in Non-Political Discussion Forums. Javnost – The Public 15(2), 17–36 (2008)
11. Habermas, J.: The Structural Transformation of the Public Sphere: An Inquiry into a Category of Bourgeois Society. Polity Press, Cambridge (1989)
12. Habermas, J.: Further reflections on the public sphere. In: Habermas and the Public Sphere, pp. 421–461. The MIT Press, Cambridge (1992a)
13. Habermas, J.: Concluding remarks. In: Calhoun, C. (ed.) Habermas and the Public Sphere, pp. 462–479. The MIT Press, Cambridge (1992b)
14. Habermas, J.: Between Facts and Norms: Contributions to a Discourse Theory of Law and Democracy. Polity Press, Cambridge (1996)
15. Habermas, J.: On the pragmatics of communication. MIT Press, Cambridge (1998)
16. Habermas, J.: Truth and justification. MIT Press, Cambridge (2003)
17. Habermas, J.: Political communication in media society: does democracy still enjoy an epistemic dimension? The impact of normative theory on empirical research. Communication Theory 16(4), 411–426 (2006)
18. Hine, C.: Virtual methods and the sociology of cyber-scientific knowledge. In: Hine, C. (ed.) Virtual Methods: Issues in Social Research on the Internet, pp. 1–16. Berg, Oxford (2005)
19. Jankowski, N.: Creating Community with Media: History, Theory and Scientific Investigations. In: Lievrouw, L.A., Livingstone, S. (eds.) The Handbook of New Media: Social Shaping and Consequences of ICTs, pp. 55–74. Sage, London (2006)
20. Kelly, J., Fisher, D., Smith, M.: Debate, Division, and Diversity: Political Discourse Networks in USENET Newsgroups'. Conference Paper, Second Conference on Online Deliberation: Design, Research, and Practice DIAC 2005, May 20-22, vol. 6. Stanford University (2005), http://www.online-deliberation.net/conf2005/viewabstract.php?id=27 (accessed October 6, 2008)
21. Misnikov, Y.: Discursive qualities of public discussion on the Russian Internet: testing the Habermasian communicative action empirically. In: De Cindio, F., Macintosh, A., Peraboni, C. (eds.) From e-participation to Online Deliberation, Proceedings of the Fourth International Conference on Online Deliberation, OD 2010, pp. 60–74. University of Leeds and Universita Degli Studi Di Milano (2010), http://www.od2010.dico.unimi.it/docs/proceedings/Proceedings_OD2010.pdf

22. Misnikov, Y.: How to read and treat online public discussions among ordinary citizens beyond political mobilisation: Empirical evidence from the Russian-language online forums. Digital Icons: Studies in Russian, Eurasian and Central European New Media, Leeds 7, 1–37 (2012), http://www.digitalicons.org/issue07/files/2012/06/7.1_Misnikov.pdf

23. Negt, O., Kluge, A.: Public Sphere and Experience: Toward an Analysis of the Bourgeois and Proletarian Public Sphere. University of Minnesota Press, Minnesota (1993)

24. Putnam, R.: Bowling alone: the collapse and revival of American community. Simon and Schuster, New York (2000)

25. Rheingold, H.: The Virtual Community: Homesteading on the Electronic Frontier, Revised edn. The MIT Press, Cambridge (2000)

26. Sanders, K.: Communicating politics in the twenty-first century. Palgrave Macmillan, London (2009)

27. Schmidt, H., Teubener, K. (Counter)Public Sphere(s) on the Russian Internet. In: Schmidt, K., Teubener, K., Konradova, N. (eds.) Control + Shift: Public and Private Uses of the Russian Internet, pp. 51–72. Books on Demand, Norderstedt (2006), http://www.ruhr-uni-bochum.de/russ-cyb/library/texts/en/control_shift/Schmidt_Teubener_Public.pdf

28. Schneider, S., Foot, K.: Web Sphere Analysis: An Approach to Studying Online Action. In: Hine, C. (ed.) Virtual Methods: Issues in Social Research on the Internet, pp. 157–170. Berg, Oxford (2005)

29. Sinekopova, G.: Building the Public Sphere: Bases and Biases. Journal of Communication 56(3), 505–522 (2006)

30. Wiklund, H.: A Habermasian Analysis of the Deliberative Democratic Potential of ICT-Enabled Services in Swedish Municipalities. New Media & Society 7(2), 247–270 (2005)

# Experimenting LiquidFeedback
# for Online Deliberation in Civic Contexts

Fiorella De Cindio and Stefano Stortone

Department of Computer Science, University of Milano
Via Comelico 39/41, 20135 Milano
{fiorella.decindio,stefano.stortone}@unimi.it

**Abstract.** The growing distrust in political institutions is accompanied by new opportunities for civic involvement through online technological platforms. LiquidFeedback is one of the most interesting, as it embeds innovative features to support online deliberative processes. This software has been designed as an intranet tool for closed and homogeneous groups but it has also recently been used in large civic context, involving generic citizens. Aim of the paper is discussing the potential of LiquidFeedback for these purposes, by presenting the preliminary analysis of the "ProposteAmbrosoli2013" initiative carried on, in occasion of the recent elections in the Lombardy region (Italy).

**Keywords:** LiquidFeedback, online deliberation, democracy, civic participation.

# 1    Introduction

The "endless" crisis of the western models of economy and democracy imposes a renewed effort to imagine and develop new forms of civic engagement (see for instance [13]). The persistent demands coming from the civil society organizations as well as from international organizations [4, 2] find more and more the concrete support of the ICTs. New software tools have been developed to facilitate knowledge sharing and the organization of new practices of crowdsourcing and collaboration. These tools are already being used by public bodies for opening government (see, e.g., [11]) and by the emerging grassroots organizations [3], to build up consultative and deliberative processes.

One of the most popular software tools for idea gathering is Ideascale (ideascale.com), already adopted in 2008 to support President Obama's Open Government Initiative, and afterward widely used worldwide. However, Ideascale has weak deliberative mechanisms to foster collaboration among participants: each proposal can be commented, voted, but not co-built. This enforces a competitive game among the proposals, as we observed in the case described in [10]. In this direction, a richer application is TOM (Estonian acronym of "Today I Decide"), developed within a state-initiated e-participation project launched in Estonia in 2001 and then proposed at the EU level (under the label TID+, http://tidplus.net)[1]. TOM is focused on

---

[1] Since 2007 TOM has been embedded into the broader participatory website www.osale.ee

M.A. Wimmer, E. Tambouris, and A. Macintosh (Eds.): ePart 2013, LNCS 8075, pp. 147–158, 2013.
© IFIP International Federation for Information Processing 2013

legislative proposals made by citizens through a deliberative process based on discussion and vote. After a fairly active beginning, participation gradually decreased, mainly due to the scarce commitment by the Government and little cooperative features for participants [8].

LiquidFeedback (LQFB in the following) is an open-source software that is recently generating much interest (e.g., [14]) precisely because of its innovative features, which are similar but more articulated than TOM/TID+: it also embeds a deliberative process through which proposals are not only debated and voted, but also supported, and written in a collaborative way, or questioned. In case of alternative options, proposals are voted using the Schultze method (see afterwards), a revised version of the Condorcet's one [15]. LQFB provides another innovative feature, the transitive proxy voting: participants can delegate (and then revoke) other members to make proposals and vote on their behalf in specific thematic areas and/or issues in which they are particularly keen on and trustworthy. These proxies can in turn choose other participants to transfer their votes again.

LQFB was conceived and designed to support the internal decision-making process of the German Pirate Party [7]. However, it also stands for representing a "political" platform whose aims is to reform democracy using technological means. Specifically, it does it by fostering an original mix of - rather than a competition between - direct and representative democracy. A liquid democracy, indeed.

Besides political parties and movements, LQFB is today promoted by a nonprofit association - Interaktive Demokratie[2] - and has broadened its application fields. It is now adopted also by civil society organizations (e.g., Slow Food Germany) and local communities: e.g., since November 2012, the County of Friesland[3] is testing LQFB for supporting civic participation and public deliberation. LQFB is a recent product and there is still no international literature that provides scientific insight about it.

Interest on LQFB has recently grown remarkably in Italy as well, where Internet is playing an extraordinary role in sustaining and supporting civic engagement against corruption and political decline [6]. The first Italian localization of LQFB is due to the Italian Pirate Party, but its widespread popularity on national media is related with its use by several local groups of the MoVimento 5 Stelle (5 Stars Movement, M5S in the following), a political movement created in 2009 by the comic actor Beppe Grillo after and through an intense use of the web (mainly his blog, daily visited by hundreds of thousands users) and social network sites, to oppose the moral decline of the Italian political class. Direct democracy, intense civic participation and the use of ICTs for public purposes, are the key issues for the M5S. It increases its popularity and rapidly reaches a major role in the political arena: it is now the second political party in Italy.

Pushed by the renewed political scenario, LQFB has recently been used within initiatives open to generic citizens. The first trial, called *Libera Sicilia*, took place in occasion of the Sicilian regional elections (September 2012) by a small party of the left coalition: the goal was to collect citizen ideas for its political program. Shortly later, the popular TV show *Servizio Pubblico* (Public Service) launched a much

---

[2] http://www.interaktive-demokratie.org/
[3] https://www.liquid-friesland.de/lf/index/index.html/

broader initiative, called "Liquid Party": however, the goal of gathering ideas from the audience of the show was not at all clear. No one of these two trials was significant enough to test the possibility for LQFB to enable purposeful and extensive initiatives of civic participation.

An experiment with such characteristics and goals has been undertaken by the RCM Foundation[4] and by the University of Milan in occasion of the anticipated regional elections in the Lombardy region, scheduled in February 2013. This paper describes and analyses this initiative, that we call hereinafter ProposteAmbrosoli2013. In particular, it presents the project timeline and the design choices (section 2) and a preliminary analysis of its outcomes (section 3). The conclusions develop some insights over the question if LQFB can foster online deliberation in civic contexts.

## 2     LiquidFeedback for Civic Participation: Design Choices

The Lombardy regional Council resigned on Oct.26th, 2012, as a result of massive corruption scandals which affected many of the leading politicians, including the Governor who has been in charge for 17 years. In the context of a large political disaffection, the primary elections of the left-coalition chose Umberto Ambrosoli – a criminal lawyer with a civil profile rooted in his father's history[5] – as candidate for running as Governor of the Region. He had to compete with the candidate of the right-coalition, Roberto Maroni, former Ministry of the Interiors in the Berlusconi's government. Largely supported by several member of the civil society, Umberto Ambrosoli is a relatively young (40 years old) independent candidate, not well-known outside the city of Milan, but still politically active.

The first talk for promoting a LQFB-based participatory initiative, so enforcing his electoral profile (and, implicitly, competing with the M5S growth too) occurred on Nov.17th. The decision of doing it arrived on Dec.18th, when Ambrosoli won the primary elections. Since the election day was scheduled for Febr.24th, the time for designing the website, configuring the software, and launching the initiative (on Jan.3rd) was then very short: just two weeks, including a couple of days for the beta testing. Nevertheless, this short period was characterized by an intense discussion over the design choices and a coordinated activity between the developers, the candidate and his staff. A direct contact with the system administrators of the Libera Sicilia website was particularly useful to learn from their experience.

Before presenting in §2.2 the main design choices done for configuring the website www.proposte.ambrosolilombardia2013.it (website, hereinafter), let us introduce the LQFB basic concepts and its relevant terminology.

### 2.1     LiquidFeedback Basic Concepts

LQFB is a purely deliberative tool, with no free discussion and forum-like facilities. It has a rich and articulated structure, which is not easy to catch through its extremely

---

[4] RCM Foundation has been established since 1994 as a spin-off of the Civic Informatics Laboratory of the University of Milan.

[5] see. e.g., http://en.wikipedia.org/wiki/Giorgio_Ambrosoli

"essential", almost text-based, user interface. To make the tool (more) within everybody's reach, an online help, developed in [12], was implemented in the section "Liquid Help" of the website. The Fig. 1 is adapted from it and represents, respectively: (a) the structure of the "issue" (or proposal) which is the basic concept/object in LQFB (bottom left side of the figure); (b) the state chart representing the states through which an issue evolves from its creation to its approval or rejection (right side); (c) the organization of the issues in a "tree" structure consisting of thematic sections and areas (top left). We use the terminology of the LQFB 2.2 version of the official LQFB distribution, which provides the English, German and Italian interfaces.

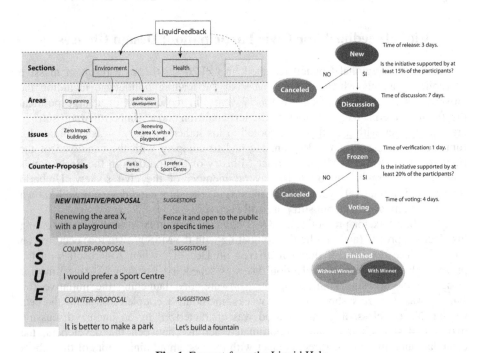

**Fig. 1.** Excerpt from the Liquid Help

1. The *issue* consists of a (preliminary) proposal to solve a problem. When created, the issue gets an identifier, e.g., i252, where "i" stands for "initiative". This means that LQFB does not distinguish between the issue and the original proposal. Any proposed initiative can be disputed by other users through the proposition of new initiatives that get different identifiers. Proposals and counter-proposals can be supported and can collect suggestion(s) which prompt the authors to reformulate their proposals. Examples in Fig. 1 (bottom left) can help to understand the relation among issues, initiatives and suggestions.
2. Each issue goes through a deliberative path, consisting of subsequent states: *New, Discussion, Frozen, Voting.* The state transition occurs according to conditions depending on time (e.g., after four days of discussion) and/or a "quorum" (e.g., if

the proposal gets at least the 20% of supporters, out of the whole participants potentially interested in that issue). The time and quorum parameters are chosen at configuration time and can be changed, e.g., to match with an increased number of registered users. Proposals which get sufficient support are firstly frozen (to allow participants to read the final version) and then voted. All the proposals facing with the same issue are voted together: voters express positive, neutral or negative opinions on them, together with priorities. Results, i.e., "winning" (or approved) proposals, are calculated with the Schultze algorithm.

The above LQFD deliberative path somehow recalls, but looks richer of, the one included in the above mentioned Estonian e-participation project.

## 2.2    Design Choices

Consistently with the guidelines for the design of deliberative digital habitat presented in [5], the main design choices concern the "participatory contract" that binds the various social actors: in this case, the candidate, owner of the website, and the citizens who advance proposals. This "participatory contract" must be realistic and trustable to both sides, and then articulated by specifying: the participants' authentication policy; the setting of the parameters which define the conditions regulating the transition of proposals from one state to another; the embedding of LQFB into a richer website. We briefly discuss them here below.

a) *The definition of the participatory contract:* participants were asked to provide specific proposals to refine and detail the (already published) candidate's political program, whose organization in thematic areas was reflected into the LQFB structure (sections and areas). To make the "game" trustable and attractive to citizens, the candidate committed himself to provide feedback about the approved proposals, either accepting or rejecting them. The platform was open to any citizens, not only to Ambrosoli's supporters. On the other side, citizens were asked to look at the candidate's program and at the functioning of LQFB, before formulating proposals. The importance of the participatory contract was emphasized by publishing it with major evidence in the website home page (through a big button "Read the Participatory Contract"). The RCM Foundation played as trusted third party, warrantor of the agreements.

b) *The participants' authentication policy:* in LQFB, participants' registration occurs upon an invitation from the administrator of the platform. To get it, citizens had to fill a very detailed form including the fiscal code (which is in Italy each one's personal ID). This guarantees a strongly committed community of concerned citizens and allows LQFB to work without any moderation facility.

c) *Configuration parameters setting:* LQFB configuration includes the setting of a wide set of parameters which shape the deliberative path of the proposals, by regulating the transition from one state to another. These include: (1) the first quorum for the proposal to enter in the "discussion" state; (2) the second quorum for going to vote; (3) the largest duration of each phase and (4) the minimum number of positive votes for the proposal to be approved. These choices influence the amount of proposals which are finally approved. In the context of a (short and competitive) electoral campaign, the objective was to fulfill participants' expectation to see their proposals considered but, at the same time, to foster some collaboration and aggregation among participants, and to avoid too many proposals for the candidate to consider. Finally, the two quorums were respectively set to the 10% and 15%; the maximum duration of the deliberative path of a proposal was set to 15 days; the minimum number of positive votes each proposal needs was three.

d) *Embedding LQFB into a richer website:* since LQFB has a very spartan interface, a more user-friendly website embeds it. It runs on the open-source software platform openDCN (openDCN.org), which also provides social media sharing facilities. This "case" website has TABs which link to its various sections. For the purpose of this paper it is worth mentioning: (a) the *LiquidFeedback* section, actually running on a different server; (b) the *Liquid Help* section; (c) the so called *Diary of Participation*, a kind of blog, where each single winning proposal was published by its proposer; it also hosts the feedback from Ambrosoli, either as comments to proposals or as autonomous posts.

## 3    Analysis

The following, still preliminary, analysis of the initiative is mainly based on the data coming from the registration and LQFB databases, collected in the period between Jan.1st 2013, and Febr.22nd, when the electoral period closed. We will also take into account data from the logfiles of the two websites (one running LQFB, the other running openDCN). Finally, we will highlight some of the results of a survey administered online on Febr.22nd and returned before the results of the elections.

Tab. 1 summarizes the participatory activity in ProposteAmbrosoli2013. During the above period (53 days), 1320 citizens filled the form to be invited to participate in LQFB. 1120 (the 85%) completed the procedure and activated their profile: we will call them "participants". The remaining 15% could have been "victim" of the demanding registration procedure. The picture of the participant's population, as it comes out from enrollment data, shows a prevalence of middle-aged men, while young people between 18 and 24 are under-represented (4,3%).

**Table 1.** Participatory activities in ProposteAmbrosoli2013

| Actions | Nr.. | Participants (1120 enrolled) |
|---|---|---|
| propose | 239 | 134 |
| suggest | 225 | 87 |
| support | 1099 | 517 |
| vote | 1002 | 298 |
| at least one action | ---- | 609 |

239 proposals were created by 134 participants (the 12%): the 90% (121) of them created 1, 2 or at most 3 proposals, which represent the 69% of the overall proposals. This first category of "standard" proposers is complemented by a group of 13 "super-active" proposers who did the remaining 75 proposals (31%). The act of proposing ideas were then quite well distributed (see Fig. 2) over the active participants' population. Participation does not only consist in submitting, but also in debating, improving and supporting already submitted proposals: 87 participants contributed to improve the quality of the proposals with 225 suggestions; 45 of them were also proposers, while 42 were not. Proposals were finally supported by 517 participants, ranging from 1 to 61 supports each and 1099 in total; 345 supporters were neither proposers nor contributors. The activities performed in the initial steps of the whole deliberative process allowed 113 out of the 239 submitted proposals (the 47%) to fulfil the policy settings and reach the voting phase. These 113 finalists came from 78 different participants, without significant distinction between "standard" or "super-active" proposers.

Voters were less than supporters: 298 participants expressed 1002 votes for the finalist proposals. One third of the proposers of finalist proposals did not even voted their own proposal. 90 of the voters were "virgin" of any other activity, 239 were not proposers. The voting phase was also characterized by the absence of disagreement: 876 votes were positive, only 22 negative and 104 were neutral. That is to say, few participants disagreed on the proposals or deemed important to vote against them: only two of the voted issues had counter-proposals, and 109 of the 113 finalists proposals (the 96,5%) were approved while only four did not.

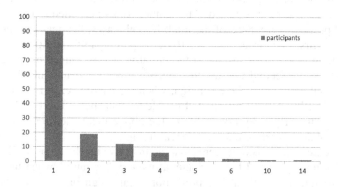

**Fig. 2.** Distribution of proposers according to the number of their proposals

Among the approved proposals, one stood out from the rest because of the high number of supporters and voters. It gathered 180 supporters and 113 voters, while the average of votes for the other proposals was 8,09, with an upper bound of 28 votes. This situation is a clear case of lobbying, as it was the coordinated action of an interest group to sustain a specific proposal. This (very well-articulated) proposal was posted by the leader of a health association and was about its mission. The proposer invited hundreds of friends and members of the association to participate to LQFB and support the proposal. We can imagine that he gave them directions to perform the appropriate actions at the appropriate time: firstly, by supporting, and then voting "their" proposals. Such a huge amount of supporters and voters was not really necessary to fulfill the policies and had the effect of unveiling the lobbying group.

Delegation, one of the LQFB key-action, deserves special attention since basically nobody used it. In the survey, we investigated the reasons of such behavior, with the following result: the 25% of the respondents just did not know about this action; the 20% did not understand its meaning, the 13% found it useful but did not whom to delegate, while the 26% simply preferred to vote personally. Only three of the respondents (2%) used the delegation feature. The 14% did not answered at all. We believe that this result was because delegation is an innovative and unexpected feature within an initiative of civic participation, and it is also unusual in the web 2.0 where people are used to vote everything s/he "likes". More time and some explicit action to enforce it, could have overcome these hindrances and favor its use.

Up to now, we studied the behavior of the active users. Now we look to the 511 citizens (of the 1120, the 46%) who enrolled in LQFB, but never performed any of the above actions. Comparing their account activation date and their last login, we have found that 404 of the 511 never logged in again after the registration. We can suppose that either they were blocked because of the low usability of the platform (as the open answers of the questionnaire suggest) or they enrolled mainly because of curiosity (due to the media attention on the platform). The motivations of this behavior need to be further investigated: was it really passive or was it coupled with reading activities which do not require to log in? What about the motivations of the other 286 citizens who also never logged in again after the first day but performed one single action?

Besides the raw values, the "participation trends" are also worth of attention. Fig 3 and Fig. 4 show that new enrollments and new proposals were concentrated in the first three weeks: during this period 700 members (63%) enrolled in the platform and created 200 proposals, the 84% of the total. In both cases, the peaks occurred in two occasions: the first one, around Jan.4th 104 new participants and 30 new proposals), after the issuing of the press release of the initiative and its launch on the candidate's Facebook page; the second one around Jan.14th (48 participants and 19 proposals), after the official opening of the campaign, when the candidate, in front of thousands of people and in live streaming, invited people to contribute. The further enrollment peak in Fig. 3 in early February is due to the above mentioned lobbying case on a single proposal and therefore does not appear in Fig. 4.

Apart the case of lobbyism, it seems that the initiative reached most of the interested citizens, who quickly started to contribute, at its very beginning, when the Ambrosoli electoral staff did the most intense promotional campaign on the candidate's social media channels. After that, they were more and more absorbed by the hard electoral campaign, thus reducing their commitment to the initiative. Moreover, as the proposals began to finish their deliberative path in LQFD, and those approved were published in the *Diary of Participation*, participants' attention moved from LQFB towards the "case" website. This trend is registered by the statistics of the two servers (Fig. 5) which reproduces the trend of Fig. 3 and Fig. 4, but shows that the "case" website server lost less Unique Visitors and Pages Visited than the LQFB server.

To conclude the analysis of the participatory process, we have to say that 92 of the 120 winning proposals were published by the proposers in the Diary of Participation. Ambrosoli commented three of them separately, while he discussed in four comments other 22 proposals, somehow related each other. In the whole, 25 of the 92 published proposal (27%) got a feedback. Nevertheless, in his last post, close to the Election Day, he confirmed the commitment to consider all the approved proposals, after the elections, when he would govern the Region. Electoral results were different: on Febr.26th Roberto Maroni won the elections with the 42,81% of the votes, while Ambrosoli got the 38,24% of the votes.

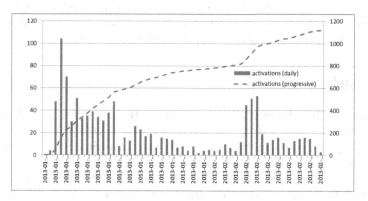

**Fig. 3.** Trend of enrollment of participants

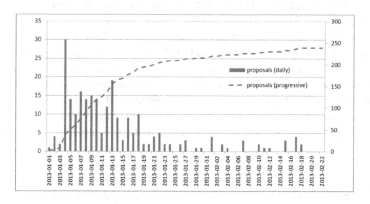

**Fig. 4.** Trend of creation of proposals

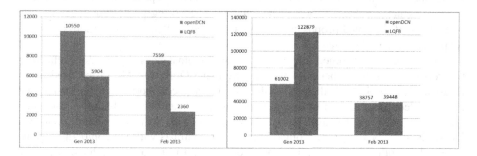

**Fig. 5.** Number of Unique Visitors and Pages Visited in openDCN and LQFB

Despite all, the decreasing participation does not seem to mean a negative opinion about the initiative. In fact, if we look at the results of the survey, over a scale from 1 to 6, more than three fourths of the respondents gave a positive evaluation (between 4 and 6) to the usefulness of four actions of LQFB: proposing, suggesting, supporting and voting; more than the half rated them between 5 and 6. The questions: *"Is LQFB useful to generate valid, reasonable and shared proposals?"* and *"Can LQFB be used to build an effective participatory government?"* got similar good results. Despite the large criticism with regards to the unfriendly user interface, explicitly expressed in the open answers, LQFB is widely considered as a valid deliberative tool.

## 4    Conclusion

In the paper on "Web Science", Hendler, Shadbolt, Hall, Berners-Lee, & Weitzner [9] recognize the role of the web to "encourage more human engagement in the political sphere." They also point out the need of carrying on experiences in real-life settings so that "successful models evolve through trial, use, and refinement." One relevant phase in the proposed applications' life-cycle is therefore the analysis of the real-life trials, which has to figure out what worked quite well, what didn't. When possible, the analysis should compare similar experiences, but this may be difficult when facing with innovative applications. This is precisely the case we have studied in this paper: the use of LQFB for civic participation and public deliberation.

In this last section, we firstly sketch some conclusions from the analysis presented in section 3. We then integrate this "internal" assessment with some elements of comparison that can be drawn from the two cases: Libera Sicilia (whose administrators provided us with some data from their logfiles) and the County of Friesland, through direct online inspection and one indirect source.

The first overall remark is that the whole set of deliberative features of LQFB were used less than one could expect. We already discussed about the missed use of delegation. We also discussed the reasons why the setting of the configuration parameters left the quorum deliberately low. The third group of seldom used deliberative features concerns the voting phase. The short time of the pilot and the quite homogeneous population involved in it (due to the electoral nature of the initiative) may be the reasons for the few counter-proposals and negative votes. Therefore, the Schultze algorithm for rating alternative proposals was not tested, and the vote actually reduces to a "yes/no" choice. The voting phase thus loses its role (the 96,5% of the voted proposals were approved) and often voters were less than the supporters of the proposals.

Because of the combined effect of all these circumstances – ultimately related to the very short electoral period – we can say that LQFB was "de facto" used as an idea-gathering tool. Nevertheless, its deliberative and collaborative nature supported the fair selection of an half of the submitted proposals and enabled some cooperation around them: as Tab. 1 shows, participants were not only willing to submit their own ideas, but also open to support others' ones. This contrasts with the competitive game enforced by other idea gathering tools, observed, for instance, in Ideascale [10], where the activity of participants is often addresses not only to promote their own ideas, but also to vote against the competing ones.

Further insights can be drawn exploiting the little we know about the Libera Sicilia and the County of Friesland cases.

Libera Sicilia and ProposteAmbrosoli2013 were similar as they were both performed in a regional electoral context to involve citizens in the definition of the political program of one candidate Governor. In Libera Sicilia participants were much less than in ProposteAmbrosoli2013 (315 vs. 1120) and only 45 proposals (vs. 239) were created in a similar period of time (6 weeks vs. 7 weeks). The two initiatives share a similar percentage of proposals admitted to vote (46% vs. 43%), mainly due to the similar quorums (20%-20% vs. 15%-20%), but in Libera Sicilia, proposals got fewer votes per voted proposal than in ProposteAmbrosoli2013 (4,09 vs. 8,09). These different outcomes would more probably depend on the higher electoral relevance of Ambrosoli and his political coalition, with respect to the Sicilian candidate. However, we believe that citizens were also attracted by the more trustable "participatory contract". In Libera Sicilia, the LQFB section was promoted by the misleading slogan that citizens would have developed the political program of the candidate. Unfortunately, the program was already written and published online. The "participatory contract" thus became unrealistic and not trustable. In ProposteAmbrosoli2013, instead, participants were asked to provide specific proposals in order to refine, specify and detail the candidate's political program, whose thematic sections were reflected into the LQFB structure. Moreover, through short but effective videos, the candidate substantiates his commitment into the initiative and his interest in considering citizens' suggestions.

The case of Liquid Friesland seems to confirm the importance of a strong "participatory contract". Here, the County Council adopted a resolution that commits it to discuss by law all the proposals approved through the LQFB deliberative process. In the first two and a half months, 500 out of 100.000 inhabitants joined LQFB (and we suppose they further increased in the meantime) and almost 50 proposals have been created to date. As in ProposteAmbrosoli2013, there has been a progressive decreasing activity in terms of proposals and votes. The bigger difference is in the higher number of citizens (up to 80) voting each single issue, as well as in the presence of several negative votes, something not observed in ProposteAmbrosoli2013. These are symptoms of the existence of contrasting positions and of a not homogeneous population. This also generates some counter-proposals, enabling the actual use of the Schultze algorithm in the voting phase. Liquid Friesland seems to encourage the use of LQFB by a local political institution willing to involve its citizens in a decision-making process with actual impact in the real life.

In conclusion, we believe that the preliminary analysis of the ProposteAmbrosoli2013 case study, carried on in this paper, motivates the increasing interest in LQFB. On the one hand, a more qualitative investigation is now going on in cooperation with the University of Trento and the Ahref Foundation (www.ahref.eu/en). On the other hand, while similar initiatives are blossoming in Italy, the Ambrosoli's platform is being re-activated for supporting his activity as member of the Regional Council of Lombardy. All this will provide additional empirical data to understand if and how LQFB can effectively foster online deliberation in civic contexts.

**Acknowledgement.** We wish to thank Umberto Ambrosoli and his staff; the RCM Foundation staff, Davide Mezzera, and all the people mentioned in the Credit Section of the website. We are also grateful to the anonymous referees for their useful comments.

# References

1. Ambrosoli, U.: Qualunque cosa succeda. Sironi editore, Milano (2009) (in Italian)
2. Caddy, J., Vergez, C.: Citizens as partners: Information, consultation and public participation in policy-making. OECD Publishing, Paris (2001)
3. Castells, M.: Networks of Outrage and Hope: Social Movements in the Internet Age. University of California, Berkeley (2012)
4. Council of Europe, Committee of Ministers, Rec, 19 of the Committee of Ministers to member states on the participation of citizens in local public life (2001),
   https://wcd.coe.int/com.instranet.InstraServlet?command=com.instranet.CmdBlobGet&InstranetImage=871858&SecMode=1&DocId=234770&Usage=2
5. De Cindio, F.: Guidelines for Designing Deliberative Digital Habitats: Learning from e-Participation for Open Data Initiatives. The Journal of Community Informatics 8(2) (2012); Davies, T., Bawa, Z. (eds.) Special Issue: "Community Informatics and Open Government Data"
6. De Cindio, F., Schuler, D.: Beyond Community Networks: From Local to Global, from Participation to Deliberation. The Journal of Community Informatics 8(3) (2012); Horelli, L., Schuler, D. (eds.) Special Issue: "Linking the Local with the Global within Community Informatics"
7. Domanski, D.: Democratization through social innovation - pirate party Germany and new methods of civic participation. Paper Presented at The Second ISA Forum of Sociology, Buenos Aires, Argentina, August 1-4 (2012)
8. Glencross, A.: E-Participation in the Legislative Process: Procedural and Technological Lessons from Estonia. eJournal of eDemocracy & Open Government 1(1), 21–29 (2009)
9. Hendler, J., Shadbolt, N., Hall, W., Berners-Lee, T., Weitzner, D.: Web science: An interdisciplinary approach to understanding the web. Communications of the ACM 51(7), 60–69 (2008)
10. Lanfrey, D., Solda-Kutzmann, D.: Progetto ConsultazionePubblica.Gov.It. In: "I Media Civici in ambito parlamentare", Senato della Repubblica (May 2013) (in Italian), http://www.senato.it/295
11. Lathrop, D., Ruma, L. (eds.): Open Government. Collaboration, Transparency, and Participation in Practice. O'Reilly, Sebastopol (2010)
12. Mezzera, D.: Realizzazione di un ambiente di deliberazione online basato su LiquidFeedback. BA thesis, Università di Milano (December 2011) (in Italian)
13. Revelli, M.: Finale di partito. Einaudi, Torino (2013) (in Italian)
14. Schuler, D.: Creating the World Citizen Parliament. ACM Interactions XX.3, (May+June 2013)
15. Schulze, M.: A new monotonic, clone-independent, reversal symmetric, and condorcet-consistent single-winner election method. Social Choice and Welfare 36(2), 267–303 (2011)

# Author Index